Church, State, and Citizen

Church, State, and Citizen

Christian Approaches to Political Engagement

Edited by

SANDRA F. JOIREMAN

OXFORD
UNIVERSITY PRESS

2009

OXFORD
UNIVERSITY PRESS

Oxford University Press, Inc., publishes works that further
Oxford University's objective of excellence
in research, scholarship, and education.

Oxford   New York
Auckland   Cape Town   Dar es Salaam   Hong Kong   Karachi
Kuala Lumpur   Madrid   Melbourne   Mexico City   Nairobi
New Delhi   Shanghai   Taipei   Toronto

With offices in
Argentina   Austria   Brazil   Chile   Czech Republic   France   Greece
Guatemala   Hungary   Italy   Japan   Poland   Portugal   Singapore
South Korea   Switzerland   Thailand   Turkey   Ukraine   Vietnam

Published by Oxford University Press, Inc.
198 Madison Avenue, New York, New York 10016

www.oup.com

Oxford is a registered trademark of Oxford University Press

Library of Congress Cataloging-in-Publication Data
Church, state, and citizen : Christian approaches to political engagement /
[edited by] Sandra F. Joireman.
p.   cm.
Includes index.
ISBN 978-0-19-537846-7; 978-0-19-537845-0 (pbk.)
1. Church and state.   2. Christianity and politics.   I. Joireman, Sandra Fullerton.
BV630.3.C49 2009
261.7—dc22   2008038533

9 8 7 6 5 4 3 2 1

Printed in the United States of America
on acid-free paper

Acknowledgments

This book evolved out of a panel at the 2004 American Political Science Association meeting on different Christian approaches to the state. Brent Nelson organized the panel, and Dan Philpot and Effie Fokas were participants. Though none of the three are contributors to this volume, their insights gave impetus to the vision for the book project. I am grateful to colleagues Mark Husbands and Edith Blumhofer for theological and historical consultations. Derek Keefe deserves special thanks for lending his copious knowledge of church history at key moments in the development of the manuscript. David Peyton, Sarah Baggé, and Katie Graham all contributed able and enthusiastic research assistance. Theo Calderara and Tim Lomperis were both a source of helpful comments and unflagging encouragement in moving this manuscript forward from idea to finished book. In writing and editing this book I have learned much, and I am grateful to each of the contributors for their participation in this project.

Contents

Contributors

MARK R. AMSTUTZ is professor of political science at Wheaton College in Illinois, where he teaches courses on international relations, U.S. foreign policy, and third world politics. Amstutz is the author of numerous articles and books, including *The Rules of the Game: A Primer on International Relations* (2008), *International Ethics: Concepts, Theories, and Cases in Global Politics*, 3rd ed. (2008), *The Healing of Nations: The Promise and Limits of Political Forgiveness* (2005), and *International Conflict and Cooperation: An Introduction to World Politics*, 2nd ed. (1999).

LEAH SEPPANEN ANDERSON is an assistant professor of political science at Wheaton College in Illinois. Anderson researches and teaches on European and postcommunist politics, social policy, and gender and politics. Her personal connection with Anglicanism began as a young adult, when she started attending (and was later married in) the Episcopal Church. She is currently a member of an Anglican church in Wheaton, and she has published most recently in *East European Politics and Societies* and *The International Journal of Public Administration*.

SANDRA F. JOIREMAN is associate professor of politics and international relations at Wheaton College in Illinois. Joireman received her M.A. and Ph.D. in political science from the University of California, Los Angeles. She is the author of *Property Rights and Political*

Development in Ethiopia and Eritrea (2000) and *Nationalism and Political Identity* (2003) and has written numerous articles on property rights and legal development, most recently in *World Development, Comparative Politics, Constitutional Political Economy,* and *Commonwealth and Comparative Politics.*

TIMOTHY J. LOMPERIS is professor of political science at Saint Louis University. Lomperis has published extensively on the Vietnam War, in which he served two tours of duty in the U.S. Army. More recently, he has published journal articles on Iraq. He grew up in India as the son of Lutheran missionaries.

TIMOTHY SAMUEL SHAH is senior research scholar at the Institute on Culture, Religion and World Affairs at Boston University, adjunct senior fellow for religion and foreign policy at the Council on Foreign Relations, and formerly senior fellow in religion and world affairs at the Pew Forum on Religion and Public Life. Shah's work on religion and politics has appeared in the *Journal of Democracy, SAIS Review of International Affairs, Political Quarterly,* and *Foreign Policy.* His Harvard government department Ph.D. dissertation was awarded the Aaron Wildavsky Award for Best Dissertation in Religion and Politics by the American Political Science Association in 2003.

ROBERT B. SHELLEDY is the coordinator of social justice ministry for the Archdiocese of Milwaukee and an adjunct professor of political science at Marquette University. Shelledy has a B.A. in political science from Marquette University, a J.D. from the Northwestern University School of Law, and a Ph.D. in political science from the University of Wisconsin, Madison. His dissertation was entitled *Legions Not Always Visible on Parade: The Vatican's Influence in World Affairs.*

JAMES W. SKILLEN is president of the Center for Public Justice and editor of the biweekly *Capital Commentary* and *Root and Branch: The Religion and Society Report.* A graduate of Wheaton College and Westminster Theological Seminary, Skillen holds an M.A. and Ph.D. from Duke University in political science. His most recent books are *With or Against the World? America's Role among the Nations* (2005) and *In Pursuit of Justice: Christian-Democratic Explorations* (2004).

STEPHEN SWINDLE is associate professor of political science at Lee University in Cleveland, Tennessee. Swindle received his Ph.D. from the University of California, San Diego, and has held previous academic positions at the

Norwegian University of Science and Technology, Brigham Young University, and Southeast Missouri State University. His primary research interest is democratic institutions, primarily in relation to their effect on political representation. His research has been published in the *American Political Science Review*, *Comparative Politics*, and *Party Politics*.

Church, State, and Citizen

1

Introduction

Sandra F. Joireman

Religion in general, and Christianity in particular, has remarkable vigor in American politics. It motivates individuals to act on both domestic and international policy issues and encourages a wide range of political behavior, from voting to lobbying or protest. The faith of various Christian politicians has been both a subject of public interest and an issue in political campaigns. In the United States, the public expects that candidates will declare their religious beliefs in any description of qualifications for political office. This is unusual in the politics of developed countries.[1] The recent emphasis within the popular press and some academic writings on the importance of the Christian vote or the Christian political lobby can lead one to the impression that there is one type of Christian voting behavior or one kind of Christian political lobbying. Yet careful observers of Christian political behavior have noted that in the past few years there has been increasing variation among different factions of North American Christians over specific policies (Guth et al. 2005). Moreover, Christians of a variety of persuasions are becoming involved in policy areas that have not previously been thought to be of concern to Christians, such as international human rights issues (Hertzke 2004). This diversification of political advocacy illuminates what has always been present within Christianity—an array of positions regarding the role of the state and the role of the individual Christian citizen within the state. There is no one "Christian" approach to politics. Rather, Christians evince multiple approaches to the state and political action, extending from the extreme of rejection of state authority to support of everything a state decides, based on the belief that it has been sovereignly appointed to its role.

In his 1951 book, *Christ and Culture*, H. Richard Niebuhr articulated five ways that Christians thought about how to understand themselves in relation to the world. "Culture" to Niebuhr was more encompassing than popular practices and trends; he used the word *culture* to denote the social and political spheres. His categorization illustrated divisions among Christians in terms of how they view the world. Niebuhr noted, "So great . . . is the variety of personal and communal 'beliefs in Jesus Christ,' so manifold the interpretation of his essential nature, that the question must arise whether the Christ of Christianity is indeed one Lord" (Niebuhr 1951: 12–13). Niebuhr's work was an epiphany for many, a moment in which it became clear why there could be such oppositional political opinions among people sharing the same core beliefs. Niebuhr influenced the thinking of generations of Christians, both scholars and popular readers. This book stands on Niebuhr's shoulders, as contributors describe Christian approaches to the state from several traditions. While we stray intentionally from Niebuhr's limited categorizations of Christian political belief, we seek to clarify both the theology and the practice of Christian approaches to the state and citizenship. In so doing, we undertake the goal of articulating complex and nuanced Christian beliefs about government and the proper role of the Christian as a political actor and citizen.

Often, Christians disagree about what appropriate political action might look like for reasons that are rooted in theological positions formed by particular historical moments. These theological differences have evolved in local contexts, prompting adherents to form contextually sensitive viewpoints on politics that have relevance today. Understanding the theology and history behind political beliefs is the first step toward more informed discussions, and even constructive disagreements, about and between these traditions.

The Changing Map of Christian Faith

Christianity is diverse. Nowhere is that more apparent than in the United States and Canada, where waves of immigrants transplanted their own particular expression of Christianity. In any given city or town in North America, it is possible to find ten or more different Christian traditions. To an outsider, these different churches or denominations appear similar. They share a core theology regarding the Trinity, God's role in creating the world, and Jesus' death and resurrection. Agreement exists on many statements in the Apostles' Creed, but the validity of the Apostles' Creed as a summation of Christianity and its use are debated. There are immense differences between Christian traditions in worship practices, the frequency and nature of Communion, formality, use of sacraments, the nature of preaching, use of the liturgical calendar, and beliefs about the accepted sources of revelation. There are also differences in styles of governance, decision making, and the weight given to tradition and history. Variations in the form of worship can be so extreme that a Christian from one tradition may feel not only ill at ease with the services in another tradition but also confused. Dissimilarities among the Christian worship traditions are indicative of differences we see in other aspects of the faith. One of the goals of this book is to identify, for both Christians within these traditions and readers who are not, where the points of difference lie and their causation. We believe this will benefit constructive dialogue among Christians, as well as between Christians and those with other beliefs.

Christianity is changing. Its geographic center is shifting away from North America toward the global South. As the geographic center changes, so does the nature of the dominant form of Christianity, because the Pentecostal and evangelical movements are seeing the most growth. As we search for a greater understanding of Christianity and its implications for political action, we need to remember that the patterns of interaction between individual Christians and the state that we see in North America will be replicated in other settings around the world where theological positions are shared but the context is different. Although the role of religion in U.S. politics may appear peculiar when it is compared with religious expression in European states, where the percentages of practicing Christians in the population are relatively low, it is familiar to those who study religious influences on politics in the developing world, where religion has more salience.[2] As Christianity is experiencing its greatest growth in the global South, it is there we should expect to see a growing role for faith-related political action. Strong theological voices from Africa, Asia, and Latin America are already defining the terms of key issues and conflicts within the Christian tradition (Jenkins 2002). Nowhere is this more apparent than in the African bishops' role in the current Anglican controversy in the United States. It is also evident in the Catholic tradition because a growing church in the global South has meant that issues such as debt relief are being articulated as Catholic concerns in North American churches. Theologies may initially be established in a Western context, but in those traditions that are flourishing overseas, theologies are being reinterpreted in ways that stretch the control over orthodoxy that is a historical artifact of the Western church. Understanding how theology affects politics in the North American context is important for any attempt to predict the political effect of the growth of Christianity on the global South.

On State and Nation

The political scientists who have contributed chapters to this book are all Americans and, for the most part, are writing from within the American context and from within their own theological traditions. However, as comparativists and specialists in international relations, they bring understandings of the concepts of state, nation, political action, and the nature of the global church that are intentionally broader than the American context and historical setting. Only one of the traditions considered in the following chapters, Pentecostalism, developed primarily in the United States. The rest were formed in political and historical contexts outside North America, which has influenced their theologies of political engagement.

To those studying international politics, the terms *state* and *nation* are not interchangeable. A state is a legal entity, a territory with a people inside its borders and a government that has the recognition of the United Nations. Max Weber has famously called the state "a compulsory association which organizes domination. It has been successful in seeking to monopolize the legitimate use of physical force as a means of domination within a territory" (Weber 1994: 310–311). Weber indicates that what distinguishes a state from other organizations is that it can use force to control its population, defend its borders, and mount challenges to the sovereignty of other states. He is clear in his definition that the ultimate form of control is violence and that the state has a legitimate claim on its use. This expression of political authority echoes Romans 13, the critical New Testament passage regarding the role of the state.[3]

> For rulers hold no terror for those who do right, but for those who
> do wrong. Do you want to be free from fear of the one in authority?
> Then do what is right and he will commend you. For he is God's
> servant to do you good. But if you do wrong, be afraid, for he does
> not bear the sword for nothing. He is God's servant, an agent of
> wrath to bring punishment on the wrongdoer. (Romans 13: 3–4, New
> International Version)

The state is a political entity. It has authority and can legitimately use force, for good or for ill. Yet, the realm of the political is more encompassing than that of the state alone, and some political positions developed by Christians are not based on a theology of the state alone but on understandings of citizenship and the responsibilities that come with it.

A nation is a psychological or emotional attachment to a particular group of people. It is a shared fundamental identification. For example, we use *nation* correctly in the sense of Navajo nation, meaning a group of people with a shared identity that takes precedence over other interests and values. We can think of states that contain many nations, that is, groups of people whose primary affiliation is to a smaller political group. Patriotism is a particular expression of nationalism—a feeling of allegiance to the state and solidarity with those living in the state. Not every state elicits this sort of allegiance from its population, although according to Ernst Haas, the strongest and most effective states work toward encouraging an emotional attachment to the state among the population (Haas 1997). Rwanda fell into violence because allegiance to the ethnic group (nation) was stronger than allegiance to the state.

The distinction between state and nation becomes important when we look at Christian political theology. For example, in this volume James W. Skillen discusses instances in which nations of people adopted an understanding of themselves as the "new Israel." In these instances, the boundaries of national or group identity were determined by a theological belief in predestination. On the other hand, an Anabaptist understanding of the state results in great discomfort with any expressed allegiance to the state or nation.

Developing Themes

The chapters that follow present seven different Christian approaches to understanding the state that have been influential in North America. These particular traditions were chosen to demonstrate the breadth of positions regarding the appropriate relationship between the church and the state. Each approach is authentically Christian, and the range of traditions represented, though not exhaustive, captures much of the disparity within the larger Christian tradition.[4] In addition to specific denominations, there are also important Christian movements represented here: Anabaptism, evangelicalism, and Pentecostalism. The latter two movements in particular have had a tremendous impact on American politics and will continue to influence political expression in the United States and around the world in contexts such as Asia and Africa.

The chapters in this book follow a loose chronological order and demonstrate how ideas about the appropriate role of the state and its importance changed significantly over time. In the last two chapters on evangelicalism and Pentecostalism, the focus changes toward a political activism and understanding that is more individualistic and pietistic, less reliant on a clearly articulated theological position. This shift is noteworthy because of the tremendous influence that Pentecostalism and evangelicalism have had in the past decades. To the extent that these are the Christian traditions growing most rapidly in the world, we are seeing more Christians with increasingly individualistic and theologically unreflective approaches to political action.

This book's chapter authors are all writing from within the tradition they discuss with three specific tasks. Their first goal is to identify the history leading to the formation of the tradition. Their second task is to identify that tradition's theological distinctives, which are often linked to the historical moment when the tradition was formed. Their final and perhaps most significant task is to discuss how these theological beliefs regarding the appropriate role of the state and the citizen influence political action. The point of these three tasks is to show the different theological demands with their resulting political actions and to help both Christian and non-Christian observers understand what they are looking at when they see radically different political actions all explicitly or apparently motivated by faith.

Beyond these three clear goals, the chapters weave in several subthemes related to Christian understandings of state and citizenship. Although each Christian group recognizes the Bible as fundamental to their beliefs, each treats it differently. For example, should the whole Bible be viewed as equally authoritative for the life and theology of the church (Reformed, Lutheran)? Or should the New Testament, in particular the life of Christ portrayed in the Gospels, be the hermeneutic lens through which the rest of scripture is interpreted (Anabaptist)? Should individuals be encouraged to confidently interpret the Bible on their own (Pentecostal)? No Christian tradition would deny the importance of scripture, but it is treated differently in each.

Each chapter also addresses the proper understanding of government and the hierarchy of authority and identifies how a believer should understand the responsibilities of the church, the state, and the citizen. The Catholic tradition has much to contribute to this discussion because the Catholic Church preexisted the institution of the modern state and has had to adapt to its modern significance. Some Christian groups have a very low view of the state, such as the early Swiss Anabaptists, who argued that government is "outside the perfection of Christ." Others, such as Anglicans, believe that it is the responsibility of the state and the church to cooperate in constructing the polity.

A related question that comes out of these religious traditions is how we judge the actions of a government. Do we follow Martin Luther's argument and judge governments not by the high standard of Christian love but by the lower standard of justice? Many of the chapters provide a particular understanding of war flowing out of the tradition's understanding of the state. Here we discover clear differences between Christian understandings of what the social contract entails. The Reformed tradition is the most hopeful regarding the use of the state in doing good and helping to create the Kingdom of God on earth. Other traditions fall into a continuum regarding their position on the use of the state for good and the role that citizens might play within it.

The authors articulate a limited role for government.[5] They may differ over where to place the limits of government, but boundaries for the appropriate role of the state are present in every tradition. This idea of limited government has its foundations in the Christian doctrine of *imago dei*, the belief that human beings are made in and bear the image of God. If it is accepted that citizens of a state are made in the image of God, then the protection of basic human rights follows. This affirmation does not imply the full panoply of internationally recognized legal norms, but an implicit social contract—the exchange of protection for obedience. As Christianity permeated the political cultures of Western Europe, more individual protections developed. Christianity, specifically Protestantism, laid the foundations for democracy to flourish through an increased emphasis on the importance of individual conscience and the priesthood of all believers. Peter Berger rightly notes that these two beliefs led to an emphasis on literacy and education so that church members could read and understand the Bible for themselves. This increase in literacy and education fostered societies in which democracy could thrive (Berger 2004).

Moreover, political scientists have noted the importance of associational life to democracy (Putnam 2000). The divisive nature of the Protestant experience had the beneficial side effect of creating a rich associational life as Protestantism moved out of Europe and into North America and what was the colonized world through missionary activity and immigration. Protestants met together in Bible studies, small groups, aid societies, and sports leagues through their churches and denominations, creating a strong and varied associational life, or civil society. This associational element of Christianity creates conditions conducive to democratic development (Woodberry and Shah 2004).

Theological Traditions

The following chapters demonstrate that Christianity provides a theological foundation for the state, although moving beyond this broad statement to the specifics of the social contract unearths disagreements between the traditions. Catholicism must come first in an analysis of church traditions, as it is impossible to understand the Reformation and what followed without a discussion of Catholic beliefs on hierarchy, authority, and the appropriate role of the state. Lutheranism and the Reformed tradition were the two major branches of the Protestant Reformation that began in Europe in 1524. Anabaptism, as the "radical fringe" of the Reformation, began at about the same time. Anglicanism was born of a political struggle shortly after the Reformation and had little to do with theology, yet over time it developed into a distinct branch of Protestantism.

All these faith traditions emerged in Europe and were exported to North America via immigration and to the rest of the world through missionary activity and colonization. Evangelicalism bridges the European and North American continents because its roots are both in the Wesleyan movement in England and in the Great Awakening in the United States. Pentecostalism is peculiarly American and, not surprisingly, bears the stamp of American individualism in its theology.[6] It emerged out of the Holiness movement of John Wesley and had its signature emersion in the Azusa Street Revival of 1906. Since that time, Pentecostalism and the charismatic movement indirectly spurred the popularity of nondenominational churches in the United States and attracted hundreds of thousands of followers in the global South.

In chapter 2, Robert B. Shelledy discusses the Catholic perspective on the state and tracks its changes through time. He emphasizes the struggle the Catholic Church has had with wanting to establish Catholicism as the state religion while, in different contexts, desiring the promotion of religious pluralism. Shelledy notes that Vatican II changed how the church interacted with states. *Gaudium et Spes* freed the church from working exclusively through the state in each country and allowed it to permeate society in unique ways. The result is a Catholic Church that has become serious about religious freedom around the world and sensitive to the common good, broadly conceived. The Catholic Church has become an advocate for the political and economic well-being of individuals living in the developing world. Shelledy also points out the effect that Catholic social thought has had on bringing the Catholic Church into the modern era.

Martin Luther challenged the authority of the Catholic Church to interpret scripture for all its members. Luther's emphasis on the Bible, captured in the famous epithet *sola scriptura,* formed the basis of all of his theological and political contributions. Luther was familiar with the Augustinian formulation of two realms of authority, the temporal and the spiritual. Yet Luther moved beyond this dualism, arguing that these two worlds could not be completely separate. In chapter 3, Timothy J. Lomperis argues that Luther's understanding of the temporal and spiritual worlds as intertwined amounts to a "fused paradox" that compels Christians to lead lives of service in a world controlled by the devil. Lomperis traces the contemporary manifestations of this theological belief in the strong commitment to education and service among American Lutherans.

Whereas Luther had a clear belief in the devil and his control in the world, the other major strand of the Reformation, the Reformed tradition, focuses on evil in its human manifestation of sin and the "total depravity of man."

In chapter 4, James W. Skillen identifies unique political problems caused by the strong emphasis on predestination in the Reformed tradition. Skillen posits that the emphasis on predestination has historically been linked to groups believing that they are somehow ordained by God to be the new Israel. The danger of "chosen people myths," well documented in the literature of comparative politics, suggests perilous consequences, from exclusion to genocide (Smith 1992). Skillen argues for a Reformed political perspective that moves beyond predestination and the depravity of man and focuses on creation. If human beings are made in the image of God and every sphere of life can be reformed to better mirror God's image, then Christians have a particular role in governing to reform, so as to bring creation more in line with God's character. Skillen questions whether this can be done through the modern system of nations and states that we have. He argues that although the goal of the Reformed Christian in governance is clear, the institutions for achieving that goal are unspecified. Skillen's emphasis on creation as a theological distinctive of the Reformed tradition provides a new perspective on how Christians can envision their role in governance and politics.

Anabaptists read the Bible with a hermeneutic that privileges the life of Christ. Anabaptist political thought is often narrowed to pacifism, its most obvious political marker, but Anabaptists also have a complex understanding of citizenship and a unique view of the role of government. The Anabaptist break with the Reformation took place over the appropriate roles of the church and the state, specifically related to baptism, tithing, and the swearing of oaths. Today, Anabaptists in a variety of denominations still struggle with the appropriate role of the state. In chapter 5, I present a contemporary Anabaptist view of government: that it has a role of providing order so that the mission of the church can be fulfilled. This conception of the rightful place of government in service to the church sets Anabaptists apart from other Christian traditions. Anabaptists believe that the church should be the primary community for the Christian. This opinion has led to both pacifism and an understanding of citizenship in heaven that affects their political behavior in ways ranging from ambivalence about politics to protest against policies viewed as harmful to the worldwide church.

Only a few years after new Christian churches originated in the Reformation, ecclesiastical change continued in Europe with the birth of the Anglican Church in England. King Henry VIII did not agree with Martin Luther and did not support what was happening with the church in Germany. However, the establishment of an autonomous church in England had more to do with English politics and the future of the Tudor monarchy than with theological disagreements. Anglicanism developed theologically under Elizabeth I, embracing a strong support of the state by the church. In chapter 6, Leah Seppanen Anderson argues that conceptually, the state and church were to cooperate to provide "good governance and sound religion." As Anglicanism expanded through the British colonial project, it became more diverse, and the church changed to accommodate its varied constituencies. The first shoots of evangelicalism sprang up within the Anglican Church through the work of John and Charles Wesley in the 18th century. Although the work of the Wesleys later gave rise to Methodism, they never formally left the Anglican Church; they argued that the revivalist movement was well within the bounds of Anglicanism. Many evangelicals since have found a haven in Anglicanism, yet it is precisely the strain caused by the conservative evangelical branch of Anglicanism that has led to the present major conflicts within the global Anglican communion. The Anglican Church struggles to maintain the diversity resulting from its tremendous growth outside England in the 20th and 21st centuries.

Evangelicalism leavens each of these traditions in some form as a "tendency" demanding the primacy of biblical authority, personal salvation, and sharing the gospel message with others. In chapter 7, Timothy Samuel Shah traces the history of evangelicalism from its "prehistory" in the 17th-century Dutch Mennonites, through the life and work of John Wesley and the Great Awakening, into the contemporary era. Though, as with some of the other traditions detailed in this book, there is no unified tradition of political thought within evangelicalism, Shah notes that one can see certain political predispositions in the evangelical tradition that privilege the preaching and spread of the gospel over political goals. Yet by the 18th century, we can identify trends in evangelical political action that followed certain themes: a belief that the state should protect religious freedom, a concern with the virtue of the citizenry, support for limited government, and political action to alleviate human suffering.

Evangelicalism and Pentecostalism are both movements that draw adherents from particular denominations but can also claim supporters across a variety of Christian traditions. Pentecostalism has become one of the most rapidly growing Christian traditions, particularly outside Europe and North America (Barrett et al. 2001). Pentecostalism emphasizes the active role of the Holy Spirit in the life of a believer and the "second work of grace"—the baptism in the Holy Spirit. For Pentecostals, reading scripture is supplemented by the revelation that the Holy Spirit gives to the individual believer. In chapter 8, Stephen Swindle astutely notes that the authority given to individual revelation precludes a coherent view of the appropriate role of Christian citizenship in relation to the state, as each believer may be led by the Spirit to a distinct opinion. The status given to individual interpretation makes Pentecostal political behavior varied and unpredictable. The political unpredictability of Pentecostalism is also found in nondenominational churches that might not call themselves Pentecostal but privilege the role of individual revelation in a similar manner.

In the concluding chapter, Mark Amstutz discusses the similarities in political approaches that exist in the traditions that are discussed in the book. He draws out four themes: the dignity of person, the universality and persistence of human sin, the need for a limited state, and the church's priority of proclaiming the gospel. Amstutz reminds readers that no single tradition expresses fully the divine strategy of redemption and that they are not fixed, but dynamic and responsive to a changing world.

The following chapters are not written by theologians. They are not authoritative statements of faith. Rather, they are informed reflections on the political implications of theological beliefs written by political scientists within these traditions. Each of the authors has tried to capture the essence of his or her Christian tradition, which is not an easy endeavor for denominations or movements that intentionally construct a broad theology of politics to promote inclusion. Different opinions and disagreement with those articulated are to be expected, particularly in terms of the perceived political implications of the traditions. Our hope is that these essays contribute to a fruitful conversation on the diversity of political manifestations of Christian faith and how the changing composition of the church might affect theological development in North America and elsewhere.

NOTES

1. It is not exclusively the case for Christians, and the impact of other religions in American politics and in the lives of politicians can also be noted.

2. See, for example, the work of Stephen Ellis and Gerrie Ter Haar on the role of religion in Africa (Ellis and Ter Haar 2004).

3. Romans 13 was certainly not referring to the modern state as we now know it, an entity that came into existence with the Treaty of Westphalia in 1648. However, it is referring to political authority more generally.

4. There is an intentional focus on the Western church in this book and no attempt here to integrate the position of the Eastern church on the role of the state after the Great Schism of 1054. One could make an argument for presenting even more denominational positions, but they begin to collapse into one another. Though there are some fine points of division, for example, within the Reformed tradition, Skillen's chapter captures a broad outline of beliefs that would be recognizable to Presbyterians and those in the Reformed churches.

5. Although we see in the Catholic tradition a changing position that has embraced the notion of religious freedom after Vatican II. Prior to Vatican II, the limits on the state were less obvious.

6. Though there are examples of Pentecostal experiences in churches all over the globe around the turn of the 20th century.

BIBLIOGRAPHY

Barrett, David A., George Kurian, and Todd Johnson. 2001. *World Christian Encyclopedia*. 2nd ed. 2 vols. New York: Oxford University Press.

Berger, Peter L. 2004. "The Global Picture." *Journal of Democracy* 15(2): 76–80.

Ellis, Stephen, and Gerrie Ter Haar. 2004. *Worlds of Power: Religious Thought and Political Practice in Africa.* New York: Oxford University Press.

Guth, James L., Lyman A. Kellstedt, John C. Green, and Corwin E. Smidt. 2005. "Religious Coalitions in American Politics." *Books and Culture* 11(6): 32.

Haas, Ernst B. 1997. *Nationalism, Liberalism and Progress.* Ithaca, NY: Cornell University Press.

Hertzke, Allen D. 2004. *Freeing God's Children: The Unlikely Alliance for Global Human Rights.* New York: Rowman and Littlefield.

Jenkins, Philip. 2002. *The Next Christendom: The Rise of Global Christianity.* New York: Oxford University Press.

Niebuhr, H. Richard. 1951. *Christ and Culture.* New York: Harper and Row.

Putnam, Robert D. 2000. *Bowling Alone: The Collapse and Revival of American Community.* New York: Simon and Schuster.

Smith, Anthony D. 1992. "Chosen Peoples: Why Ethnic Groups Survive." *Ethnic and Racial Studies* 15(3): 436–456.

Weber, Max. 1994. "The Profession and Vocation of Politics." In *Political Writings.* New York: Cambridge University Press.

Woodberry, Robert D., and Timothy S. Shah. 2004. "The Pioneering Protestants." *Journal of Democracy* 15(2): 47–61.

2

The Catholic Tradition and the State: Natural, Necessary, and Nettlesome

Robert B. Shelledy

Max Weber defines the state as a "human community that (success-fully) claims the monopoly of the legitimate use of physical force with a given territory" (Weber 1946: 78). This particular political institu-tion is the foundation of the modern international political system, which scholars conventionally date back to the Peace of Westphalia in 1648. Although academics might quibble over the exact date, that period marked a transition from feudal to modern authority patterns (Krasner 1993; Philpott 2001). A consistent presence throughout this period of transition was the Catholic Church. However, there have been significant changes in the Catholic perspective on the state from the medieval period to the current day.

According to Catholic teaching, the state is a natural and necessary element of our lives. The efforts of the state should be directed toward the common good: respecting and protecting human rights and provid-ing order. Although the Catholic Church currently accepts and affirms the state, it originally resisted the emergence of sovereign states as Europe transitioned to modernity. This resistance has subsided, giving way to the Catholic Church's current affirmation of the state, yet some tensions remain. As a transnational organization with its administra-tive center in Rome, the Catholic Church will always be in conflict with any entity that claims exclusive control over a given geographic area, as it asserts its authority over its members in the same regions.

The first section of this chapter highlights the difficulties in for-mulating a "Catholic perspective" on the state. The second describes the ideal state from a Catholic perspective and traces a broad historical overview of the modern state's development and the Catholic Church's reaction. The third discusses divergences within Catholic perspectives, as well as divergences between Catholicism and other religious perspectives. The chapter concludes with a reflection on the Catholic understanding of solidarity, its implications in terms of nationalism, and the limitations of state prerogatives in international relations.

Historical Background

In *Finnegans Wake* the novelist James Joyce refers to the Catholic Church as "here comes everybody." The Catholic Church is an extremely large worldwide religious organization of approximately 17 percent of the world's population, making Catholicism the world's second largest religion (Nichols 1981: 21).[1] Catholicism is distinguishable from Islam, Buddhism, Hinduism, and other branches of Christianity by its organizational structure, which is a formal hierarchy with a well-defined social structure. The central feature of this structure is the division of the "whole earth's surface into territorial units . . . governed or ruled, through papal authorization, by a residential bishop or a person of equivalent or near-equivalent rank" (Vallier 1972: 130). Every Catholic is responsible to his or her bishop, who in turn is responsible to the pope, who is head of the church.

Despite its religious nature, the Catholic Church is similar to other bureaucracies in that members are capable of a high degree of independent action (Barnett and Finnemore 1999). For example, just as the foreign policy of a country varies across different branches of its bureaucracy (Allison 1971), so, too, Catholic "policy" varies across the church. There can be a diversity of goals among the efforts of the pope himself and other groupings within the Vatican, such as the Secretariat of State and the Pontifical Council for Justice and Peace. The Catholic Church may also work through and with individual bishops or national bishops' conferences to advance its policy goals.

In addition to these organizational issues, Catholicism provides a large body of theological reflection on the state. All Christian denominations draw on the long Catholic tradition of reflection about the relationship of the church and political authority. Following in this tradition, in 1891, when confronted with the Industrial Revolution and mass democratic movements, Leo XIII wrote the encyclical *Rerum Novarum*. This was the beginning of a series of papal encyclicals on the economic, political, and social order of the world that form the core of Catholic social doctrine.[2] Premised on the inherent dignity of the human person and the idea of the common good, Catholic social doctrine seeks to build a more just society and provide criteria to guide Catholics' participation in public life.[3]

Even so, neither Catholicism nor Catholic social doctrine is monolithic but, rather, complex and differentiated (Tergel 1998: 112). Therefore, one should keep in mind what Michael Fleet calls "instances of the Church": the Catholic Church is both a whole organization and a conglomeration of many different parts, each capable of acting independently, developing its own constituencies, and cultivating its own resources.[4]

Catholicism has inspired such diverse organizations as the pacifist Catholic Worker movement and the traditionalist Opus Dei. Individual Catholics vary in their political beliefs to such an extent that Catholics served in government in both Franco's Spain and Ortega's Nicaragua. These examples should give one pause before articulating a Catholic perspective on any topic. This is even truer when the topic is as complex as the modern state. In an effort to avoid becoming mired in complexity and to circumvent the many ecclesiological debates over who truly makes up the Catholic Church, the official hierarchy, the faithful, and the tradition, we do well to paraphrase Henry Kissinger's quip about Europe, "If one wants to talk to the Catholic Church, one calls the pope." This chapter concentrates on the "official" Catholic Church: that of the formal hierarchy and particularly the pope. With these caveats in mind, the next section traces the Catholic view of the ideal state.

A Catholic Perspective on the State

Readers should keep in mind Terry Nardin's insight that the significant divide in modern political thought is not between left and right; it is between those who see the state as an instrument for promoting particular purposes, a conservative view, and those who see it as a framework within which people can pursue their own self-chosen purposes, a liberal view.[5]

The Catholic Church takes the conservative view in that the state "is and must be a positive and irreplaceable component of civil life" (Compendium [2005] #393 citing #1897 of the Catechism [2000]).[6] The state is responsible for promoting the particular purpose of the common good. As stated in greater detail later, historically the Catholic Church has also considered the state responsible for promoting Catholicism.

The thought that the state has a positive role is a more benign view of the state than the tension that Luther observes, according to Timothy J. Lomperis in chapter 3 of this book. In Catholic belief, the world is not "in the grip of the devil" but merely marred by sin. Although merely a matter of degrees, Catholic belief is more optimistic about humans' ability to achieve some measure of justice here and now than Lomperis's analysis of Luther.

This role of the state as positive and irreplaceable is the logical implication of the premise in Catholic thought that human beings are inherently social. Humans can find their truest earthly fulfillment only in relationship with others. This general orientation underpins much of Catholic social doctrine. The state then pursues the common good through global solidarity and a preferential love for the poor.

In Catholic teaching, the state is "founded on human nature and hence belongs to the order designed by God" (*Gaudium et spes:* paragraph 74). The state is both natural and necessary because people are inherently social beings, and only in relationships do people live out their calling to love God and their neighbor. Therefore, participation in all aspects of society is vocational for Catholics.

From a Catholic perspective, the state has a positive role beyond the mere provision of physical security. The state has a responsibility to promote the common good, which "embraces the sum of those conditions of the social life whereby men, families and associations more adequately and readily may attain their own perfection" (*Gaudium et spes:* paragraph 74). There is a presumption that the state will be involved in solving social problems. Catholic teaching is therefore at odds with a libertarian view of the state in which "government is the problem."[7]

This theoretical formulation corresponds with a long history of Catholic Church involvement with states and their precursors. This involvement was often antagonistic but has changed throughout the development of the present global system. Interestingly, the Vatican itself has been a formally recognized state through much of this history.

Since the Middle Ages, the Vatican has been a central actor in European politics (Hall 1997; Philpott 2001). More than a thousand years ago, Pepin, the king of the Franks, granted the pope the Papal States, and since that time, with only one major interruption, the popes have been the temporal rulers of parts of modern-day central Italy (Graham 1959: 157). During most of this time, the Catholic Church resisted the emergence and existence of the state. The Catholic Church approved of a state only when it upheld the Church's authority and enforced the faith (Philpott 2004). Under pressure from liberalism, mass political movements, industrialization, and communism, the Catholic Church begrudgingly shifted its position and accepted states.

From Christmas Day 800 A.D. through the Reformation and the Treaty of Westphalia (1648), Europe was ruled under the "two swords" of emperor and church. In the words of St. Augustine, humans were citizens of two cities, one earthly and one heavenly. All of European society was viewed as ordered into a system of ends and purposes and therefore maintained the potential for complete unity and harmony (Hanson 1987: 26). Christendom enveloped the entire European world (or civilized world, as it was called) and was subject to the "universal monarchy" of the papacy. Although history rarely achieved this serene ideal, it did record actions at least partially intended to be a reflection of it, such as Concordat of Worms.

The unity of Christendom was undergirded by the assertion of absolute sovereignty of the church in both temporal and spiritual matters. There was one church and one emperor subject to the spiritual authority of the church. Popes raised and led armies in defense of papal territory and had all the attendant problems of contemporary temporal rulers. Papal statecraft even provided certain examples for Machiavelli's *The Prince*.

Secular rulers, the Reformation, and the rise of the modern state challenged medieval Christendom. Rulers questioned the authority of the papacy in several different ways. One of the most explicit challenges was the investiture conflict, in which Emperor Henry IV asserted that he could appoint bishops. The pope disagreed, and this led to the Henry's eventual excommunication and submission. Yet, even today some secular states, such as China, have asserted the right to appoint Catholic bishops (Leung 1992; Reese 1996: 232–241).

Martin Luther's posting of his Ninety-five Theses in 1517 was an even greater confrontation to church authority than were secular rulers. The church's inability to recognize and reform internal laxity and corruption led to a division of Christianity into numerous denominations. Christianity's division contributed to almost a hundred years of warfare, most of which was fought on "religious" grounds and shattered the medieval political order (Philpott 2001).

In what became the political sphere of human activity, the unitary, hierarchical structure of medieval life yielded ground to a system in which independent units or states were dealt with as de jure equals and not along an elaborate ladder of lords and vassals (Graham 1959: 102). Temporal rulers asserted their independence by claiming greater and greater discretion within their territory, seeking even to conquer parts of the Papal States.

The period from 1779 to 1965 witnessed the Catholic Church resisting many aspects of modern states, including the demand for secularity, total allegiance, democracy, and religious freedom. The French Revolution of 1789 ushered in almost a hundred years of steady decline in the material fortunes of the Catholic Church. This decline continued through the nineteenth century as Spanish, Austrian, French, and Italian troops occupied parts of the Papal States. Even so, as late as 1859, the Papal States consisted of 17,218 square miles, roughly the size of Switzerland, and had a population of more than three million people (Cardinale 1976: 99). These material challenges were part of the Catholic Church's ideological struggle with liberalism.

Liberalism, even in the eighteenth and nineteenth centuries, is difficult to define. Liberalism's core tenets prior to the 1870s were "a belief that progress, leading to final perfection, could be achieved by means of free institutions, such as freely elected parliaments, accountable ministers, independent judiciaries, freedom of speech, press, religion, assembly, careers open to talent, the protection of property, and due process before the law" (Steinfels 1994: 23).

Liberalism encouraged greater democracy and greater participation in political life. The fifty years between 1870 and 1920 saw an increase in the opportunities for mass political activity, in large part because of industrialization, a movement into urban areas, and an extension of the franchise.

Prior to the development of mass political activity, church authorities handled Catholic political activity in or through direct negotiations with the particular state governments. The church was one of a few elite institutions that governed during the previous era. The liberal confrontation with ancient institutions included a challenge to the Catholic Church and to the temporal power of the pope. There the alliance of throne and altar was questioned. In addition, for various reasons, certain liberals were extremely anticlerical.[8]

Throughout the 1800s, the church struggled with liberalism both externally and internally. While hailed as a liberal at the time of his election, rather than embracing liberalism as expected, Pius IX recoiled from the events of the Revolution of 1848 and reasserted the church's antiliberal stance. Pius IX enshrined this position in the *Syllabus of Errors* of 1864, which Whyte describes as "a comprehensive denunciation of liberal doctrines such as freedom of speech, freedom of the press, and freedom of worship. It ended with a ringing condemnation of the idea that the Holy Roman Pontiff can and ought to reconcile himself to what is called progress, liberty and modern civilization" (1981: 36).

The nadir of this challenge for the Catholic Church was Italian unification, when in 1870, in what was called the Risorgimento, Italian troops conquered the Papal States (Crawford 1979: 153).[9] When Italian troops were on the verge of taking the Vatican, Pius IX called the First Vatican Council (1869–1870). This council promulgated the doctrine of papal infallibility, meaning that when the pope speaks formally ex cathedra on faith and morals (which is very rare), the teaching becomes Catholic dogma (Burns 1992). Two months later, Italian troops stormed Rome, ending more than a thousand years of Vatican temporal authority (Gontard 1964: 512).

The Roman Question is the term describing the controversy between the Vatican and the Italian government from 1870 to 1929 over the status of the

Vatican. Neither of the two would recognize the other's sovereignty, and each considered the other to be interfering in its internal affairs. On February 11, 1929, however, the Italian government, under Mussolini, and the Vatican, under Pius XI, signed the Lateran Treaty. Pursuant to the treaty, Italy ceded the Vatican forty-four hectares, which became the new State of the Vatican City (Kunz, 1952: 312). Italy recognized the sovereignty of the Vatican and recognized the Catholic Church as the official state religion.[10] In turn, the Vatican recognized the Italian government.[11]

During the period of the Roman Question, many Catholic leaders began to look for means to accommodate liberal ideas within a Catholic framework. The popes also made some efforts to comment on current conditions, such as Leo XIII's encyclical *Rerum Novarum* regarding the conditions of workers and their rights. In the encyclical, Leo XIII defended the right to private property and vigorously denounced socialism; however, he also wrote: "[T]he poor and badly off have a claim to especial consideration. The richer class have many ways of shielding themselves, and stand less in need of help from the State; whereas the mass of the poor have no resources of their own to fall back upon, and must chiefly depend upon the assistance of the State" (*Rerum Novarum*: paragraph 37). Despite being stateless and so-called prisoners of the Vatican, during the Roman Question, popes continued their involvement in world affairs. Most dramatically, Benedict XV made many efforts to negotiate an end to World War I and founded the precursor to modern refugee organizations (Pollard 1999: 112–139).

In the early to mid-twentieth century, in light of the growing appeal of religious freedom, the Catholic Church adopted a policy prescription of the "thesis and hypothesis" (Murray 1993: 133–134; Pavlischek 1994: 41–46). In the eyes of the Vatican, the optimal situation was the thesis: an established Catholic Church, in which "the state recognizes the role of the Catholic Church in (legislation)" (Hehir 1993: 19). The Vatican sought political allies who would establish the Catholic Church as the official church of the state.[12] The alliance of church and state has had significant implications for both the Catholic Church and those countries in which such alliances existed (Casanova 1994).[13] In other situations, different types of legal arrangements, which were referred to as the hypothesis, were permissible. In other words, in states with a Catholic majority, there should be an established Catholic Church. In states in which Catholics are a minority, pluralist arrangements are regrettably acceptable. Not surprisingly, many were suspicious of this limited commitment to religious freedom.

The twentieth century witnessed another challenge to Catholicism, communism. Communism's strictly atheistic and materialist viewpoints were anathema to the Catholic Church. The Vatican was firmly anticommunist;

resisting communism in Eastern and Western Europe, Asia, and Latin America. Ironically, this position led the Vatican first to a tolerance, if not outright promotion, of fascism but ultimately set it on the gradual path to acceptance of democracy.

Between 1850 and 1942, the Vatican had been, at best, ambivalent about the development of democracy and, at worse, an active opponent (Casanova 1994: 9). Not until 1942 did the Vatican officially accept democracy as a legitimate form of government (Pius XII 1942). As the Cold War bifurcated the world into two camps, the Vatican's strident anticommunism made it a natural ally of the Western democratic countries (Hanson 1987). These developments reflected a shift in the Vatican's attitude toward the modern world that culminated in the Second Vatican Council. The Second Vatican Council (1962–1965) was the most recent of the twenty-one ecumenical councils in the history of Catholic Christianity. John XXIII called the council for an aggiornamento ("bringing up to date") to review the "new conditions and forms of life introduced into the modern world" and the church's role in it (Komonchak 1994).[14] In Vatican II, the Catholic Church rejected an establishment model of church-state relations and the thesis-hypothesis reasoning (Dupuy 1980: 245). Instead, the church moved toward a tolerance of pluralism and the promotion of religious freedom. As part of the process, John XXIII issued the encyclical *Pacem in Terris,* in which he wrote: "14. This too must be listed among the rights of a human being, to honor God according to the sincere dictates of his own conscience, and therefore the right to practice his religion privately and publicly." The Second Vatican Council's *Dignitatis Humanae* (Declaration on Religious Liberty) confirmed this support for religious freedom and emphasis on human rights (Hanson 1987: 120; Tergel 1998: 179). It was argued that states should provide support for religious institutions and organizations because of the important role religion plays in society. These institutions and organizations need not be exclusively Catholic.

The council's efforts vis-à-vis the political world resulted in the *Gaudium et Spes* (Pastoral Constitution on the Church in the Modern World). The council asserted that not only did the Church have something to teach the modern world but also the modern world had something to teach the church. Instead of relying solely on a "state to state" relationship, the church must reach out to broader aspects of society. Catholic laity were to play a distinct role in society, with ordained clergy providing spiritual guidance. *Gaudium et Spes* emphasized the particular expertise of the laity in secular affairs and looked for the laity to bring the light of the gospel into the world. The church no longer demanded a formal organization to provide a de jure role in society. As *Gaudium et Spes*[15] states: "[S]he (the Roman Catholic Church) does not lodge her hope in privileges conferred by civil authority. Indeed, she stands ready to renounce the exercise of certain legitimately acquired rights if it becomes clear that their use raises doubt about the sincerity of her witness or that new conditions of life demand some other arrangement" (Article VI, Section 76).

Not "lodging hope in privileges conferred by civil authority" is completely opposite the strategy used by the Vatican throughout the 1800s and first half of the 1900s, when it explicitly sought state support in religious education and religious activities. Now, even though the church still has a political message, this is a by-product of the religious message of the church. J. Bryan Hehir explains, quoting *Gaudium et Spes:* "Christ, to be sure, gave his church no proper mission in the political, economic or social order. The purpose which he set before her is a religious one. But out of this religious mission itself comes a function, a light, and an energy which can serve to structure and consolidate the human community according to the divine law" (1990: 37). The Vatican sees itself as leading this light of the world and sees its mission to be the conscience of humankind. The Vatican's ideological claims,[16] based on a universal religious code, frequently conflict with those of many states. This opposition is most obvious in communist countries with atheistic ideologies, but it occurs also in countries with capitalist ideologies that emphasize economic efficiency.

Divergences

Any effort to bring together different approaches to a given topic seeks to encourage comparison among the approaches. Before moving on to that comparison, this section first addresses comparisons between a traditional international relations perspective and Catholic viewpoints. International relations' most prominent paradigm, realism, takes a statist view and presumes that states are the most significant organizations in world politics.

Religions generally, and Catholicism in particular, present a transnational challenge to this view and to the Westphalian models of sovereignty (Byrnes 2001: 9–12; Rudolph 1997: 12). Sovereignty is premised on the exclusion of other authorities, and even though the Vatican strives to exclude outside authority from certain areas of social life, as Krasner explains in his model of Westphalian sovereignty, these "areas" are not territorial. Instead, the Vatican strives to exclude other authorities from "religious" issues, a claim that aims at giving the Vatican transnational authority that is different from that of states.[17]

Although most often discussed in terms of economic integration and the European Union, the new medievalism or neomedievalism offers a different theoretical starting point for research on the influence of religious actors vis-à-vis the state (Friedrichs 2001). Religious actors are an excellent subject matter for empirical studies of authority in international relations. In addition to the transnational nature of the Catholic Church, each of the chapters in this book points to the transnational influence of different Christian traditions; for example, see Swindle's chapter 8 on Pentecostalism, which was founded in the United States and has grown in numbers and influence in Latin America and Asia.

Beyond this challenge to dominant paradigms in international relations scholarship, a Catholic perspective on the state is often questioned internally. The most notable example is the Society of St. Pius X, which was led by Archbishop Marcel Lefebvre, who died in 1991. The Society of St. Pius X disagreed with several parts of Second Vatican Council, particularly the council's rejection of the previous preference for state recognition of Catholicism to one of religious freedom (Rico 2002). The society holds to the pre–Vatican II view that ideally the state will be a Catholic one. The society has been in schism from the Catholic Church since 1988, although its members believe that it is not in schism.

Although less dramatic than the Society of St. Pius X, differing views on the implications of a Catholic view of the state are numerous. Often these differing views are matters of prudential judgment as to the best course of action in given circumstances. For example, Pius XI authorized a concordat with Nazi Germany in 1933. After the Nazis failed to honor it, Pius XI wrote the 1937 encyclical *Mit Brennender Sorge,* condemning the Nazi ideology. Pius XI's successor, Pius XII, who was elected in 1939, was less confrontational (Sánchez 2002; Kertzer 2001). Neither pope disagreed about the role of the state in society, but they did disagree on the most prudent approach to Nazism.

Another example, after Vatican II, of differing views about the implications of Catholic views of the state related to the first Persian Gulf War of 1990–1991 (Shelledy 2003). Throughout the buildup to the war, John Paul II and the Vatican remained constant in their message against the war. Even so, Catholic bishops in the countries directly involved in the war presented a broader range of opinions, which ranged from reluctant approval of the military option by the United Kingdom's Basil Cardinal Hume to pacifist rejection of all uses of the military by U.S. bishop Thomas Gumbleton. Of all Catholic bishops in the world, the most outspoken critic of the war was Raphael Bidawid, the patriarch of the Chaldean Catholic Church. George Weigel, a prominent lay Catholic commentator, argued that the approach of some U.S. bishops and the Vatican converted Catholic just-war teaching into a functional pacifism (Weigel 1991: 66).

Interestingly, from a sociological standpoint, disagreement over the implications of Catholic views has led some Catholics into political alliances with other religious actors who do not share the underlying premises about the state. For example, some Catholics found themselves politically allied with Mennonites against the 2003 U.S. invasion of Iraq, not because, as some Mennonites believed, the state should never resort to violence, but because violence was not justified in the given circumstances.

The Catholic viewpoint diverges from other Christian perspectives because of ideological and organizational differences. Ideologically, the Catholic Church views the state as having a positive role to play in society. Organizationally, the Catholic Church has a unique transnational structure and outlook that can present a challenge to the authority of states. Moreover, the Catholic Church's organization allows it to make definitive and authoritative changes in teaching, unlike other denominations that do not make theological changes from the top down.

The Catholic approach to the state is a communal one that recognizes a significant role for organizations in society, including the state. The egalitarianism of Luther's outlook and the almost entrepreneurial nature of evangelical churches are different from Catholic viewpoints. Catholic leaders across the globe raise great concerns about the rampant individualism of the modern world. Modern Catholic social doctrine arose in the ferment of 19th-century Europe, where atheistic socialism competed with individualistic capitalism.

Organizationally, the Catholic Church is also distinct. Its institutional structure provides many different points of entry into political processes. Catholics in a particular country may bypass their own government by appealing to Catholics in other countries, to their bishop, and to the Vatican. Obviously, other religious groups have a similar ability to garner transnational support, but this is most formalized in the Catholic Church. An excellent example is the Catholic Church in China, which is divided between a government-controlled Chinese Catholic Patriotic Association (CPA) and an underground Catholic Church loyal to Rome.[18] Underground Catholics have made numerous pleas for support from the Vatican, which has provided them with material and diplomatic support. This has created tension between the Vatican and the Chinese government, which does not welcome or recognize the intervention of the church.

The organizational structure of the Catholic Church reinforces worldwide Catholic solidarity. "Solidarity" in Catholic social thought is "not a feeling of vague compassion . . . at the misfortunes of so many people, [but] a firm and persevering determination to commit oneself to . . . the good of all and of each individual, because we are all really responsible for all" (*Sollicitudo rei socialis:* paragraph 38). Ideally, Catholics recognize everyone across the globe as sister and brother regardless of citizenship, race, or economic status. Again, many religions share this global outlook, but it is institutionally reinforced in the Catholic Church.

Finally, the Catholic Church's hierarchical structure allows for definitive solutions of doctrinal disputes. As was seen earlier, the Second Vatican Council resolved the debate between "thesis-hypothesis" and religious freedom viewpoints. Once "Rome has spoken" on an issue, it is formally resolved. In less hierarchical religious structures, religious disputes with political implications can linger longer unresolved. Of course, one also needs to keep in mind that the Second Vatican Council's embrace of religious freedom took place seventeen years after the adoption of the Universal Declaration of Human Rights by the United Nations and that Italy disestablished Catholicism only in 1982.

The Catholic Tradition and Contemporary Politics

Catholic perspectives on the state have two implications for politics in the early 21st century. First, Catholic social doctrine provides an intellectual framework for a communal vision of politics in opposition to more libertarian or individualistic visions. Second, Catholic views provide a global vision of solidarity instead of narrower nationalistic views. However, tensions within the Catholic Church due to its complex and differentiated nature hamper efforts to bring a "Catholic" vision forward into everyday politics.

The Catholic view of the positive role of the state supports a stronger role for the state in the economy and social life than other more conservative views. This is particularly true in the area of social welfare (see Esping-Anderson 1990). As socialist and Marxist ideologies have fallen out of favor, Catholic social thought provides an alternative approach for more communal and statist approaches to politics. The emphasis on natural law in Catholic social thought makes it accessible to non-Catholics and compatible with nonsectarian dialogues.[19]

Despite a commitment to the positive role for the state, Catholic perspectives are tempered by the transnational nature of Catholicism. Ideas of solidarity and a global common good limit a state's prerogatives in the international system. This emphasis on the global, international good has implications for a state's national interest in both security and economics. A Catholic perspective does not support a state that merely follows its own exclusive national interest. Issues of security and economic development are a concern for everyone and not just the citizens of a single country or group of countries. In the field of economics, the Catholic teaching of a preferential love for the poor also limits the acceptable policy choices of states. The Catholic Church was influential in the international campaign for debt relief and has been strong advocate for international development aid. During the Jubilee 2000 debt relief campaign, the church educated

Catholics around the world about the problems debt service payments cause in countries pursuing economic development.

Jubilee 2000 was part of a larger pattern whereby the Catholic Church has taken on the role of advocate for many states from the global South. Beginning with John XXIII's 1961 encyclical *Mater et Magistra,* through Paul VI's 1967 *Populorum Progressio,* to John Paul II's 1988 *Sollicitudo Rei Socialis* and 1991 *Centesimus Annus,* popes have raised the issue of the unjust treatment of the developing world. J. Bryan Hehir asserts that support for the least developed countries is a major part of the Catholic Church's "foreign policy" (1990: 44).

This support illustrates the broader idea of solidarity. As John Paul II stated, "[M]embership in the Catholic community is not determined by nationality, or by social, or ethnic origin" (2003). Catholic social doctrine rejects nationalism and focuses on the universal human family. However, in many nationalistic struggles, such as Ireland, Poland, and East Timor, Catholic identity has played a large role. Conversely, Catholic identity in other situations has failed to overcome different identities, most tragically in Rwanda.[20]

In spite of clear Catholic teachings regarding the positive role of the state and global solidarity, the Catholic Church continues to struggle with issues of internal pluralism. In any large organization, maintaining coherence is difficult, and this is especially true in a transnational organization where there is an inherent tension between local and central activities. Crosscutting cleavages are constantly at play. For example, there are contemporary Catholics who reject the church's view on religious freedom and oppose its assertion from Rome. In addition, the teachings of the Catholic Church are broad enough on many political issues that significant differences arise regarding the proper means to accomplish a given goal, for example, religious freedom in China. Cognizant of this possibility, the Second Vatican Council wrote:

> Often enough the Christian view of things will itself suggest some specific solution in certain circumstances. Yet it happens rather frequently, and legitimately so, that with equal sincerity some of the faithful will disagree with others on a given matter. Even against the intentions of their proponents, however, solutions proposed on one side or another may be easily confused by many people with the Gospel message. Hence it is necessary for people to remember that no one is allowed in the aforementioned situations to appropriate the Church's authority for his opinion. They should always try to enlighten one another through honest discussion, preserving mutual charity and caring above all for the common good. (*Gaudium et spes:* paragraph 43)

Beyond the "official" church, all of this points to a great deal of political pluralism among Catholics. Not surprisingly, in the 1960 U.S. presidential election, Catholics formed a solid Democratic voting bloc behind John F. Kennedy, the Catholic and Democratic candidate. That trend began to change, however, beginning with the 1972 presidential election in which Richard Nixon, the Republican incumbent, won reelection. Since then, Catholics have increasingly moved toward the Republican Party, and today the Catholic vote is almost equally split between Republicans and Democrats. For example, the Center for Applied Research in the Apostolate at Georgetown University (2004) found that about 52 percent of Catholics voting in the 2004 presidential election voted for President George W. Bush and about 47 percent of Catholics voted for Senator John Kerry. This trend has also been mirrored on a Congressional level, where Catholic members of the U.S. House of Representatives are almost equally split between Republicans and Democrats. Although beyond the scope of this chapter, several interesting questions bear further research on the voting behavior of Catholics in the United States. First, will the trend of regular church attendees continue to favor the Republican Party? Second, what will the effect of increasing numbers of immigrants in the U.S. Catholic Church be on the voting patterns of Catholics? Third, do changes in Catholic voting behavior merely reflect broader social changes, or are Catholics causing those changes?

Conclusion

Despite the analytical difficulties in discerning a single Catholic view of the state, we may safely say that the Catholic Church has accepted and affirmed the existence of the modern state. The state can and should be a positive influence in social life and has specific responsibilities for the common good. As such, a Catholic viewpoint will reject any political position that supports a minimalist state. The acceptance and affirmation of the state has some qualifications. The prerogatives of the state are limited, in particular, by the ideas of global solidarity and a preferential love for the poor. In addition, states are practically limited by the organizational structure of the Catholic Church. The Catholic Church's size and transnational nature provide a means for Catholics to bypass the state in some circumstances, which places limits on state power. The necessity of guaranteeing human rights, especially the right of religious freedom, also limits the authority of the state.

The Catholic perspective on the state provides an intellectual challenge for religiously sensitive political groups in the United States. For those on the right, it provides a view of authority based on shared beliefs and the importance of morality, but one that embraces the significant role of the state in American society. For those on the left, it provides a communal vision of politics and a religious language with which to articulate a concern for the poor. As such, the Catholic Church and Catholic social thought can provide the necessary connection between U.S. progressives and evangelicals, who, David Brooks (2005) observes, are more and more influenced by Catholic social teaching to address issues of poverty in the United States and across the globe.

NOTES

1. Even though these numbers are accurate, they represent a wide variation of actual practice and belief. The Catholic Church counts all who are baptized as Catholics as members for their entire lives unless they are excommunicated. So, for example, Italy is home to more than fifty-seven million Catholics, but only 41 percent of them are likely to attend a Catholic Church service in a given week, which is a requirement of the faith (Marchisio and Pisati 1999: 240–247; Catechism 2000: 2180). Even so, if one counts only "active" Catholics, the Catholic Church is still the largest single Christian church in the world and remains the second largest religion in the world behind Islam.

2. Catholic social doctrine is also called Catholic social teaching or Catholic social thought. It seems that *social doctrine* is now the preferred term, with the Pontifical Council for Justice and Peace's publication of the Compendium of the Social Doctrine of the Church in 2005.

3. The most recent addition to Catholic social doctrine is Pope Benedict XVI's encyclical *Deus caritas est* (December 25, 2005). In his encyclical, Benedict writes: "[T]he pursuit of justice must be a fundamental norm of the State" and "[t]he two spheres (Church and State) are distinct, yet always interrelated." Like much of Catholic social doctrine, this papal document will inspire writings by theologians, philosophers, and public commentators. The Catholic tradition of political reflection is much broader than official doctrine (for example, see the works of Jacques Maritain, John Courtney Murray, Kenneth R. Himes, Michael Novak, and Richard J. Neuhaus). For the reasons stated previously, this chapter focuses on "official" Catholic sources.

4. Personal conversation.

5. The terms *conservative* and *liberal* have their traditional political theory meanings here and not their meanings in contemporary U.S. political dialogue. The conservative view rests on the assumption that any authority is based on shared beliefs. In other words, a common set of beliefs is constitutive of authority in a social order (de Tocqueville [1835] 1956; Durkheim [1915] 1965: 236–245). The influence of authority is a function of the existence of shared beliefs, values, and practices within a given social setting (Durkheim [1915] 1965: 207; Parsons 1960). The liberal view is that the lack of shared beliefs is what makes authority crucial in social relations. In this view, authority solves the inherent problem of chaos in situations with no substantive agreement between the actors. Having a person in authority solves the predicament of disagreement over what is to be done; in other words, when actors cannot agree on a course of action, they select an actor to make the decision for them (Friedman 1973: 140). This

view of authority, often associated with Thomas Hobbes, is based on procedural and not substantive agreement. Any social interaction is part of what Terry Nardin calls a practical association, which assists not in generating shared goals but in tolerance between people (Nardin 1983: 10–14). In this view, the role of authority would be consistent with Goldstein and Keohane's assertion that ideas serve as both focal points and a social cohesive in situations where there is no unique equilibrium outcome (1993: 13–20). Authority prevents inaction or chaos caused by disagreement or uncertainty.

6. This chapter reflects the influence of Rev. Bryan N. Massingale, S.T.D., in particular his lecture "Public Service in the Context of Our Faith," delivered at Marquette University on October 24, 2005. For another view of Catholic perspectives on the state see Manuel et al. (2006).

7. "Government is the problem" is a quote from U.S. president Ronald Reagan's First Inaugural Address and is a slogan of libertarian elements of conservative political movements.

8. Whether anticlericalism was a response to the Roman Catholic Church's antiliberalism or a cause of it is a topic for another paper.

9. Literally "resurgence," but also the term used to label the process of Italian unification.

10. Italy recognized "the sovereignty of the Holy See in the field of international relations as an attribute that pertains to the very nature of the Holy See, in conformity with its traditions and with the demands of its mission in the world" (Shaw 1986: 153).

11. On February 18, 1984, Italian prime minister Bettino Craxi and the Holy See's secretary of state Agostino Cardinal Casaroli signed a new concordat that modified the Lateran Concordat of 1929.

12. For a discussion of different models of church-state relations, see Monsma and Soper (1997: 10–12).

13. Several modern states have sought to replicate this model of a "Catholic state," with Franco's Spain the most infamous example (Lannon 1987; Payne 1994).

14. A great deal of post–Vatican II Catholic scholarship addresses the extent to which the Catholic Church may accept the modern world.

15. This is the Vatican II document regarding the role of the Catholic Church in the world.

16. I am using the term *ideological* in a neutral descriptive sense (Appel 2000). The Vatican rejects the allegation that Catholicism is an ideology (John Paul II 1991: paragraph 46).

17. This is what Spruyt calls translocal authority (1994: 34–57).

18. The numerous books on religious freedom in China include Richard Madsen's *China's Catholics: Tragedy and Hope in an Emerging Civil Society* (Berkeley: University of California Press, 1998) and Jason Kindopp and Carol Lee Hamrin's *God and Caesar in China: Policy Implications of Church-State Tensions* (Washington, DC: Brookings Institution Press, 2004).

19. Evangelicals often use Catholic social thought as a basis for their political positions, which demonstrates its wider use, albeit by other believers. Nonsectarian use of Catholic social thought has been less prevalent.

20. The relationship of Catholic social doctrine and nationalism is an area that deserves further research but is beyond the scope of this chapter. One starting point is Baum (2001).

BIBLIOGRAPHY

Allison, Graham T. 1971. *Essence of Decision: Explaining the Cuban Missile Crisis.* Boston: Little, Brown.

Appel, Hilary. 2000. "The Ideological Determinants of Liberal Economic Reform: The Case of Privatization." *World Politics* 52(4): 520–549.

Barnett, Michael N., and Martha Finnemore. 1999. "The Politics, Power, and Pathologies of International Organizations." *International Organization* 53 (Fall): 699–732.

Baum, Gregory. 2001. *Nationalism, Religion, and Ethics.* Montreal: McGill-Queen's University Press.

Benedict XVI. 2005. *Deus Caritas Est.* http://www.vatican.va/holy_father/benedict_xvi/encyclicals/documents/hf_ben-xvi_enc_20051225_deus-caritas-est_en.html. Accessed February 9, 2006.

Brooks, David. 2005. "A Natural Alliance." *New York Times.* May 26.

Burns, Gene. 1992. *The Frontiers of Catholicism: The Politics of Ideology in a Liberal World.* Berkeley: University of California Press.

Byrnes Timothy A. 2001. *Transnational Catholicism in Postcommunist Europe.* Lanham, MD: Rowman and Littlefield.

Cardinale, Hyginus E. 1976. *The Holy See and the International Order.* Toronto: Macmillan of Canada.

Casanova, Jose. 1994. *Public Religions in the Modern World.* Chicago: University of Chicago Press.

Catechism of the Catholic Church. 2000. 2nd ed. Vatican City: Libreria Editrice Vaticana.

Center for Applied Research in the Apostolate, Georgetown University. 2004. "Catholic Vote in 2004 Election at 63 Percent." *The CARA Report* 10(3).

Compendium of the Social Doctrine of the Church. 2005. Washington, DC: USCCB.

Crawford, James. 1979. *The Creation of States in International Law.* Oxford, UK: Clarendon Press.

De Tocqueville, Alexis. [1835] 1956. *Democracy in America.* Ed. Richard D. Heffner. New York: New American Library.

Dupuy, André. 1980. *La Diplomatie du Saint Siège après le II Concile du Vatican: le pontificat de Paul VI, 1963–1978.* Paris: Téqui.

Durkheim, Émile. [1915] 1965. *The Elementary Forms of the Religious Life.* Trans. Joseph Ward Swain. New York: Free Press.

Esping-Anderson, G. 1990. *The Three Worlds of Welfare Capitalism.* Princeton, NJ: Princeton University Press.

Friedman, Richard. 1973. "On the Concept of Authority in Political Philosophy." In *Concepts in Social and Political Philosophy,* ed. Richard E. Flathman. New York: Macmillan, 121–146.

Friedrichs, Jörg. 2001. "The Meaning of New Medievalism." *European Journal of International Relations* 7(4): 475–502.

Gaudium et spes. 1965. http://www.vatican.va/archive/hist_councils/ii_vatican_council/documents/vat-ii_cons_19651207_gaudium-et-spes_en.html. Accessed January 12, 2006.

Goldstein, Judith, and Robert O. Keohane. 1993. "Ideas and Foreign Policy: An Analytical Framework." In *Ideas and Foreign Policy: Beliefs, Institutions, and Political Change,* eds. Judith Goldstein and Robert O. Keohane. Ithaca, NY: Cornell University Press, 3–30.

Gontard, Friedrich. 1964. *The Chair of Peter: A History of the Papacy.* Trans. A. J. Peeler and E. F. Peeler. New York: Holt, Rinehart and Winston.

Graham, Robert A. 1959. *Vatican Diplomacy: A Study of Church and State on the International Plane.* Princeton, NJ: Princeton University Press.

Hall, Rodney Bruce. 1997. "Moral Authority as a Power Resource." *International Organization* 51 (Autumn): 591–622.

Hanson, Eric O. 1987. *The Catholic Church in World Politics.* Princeton, NJ: Princeton University Press.

Hehir, J. Bryan. 1990. "Papal Foreign Policy." *Foreign Policy* 78 (Spring): 44.

Hehir, J. Bryan. 1993. "Catholicism and Democracy: Conflict, Change, and Collaboration." In *Christianity and Democracy in Global Context,* ed. John Witte Jr. Boulder, CO: Westview, 15–30.

John Paul II. 1991. *Centesimus Annus.* Washington, DC: United States Catholic Conference.

John Paul II. 2003. Papal message for Day of Migrants and Refugees. http://www.vatican.va/holy_father/john_paul_ii/messages/migration/documents/hf_jp-ii_mes_20021202_world-migration-day-2003_en.html. Accessed November 18, 2008.

Kertzer, David I. 2001. *The Popes against the Jews: The Vatican's Role in the Rise of Modern Anti-Semitism.* New York: Alfred A. Knopf.

Komonchak, Joseph A. 1994. "Vatican II and the Encounter between Catholicism and Liberalism." In *Catholicism and Liberalism,* eds. R. Bruce Douglass and David Hollenbach. Cambridge: Cambridge University Press, 76–99.

Krasner, Stephen D. 1993. "Westphalia and All That." In *Ideas and Foreign Policy: Beliefs, Institutions, and Political Change,* eds. Judith Goldstein and Robert O. Keohane. Ithaca, NY: Cornell University Press, 235–264.

Kunz, Josef L. 1952. "The Status of the Holy See in International Law. *American Journal of International Law* 46: 308–314.

Lannon, Frances. 1987. *Privilege, Persecution, and Prophecy: The Catholic Church in Spain, 1875–1975.* New York: Oxford University Press.

Leo XIII. 1891. *Rerum Novarum.* http://www.vatican.va/holy_father/leo_xiii/encyclicals/documents/hf_l-xiii_enc_15051891_rerum-novarum_en.html. Accessed January 12, 2006.

Leung, Beatrice. 1992. *Sino-Vatican Relations: Problems in Conflicting Authority 1976–1986.* Cambridge: Cambridge University Press.

Manuel, Paul Christopher, Lawrence C. Reardon, and Clyde Wilcox, eds. 2006. *The Catholic Church and the Nation-State: Comparative Perspectives*. Washington, DC: Georgetown University Press.

Marchisio, Roberto, and Maurizio Pisati. 1999. "Belonging without Believing: Catholics in Contemporary Italy." *Journal of Modern Italian Studies* 4(2): 236–255.

Monsma, Stephen V., and J. Christopher Soper. 1997. *The Challenge of Pluralism: Church and State in Five Democracies*. Lanham, MD: Rowman and Littlefield.

Murray, John Courtney. 1993. "The Problem of Religious Freedom." In *Religious Liberty: Catholic Struggles with Pluralism/John Courtney Murray*, ed. J. Leon Hooper. Louisville, KY: Westminster/John Knox Press, 127–198.

Nardin, Terry. 1983. *Law, Morality, and the Relations of States*. Princeton, NJ: Princeton University Press.

Nichols, Peter. 1981. *The Pope's Divisions: The Roman Catholic Church Today*. New York: Holt, Rinehart and Winston.

Parsons, Talcott. 1960. *Structure and Process in Modern Societies*. Glencoe, IL: Free Press.

Pavlischek, Keith J. 1994. *John Courtney Murray and the Dilemma of Religious Toleration*. Kirksville, MO: Thomas Jefferson University Press.

Payne, Stanley. 1984. *Spanish Catholicism: An Historical Overview*. Madison: University of Wisconsin Press.

Philpott, Daniel. 2001. *Revolutions in Sovereignty: How Ideas Shaped Modern International Relations*. Princeton, NJ: Princeton University Press.

Philpott, Daniel. 2004. "The Catholic Tradition and Comparative and International Politics." Paper presented at American Political Science Association Convention, Chicago.

Pius XII. 1942. Radio message for Christmas. *Acta Apostolicae Sedis* 35(1943): 6.

Pollard, John. 1999. *The Unknown Pope: Benedict XV (1914–1922) and the Pursuit of Peace*. London: Geoffrey Chapman.

Reese, Thomas J. 1996. *Inside the Vatican: The Politics and Organization of the Catholic Church*. Cambridge, MA: Harvard University Press.

Rico, Hermínio. 2002. *John Paul II and the Legacy of Dignitatis Humanae*. Washington, DC: Georgetown University Press.

Rudolph, Susanne Hoeber. 1997. "Introduction: Religion, States, and Transnational Civil Society." In *Transnational Religion and Fading States*, eds. Susanne Hoeber Rudolph and James Piscatori. Boulder, CO: Westview, 1–26.

Sánchez, José M. 2002. *Pius XII and the Holocaust: Understanding the Controversy*. Washington, DC: Catholic University of America Press.

Shaw, Malcolm N. 1986. *International Law*. Cambridge, UK: Grotius.

Shelledy, Robert B. 2003. *Legions Not Always Visible on Parade: The Vatican's Influence in World Politics*. Ph.D. dissertation, University of Wisconsin.

Spruyt, Hendrik. 1994. *The Sovereign State and Its Competitors: An Analysis of Systems Change*. Princeton, NJ: Princeton University Press.

Steinfels, Peter. 1994. "The Failed Encounter: The Catholic Church and Liberalism in the Nineteenth Century." In *Catholicism and Liberalism: Contributions* to *American Public Philosophy,* eds. R. Bruce Douglass and David Hollenbach. Cambridge: Cambridge University Press, 23.

Tergel, Alf. 1998. *Human Rights in Cultural and Religious Traditions.* Uppsala: Acta Universitatis Upsaliensis.

Vallier, Ivan. 1972. "The Roman Catholic Church: A Transnational Actor." In *Transnational Relations and World Politics,* eds. Robert O. Keohane and Joseph S. Nye Jr. Cambridge, MA: Harvard University Press, 129–152.

Weber, Max. 1946. *Essays in Sociology.* Trans. H. H. Gerth and C. Wright Mill. New York. Oxford University Press.

Weigel, George. 1991. "War, Peace, and Christian Conscience." In *Just War and the Gulf War,* eds. James Turner Johnson and George Weigel. Washington, DC: Ethics and Public Policy Center, 45–90.

Whyte, John Henry. 1981. *Catholics in Western Democracies: A Study in Political Behavior.* New York: St. Martin's Press.

3

Lutheranism and Politics: Martin Luther as a Modernizer, but for the Devil

Timothy J. Lomperis

Martin Luther, the leader of the Protestant Reformation, has often been characterized as running afoul of modern politics. Ernst Troeltsch, for example, has dismissively argued that Luther's connection with modernity lies in reactionary political parties.[1] Reinhold Niebuhr maintained that Luther developed two irreconcilable ethics: a perfectionist private or personal ethic and a cynically realistic political ethic.[2] Like Plato, who was accused of being a modern fascist, Luther's legacy to modern political science is far too important, and complicated, for such easy dismissals.

My thesis is as follows. The three core tenets of Luther's theology—justification by faith alone, *sola scriptura*, and the priesthood of all believers—created an important underpinning for an emerging modern world. Further, his sophisticated, post-Augustinian formulation of "the two kingdoms" provided a central justification for the sovereign and secular modern nation-state and its attendant system of international relations, even as it led him to oppose the just war tradition of his day. What may be described as a Lutheran method or approach to the world, however, is complicated and may be characterized as half modern and half medieval. Finally, what moves from the complicated to the regressive was Luther's persistent fear of the devil. To him, whatever the merits of a rebellion or insurrection, the ensuing anarchy, chaos, and violence was just the opening the devil needed to make his bid for global mastery. But for this fear, Martin Luther would have been a thoroughly modern man.

Moving forward, this persistent belief in the devil by Luther's modern follow-ers, supplemented by the use of Lutheran institutions in the New World as a preserve for Lutheran ethnic identities, has given American Lutherans a decid-edly more politically conservative cast than that of sister Protestant denomina-tions, and certainly than that of European Lutherans.

The Historical Background of Luther's Message

When Martin Luther nailed his Ninety-five Theses on the door of Castle Church in Wittenberg on October 31, 1517, he had no idea that he had just detonated the Protestant Reformation that would permanently divide Western Christi-anity. As a Catholic professor of theology, these theses were an invitation to academic debate among his colleagues. In his own study of the Bible, he had concluded that salvation, or justification, came only by a profession of faith in the sacrifice of Jesus on the cross for human sin and not by any human efforts in good works, even if sanctioned by the church. The topic of most of these theses related to a current campaign by the church in Rome to sell indul-gences to believers that supposedly could forgive sins and help buy the release of the souls of loved ones from purgatory. More materially, the proceeds of these indulgences were being used to finance the reconstruction of St. Peter's Basilica in Rome.

What got Luther in trouble was his further belief that the Bible was the sole authority in resolving any religious controversy. In these debates, then, Luther refused to acknowledge the hierarchical authority of the church, or even that of the pope, as sufficient. For this, Pope Leo X was persuaded to excommunicate Luther in 1521, and in April of that year, Charles V, emperor of the Holy Roman Empire who ruled over Germany, Spain, and much of Italy, ordered Luther to appear before a *diet,* or assembly, at Worms and recant his teachings. Luther appeared but refused to retract anything; he argued that the emperor as well had no authority on religious questions. Savonarola in Italy and Jan Hus in Bohemia had made similar declarations of faith against ecclesiastical authority in the pre-vious century, and both were burned at the stake. Luther, however, received politi-cal protection from Frederick the Wise, Duke of Saxony. As a German prince, Frederick viewed the sale of indulgences in Germany by a largely Italian church as meddlesome and saw Luther's questioning of both religious and political author-ity as an incipient movement that could promote greater autonomy for Germany within the Holy Roman Empire. After his defiance at the diet, Luther was spirited away to Wartburg Castle near Eisenach for protection. In this exile, he translated the New Testament from Greek and Latin into vernacular German.

Luther returned to his post at Wittenberg University in 1522. Under the duke's continued protection, he turned again to his writings; to his theological disputes with the "papists," Calvinists, Anabaptists, and humanists; and to the nettlesome issues of church organization. His Wittenberg colleague Philip Melanchthon directed an effort to distill Luther's teachings into a single statement, known as the Augsburg Confession. It was published in 1530, and it became the basis for establishing a separate, Lutheran church.

Nevertheless, because Luther pronounced himself in fundamental agreement with the Roman Catholic Church on the central doctrine of the Holy Trinity, he saw himself as a reformer, not a revolutionary.[3] To Luther, the absolute anchor to Christianity was the doctrine of the Trinity, which articulated the nature of the God in which true Christians professed their faith. The Catholic Church, Luther acknowledged, had created a global Christendom (the church universal) in its defense of the Trinity against the heresies of the early church and against the Eastern Orthodox schismatics later on. He did not see his famous theses, or the central beliefs grounding them, then, as corrosive of the basic worldwide Catholic solidarity highlighted by Robert Shelledy in chapter 2. But in the words of J. M. Porter, "[T]he historical effect of his thought was to erode the ecclesiastical and ultimately cultural foundations of medieval society."[4] This erosion becomes clear in three cornerstone beliefs of his reformation, even though Luther initially insisted that they were mere outpourings from his orthodox Catholic faith in a triune God.

First, Luther's belief in a justification by faith alone, and not by good works (especially those prescribed by the church), gave Christians the fundamental freedom of their souls. Outside institutions, like the church, the state, or even the pope himself, could not determine the internal condition of the souls of believers or their social standing as moral beings in the community. Moreover, these authorities could not levy any requirements, or "good works," for this moral standing, or even for their salvation. There was, then, in this internal freedom of the soul, and of external professions of faith, a justification for the freedom of conscience above any claims by religious or political institutions that became a central tenet of Luther's theology—and of modern liberalism.[5]

This freedom, in a sense, was sealed by *sola scriptura*, Luther's second cornerstone. When Emperor Charles V called upon Luther to recant his teachings, Luther refused. Luther was certainly not one to counsel disobedience to temporal authority, but when such an authority, like Charles V, transgressed into the spiritual realm, it was only on the basis of Holy Scripture that the emperor, or anyone else, could exercise authority in this realm. Because the emperor and his advisers could not show Luther his scriptural errors, Luther decided to stand where he was.[6] His third cornerstone, the priesthood of all believers, cemented this leveling of spiritual authority. On the matter of scripture, or anything else religious, in Luther's words, "[T]here is no true, basic difference between laymen and priests."[7] Christians can decide for themselves.

What was at root here for the emergence of modern society, at least in spiritual terms, was Luther's projection of a fundamental human equality before God. These three core beliefs tore down the walls with which the Catholic Church had hierarchically armored itself and undergirded the highly stratified medieval sociopolitical order. First, the Catholic Church declared that spiritual power trumps secular power. But to Luther, in political terms, the temporal power of the church came only for the sake of the office and of the performance of the work attached to the office, nothing more. There could be no spiritual claim of higher or prior authority from the mere office itself, be it priest, bishop, or even pope. Second, to the Catholic Church's claimed control of access to scripture, Luther responded that individual Christians cannot be suppressed by any sole right of the church to interpret scripture, because this interpretation was open to all Christians. Third, on this same basis, Luther disputed the Catholic Church's trump card that only the pope could resolve festering doctrinal disputes because he had the sole power to convene councils. Again, Luther insisted that church officials had to consult fellow believers on such disputes because holding an office per se carried no exalted spiritual authority.[8] The effect of Luther's beliefs, then, was to free Christians from the bonds of church authority and to set the stage for the emergence, from this medieval hierarchy, of the egalitarian political citizen.

The Lutheran Perspective on the State: The Two Kingdoms

Luther was not so modern as to embrace the limited view of government embodied by such modern social contract theorists as John Locke and his American intellectual protégés James Madison and Thomas Jefferson. But his doctrine of the two kingdoms has played an unheralded, but significant, role in the foundation of the sovereign nation-state of modernity. Referring to his treatise "Temporal Authority" (1523), Luther immodestly proclaimed, "Not since the Apostles has temporal government been so clearly described."[9] He more properly amended this claim to "since St. Augustine," because Luther's formulation of church and state was dualistically Augustinian.[10] Like St. Augustine, Luther embraced the classical Greek ideal that political systems are organic to human beings in their innate nature as social animals. They do not have to be contrived or "constructed," as social contract theorists contend. Unlike the Greeks, however, both Luther and St. Augustine saw political authority and spiritual authority as divinely commanded.[11] For Luther, the state began with God's protection of Cain, an authority established to prevent blood revenge and the devil from completely overcoming the world as a result of Cain's sin.[12] Continuing to follow St. Augustine, Luther did insist that real boundaries existed between political and spiritual authority, and that God effected His will in both realms: in the political, through the promotion and defense of justice, and in the spiritual, through the sacrifice and suffering of believers.[13]

Whereas St. Augustine's view of the two cities, or kingdoms, was unidimensional, however, Luther articulated three dimensions to these two kingdoms. The first was the recognizable Augustinian distinction between the kingdom of Christ and the kingdom of the world, what we would refer to simply as church and state in the modern world. The second, though, expressed a crossover between the territorial and other political responsibilities of bishops in the Middle Ages and the spiritual responsibility of political authorities "to guard against unbelief and heresy." Third, Luther proposed a separation between the activities Christians undertook for themselves and what they shouldered for their neighbors.[14]

It is in these latter two dimensions where Luther moved well beyond St. Augustine to propound an interpenetration of these two kingdoms into what may be called a "fused paradox." This is best illustrated by the paradoxical ways in which Luther called individual Christians to live in these two worlds. Christians live first in the uncoercive Word of God. In this realm, their calling is one of service and suffering, to live the Sermon on the Mount. That is, for themselves, they must endure injustice rather than fight or use violence. But for others, Christians are called to serve their neighbors in the second political realm by fighting for their welfare and fighting injustice. What separates these two worlds of politics and religion is sin, and what must heal this wound of separation is love, a love demonstrated by Christian service.[15]

This fused paradox of Luther's two kingdoms carries enormous significance for modern politics. As opposed to the reclusive monasticism of medieval Catholicism and the pious withdrawal of the Anabaptists, Luther levied an extra burden of Christian responsibility to politics and government. He noted that both Christians and non-Christians are bonded together in a country by the same responsibilities of citizenship toward the state. Both, then, must offer their services and submit to the just requirements of the political authorities. However, because Christians enjoy the experience of God's grace and healing love, they "are qualified above all others for service in secular government."[16] Lutherans, then, should not help themselves through politics, but through politics, they are called to serve and fight injustice for others. It is in politics, then, that Christians must walk the extra mile of the Sermon on the Mount.

Lutheran Education

By way of an extended example, this ethos of civic, Christian duty led Luther to very modern views on public education. Because secular authority is divinely ordained, and Christians are called to serve in the political realm, the exercise of government demanded a "high measure of wisdom and of strength to make free decisions."[17] Because it was the government that needed this wisdom to exercise this secular authority, Luther thought that the government should provide this education, in that education was the only way "to get able and skillful rulers."[18] But he saw this education in broader terms than just the cultivation of wise rulers. What in the Middle Ages had been a function of the church and its monasteries, Luther, in very modern terms, vested in the temporal authority because this authority was divinely sanctioned to begin with and could not rule without educated leaders and without citizens educated in their civic responsibilities and understandings of justice. Thus, in Luther's words, "A city's best and greatest welfare . . . consists in its having . . . well-educated citizens."[19] Indeed, Luther's broad vision on education was such that he championed the establishment of schools for girls as well.[20]

Further, though it was a divine command for parents to educate their children (Proverbs 4: 1–9), Luther recognized that many parents were either unfit or unable to educate their children, and because not everyone could afford to pay for a church-provided education, he appealed to "the Councilmen of All Cities in Germany That They Establish and Maintain Christian Schools" (1524). Indeed, Luther felt that rulers could compel education, just as they could military service.[21] In other words, Luther was one of the first to call for compulsory public education as a state responsibility.

But Luther's fused paradox of the two kingdoms introduced a controversial element to this education, at least to modern education. Besides exercising his political responsibilities, a ruler also had the spiritual responsibility of guarding and defending the realm from unbelief and heresy. To Luther, "No government is justified in ignoring the religious convictions of its subjects."[22] In fact, when Luther laid out the curriculum for such a public education, a thorough study of the Bible, its languages, and church history formed an integral part, along with history, literature, elocution, music, and mathematics.[23] To Luther, a separation of church and state did not entitle the state to separate out and omit religious subjects from its public education. The two sets of subjects should be fused into one cultural whole. Luther's modern legacy in education in the United States is a Lutheran denomination deeply committed to both primary education, in the case of the Missouri Synod, and to higher education in the form of nearly fifty Lutheran colleges and universities numbered among all the synods.[24]

Lutherans and Other Traditions

This fused paradox led Lutherans in the United States to a middle position in politics between sister Protestant groups on the one hand and Roman Catholics on the other. Unlike the main "English denominations" (Baptists, Presbyterians, Congregationalists, Episcopalians, and Methodists),[25] Lutherans could not embrace a full separation of church and state. Political life and religious life were indeed different, but they were also inseparable, and Lutherans sought to take care of this fusion for themselves. Nevertheless, Lutherans, in the United States anyway, could not go along with a Catholic preference to be a full part of the authority structure of the state, especially when it came to war or any kind of civic salvation through government. Because, as discussed shortly, Luther believed that the current age had been given over to the devil, the state could not be an instrument for religious perfectionism, as some Calvinists hoped, nor could the state wage war for purely religious purposes like crusades, as could be rationalized by the just war theory of Roman Catholicism. In their politics, Lutherans recommended the humbler path of vocational service.

Luther and War

Perhaps Luther's greatest legacy to the modern world was his forceful views on war. These views were another focal feature of his break with the medieval world. Though Luther came out of the just war tradition of the Catholic Church,[26] his views were far more stringent than what this tradition allowed as acceptable reasons for going to war. A simple just war was not enough. Luther imposed many more conditions before he would sanction a war. In his treatise "Whether Soldiers, Too, Can be Saved" (1526), Luther said that three types of people made war: subjects against rulers, rulers against subjects, and wars among equals. Because of his abhorrence of disorder, Luther made wars by subjects against rulers almost impossible. To him, simply, "Rulers are not to be opposed with violence or rebellion."[27] He did extend to the ruler the right to put down a revolt by his subjects, but even here, Luther imposed conditions. The ruler should not be so concerned about being right as he should appreciate that his suppression of the rebellion was for the sake of the community. It had to be an action that gained the support of his subjects and was done in the fear of God.[28]

For wars among equals, Luther insisted on very severe standards. Even if a contemplated war met the just war criteria, Christians still cannot fight with pride or arrogance. Christians, further, can have no part of wars fought for honor, which, to Luther, was nothing but a mask for greed. He also warned that just because a war was just would not guarantee victory. Once a war started, the activities of the combatants were difficult to control, and as far as Luther was concerned, as soon as civilians were killed and otherwise abused, victory had passed to the devil. Thus, "whoever starts a war is in the wrong." In a war among equals, then, participants escape damnation only if the war was forced on them. The best justification for a war that Luther could muster was that it might be "necessary."[29] Clearly, one recent strategy of modern warfare that Luther would be unlikely to embrace is that of preemption.[30]

On the matter of individual conscience, Luther displayed a modern sensitivity. He posed two situations regarding an individual Christian's response to a ruler's call for war. If the Christian knows for sure that this call is wrong, then he should "fear God rather than men" and refuse the call. If, however, "you do not know, or cannot find out, whether your lord is wrong," then the Christian should heed the call and serve because God will judge the ruler, not the Christian serving in ignorance.[31] In modern terms, the Vietnam War, for example, evoked a mixed response from American Lutherans. The Missouri Synod offered its forthright support. Both the Lutheran Church in America (LCA) and the American Lutheran Church (the two denominations that have since merged to form the Evangelical Lutheran Church in America) criticized certain aspects of the war and called for a negotiated settlement to the war, but neither denomination made statements of outright opposition. Following Martin Luther's views on individual conscience, however, the LCA did officially permit individual Lutherans the right of selective conscientious objection to the war, even though such a right was never agreed to by the American legal system.[32]

It was on the matter of Christians taking up arms for God, as Catholic popes explicitly commanded Christians to do in the Crusades, that Luther launched his greatest attack on the international politics of his day. Such a call, to Luther, was abhorrent. Luther's objection to a holy war lay, again, in his fused paradox, or interpenetration, of the two kingdoms. In his treatise "On War against the Turk" (1529), Luther resolved the question of whether to take up arms against the Turks (as opposed to surrendering outright for peace or to accommodating Germany diplomatically to Turkish rule or influence) in favor of fighting the infidels, but not as Christians. He specifically rejected the pope's call for "an army of Christians against the Turks" because, as Christians, we cannot resist evil with violence. He cited as evidence the command of Jesus to Peter to put away his sword in the Garden of Gethsemane, when temple soldiers arrested Jesus. Luther reasoned that against a possible Turkish invasion, there were two enemies—the devil and the Turk—which had to be resisted by "two" paradoxically fused soldiers. Only Christians can fight the devil, but the devil must be fought with "repentance, tears, and prayer," not with arms. The Turk, on the other hand, can be fought with arms, but only by the emperor and his soldiers. Thus, even wars against infidels like the Turks must be fought for justice at the emperor's command and authority, not at the call of the church or the pope. Because political authority is divinely ordained, soldiering is a legitimate occupation, even for Christians. But when Christians take up arms, they fight under political authority, not religious authority.[33] In the current days of the War on Terror, then, there are no holy wars or religious crusades for Lutherans, except against the devil.

A Lutheran Approach or Method

Before going to the devil (that is, before discussing him), there are three striking features to what may be called a Lutheran approach or method to the world and its problems that are unsettling to the modern mind set in the frieze of a separation of religion from politics. First, to Luther, this separation of these two kingdoms was not so simple because of the fused paradox, or interpenetration, of these two realms. Luther often couched the problems he confronted in dialectical opposites.[34] These paradoxes led him to espouse series of contradictions that he termed the twin truths that comprised the heart of our human existence in a world where we could at best "see through a glass darkly." Thus, in the personal dimension of the two kingdoms, for example, he said, "A Christian is a perfectly free lord, subject to none. A Christian is a perfectly dutiful servant . . . subject to all."[35] The most famous of his paradoxes was about sin and perfectibility with which he startled the world in his "Schmalkald Articles" (1536–1538): "As John says (I John 3:9, 5:8): 'Those who have been born of God do not sin and cannot sin.' And it is still the truth (as the same John writes [1:8]): 'If we say we have no sin, we deceive ourselves, and the truth of God is not in us."[36]

The political theorist Sheldon Wolin has observed about the political thought of Luther: "His thought represented a striking combination of revolt and passivity."[37] Consistency would be possible if humans lived completely in one world or the other, or at least separately in one world or the other by the nature of the activity, as it might be argued that the U.S. Constitution attempts to set up for liberal American citizens. For Luther, however, Christians are called to live in both worlds at once and must exist in the tension of this contention. What is unsettling to moderns is that to Luther this cannot be helped because the world in which Christians are called to live is a fallen one in the grip of the devil. These paradoxes are part of the price Christians must pay for this calling.

The second striking feature of a Lutheran method is the total extent to which Luther took his belief in *sola scriptura*. That is, there is not a subject under the sun discussed by Luther that is not supported by scriptural references. They literally grounded all his thinking and were the sole authority for all of his writings. Granted, as a university professor, he did make reference to other works and arguments, but all of his own answers were ultimately based on scriptural authority. This scriptural grounding certainly extended to all of his commentary on the political world as well. Translated to modern America, with Luther's idea of the fused paradox, it would not be enough, for even political authorities, to ground laws and decisions in the U.S. Constitution. Holy Scripture should be invoked as well. Thus, for Luther, the interpenetration of religion in the public space and political arena (so sharply decried by modern civil libertarians) should, in fact, be seen as an integral part of the double calling of the two kingdoms.

The fact that the Declaration of Independence acknowledges the sovereignty of "Nature's God" would be fine with Martin Luther, but the failure to recognize any divine provenance in the Preamble to the U.S. Constitution would not. He would approve of chaplains in the military, prayers of invocation in the U.S. Congress, and pledges of allegiance to a nation "under God" in public schools, but not of a court decision to remove the Ten Commandments from a county courthouse in Alabama or of the decision by many municipalities to remove Nativity scenes from town squares during the "winter holiday."

Finally, to Luther, a job is not just a job. For a Christian, it is a sacred calling. In fact, Luther argued that the very essence of Christ's call for Christians to follow Him is rooted in vocation. To imitate Christ is to bear the cross of the needs of others in service to family, and then to others, through vocation. Luther averred, "[V]ocation is the work of faith; vocation is worship in the realm of the world."[38] In sum, for all its worldliness, to Luther the world is still a sacred place for all Christians—even though it belongs to the devil. There can be no abdication from the world for Lutherans. It is their vocation to be in it, and in its politics.

The Devil and Martin Luther: The Fourth Dimension

For moderns, especially civil libertarians who hold rights to dissent, protest, and even rebellion (under certain conditions) to be sacrosanct, Martin Luther's strong views against rebellion and sedition have earned him a bad reputation.

In his three treatises on the peasant rebellion of 1525, Luther conceded that many of the peasant grievances were just, and he did call on the princes to listen to these grievances and restore justice. Nevertheless, he insisted that the peasants end their disobedience. He reminded them that it is the Christian's "duty to suffer and pray in this world, it is not to take up the sword against temporal authority." When the peasants launched a rebellion anyway, in which approximately 100,000 people were killed, Luther became vitriolic in demanding that if the peasants would not desist, they all deserved to be killed. Despite intense criticism from both other Protestants and peasant leaders, Luther refused to relent.[39]

Even on this subject, however, his doctrine of the two kingdoms led him to some more complicated positions. The peasant revolt was a political issue, in the realm of justice and law and order, but when the Emperor Charles V contemplated an armed suppression of the Protestant movement in Germany in 1531, he was transgressing into the spiritual realm. Christians, then, should not obey such a war. As a minister, Luther said that he could not counsel war, but if a war broke out started by the papists, he would accept Protestant resistance as self-defense. This would particularly be the case if the Protestant rebels were not accorded the right of a hearing.[40] Indeed, in the Torgau Statement of October 1531, Luther declared that the right to resistance against the emperor "might exist." Luther hovered at the brink, while his colleague Philip Melanchthon flatly asserted a right of *jus reformandi*, the right of the Reformation to defend itself by armed force against an irreligious act of suppression by the state.[41]

What made Luther hesitate was what can be called the fourth dimension to his doctrine of the two kingdoms. Earlier, I mentioned that Luther expanded St. Augustine's simple dichotomy of the city of God versus the city of man by adding two other dimensions. Luther's new second dimension was the crossover between the temporal duties of the church in the political dimension and the spiritual duties of the state in the religious dimension, and the third was the separation between what Christians did for themselves and what they did for their neighbors.

This fourth dimension was one of time. It is the period in which we all live, medievals and moderns, namely, the time between the ascension of Jesus into heaven (St. Augustine's finite city of man) and the time of his return (St. Augustine's infinite city of God)—an epoch, in this mean time, given over to the devil. In this current age, it is law, order, and Christian resistance to temptation that restrains the devil. Far from a neutral period in which civil societies can address and solve their problems either peacefully or with vocal and violent dissent, as they please, the devil lurks in the shadows as a palpable and constant menace to human life. At best, in this fourth dimension, the devil can only be kept at bay until Jesus returns to deal with him definitively. What can allow him to break down these restraints and gain complete mastery of this epoch is when the realm of justice is engulfed by anarchy, chaos, and violence. In Luther's own words, "God has thrown us into this world, under the power of the devil. As a result, we have no paradise here."[42] Paradise awaits all who believe in God's true kingdom, the kingdom not of this world.[43]

The Lutheran Tradition and Contemporary Politics

Luther's persistent fear of the devil, and particularly of the political disorder that gives the devil his elixir of power, is probably most responsible for the conservatism in Lutheranism so decried by Ernst Troeltsch and Reinhold Niebuhr at the beginning of this chapter.[44] Other factors have contributed as well. In the United States, Lutherans came from rural areas of Germany and Scandinavia, and initially these immigrants took up farming and other rural occupations in the Mid-Atlantic and Midwestern states, as opposed to, for example, Jewish immigrants, who in this era came from urban backgrounds and were, at least in some numbers, radical refugees from the revolutions of 1848.[45] Lutheran creeds and confessions also served as a buffer against the various liberal passions that swept across the country in the late nineteenth century: Darwinism, the Social Gospel, and the progressive movement.[46]

This conservative direction to American Lutheranism opened up a chasm with its European forebears. In Europe, Lutherans took Luther's two kingdoms to both serve society vocationally and join directly in the governing process by forming political parties. In Europe, Lutheran Germans and Scandinavians lived in countries where the language and the religion were indistinguishable in the "two kingdoms," and Lutherans took up politics and governance with enthusiasm to become champions of the "big government" social welfare state that has become the hallmark of Western European political systems.

In America, however, Lutherans faced a barrier. They came to a political system dominated by the English and their language. To preserve their identity in this ethnically alien world, Lutherans preferred to serve their own, rather than rely upon and lose themselves to this alien system. They soon built their own institutions and endeavored to keep the national, alien government limited so that it would not encroach on their own set of institutions and thereby their carefully protected identities. This grew into a particular Lutheran understanding of the separation of church and state. Regarding their political responsibilities, Lutherans would serve society and justice through their own educational institutions, charity, and vocations. But as for the state serving them, Lutherans preferred to offer the state their prayers, expecting nothing in return so as to keep it away and, instead, letting Lutheran institutions take care of their own. This way they could become Americans, yes, but remain Swedish (for example) and Lutherans at the same time.

Three cardinal features of American Lutheranism have risen up from this particular American conservatism. First, more than any other religious group in America, Lutherans developed a full infrastructure of support for their fellow believers beyond the pews of their churches. They rivaled Catholics in their schools and hospitals. They surpassed Jews in their extensive social support services. They even founded their own insurance companies. And they outdid everyone in their charities to the community as a whole. The fact that Lutheran social ministries rank first among U.S. charities in dollar amount contributions (with the YMCA and the Red Cross coming in second and third in 2001) has led Edgar Trexler to observe that "Lutherans make up the largest nonprofit social and health services network in America."[47]

Second, beyond reaching out to the larger community and world through its charities and foreign missions, Lutherans have certainly done a commendable job of taking care of their own. This success has helped to create an American Lutheran preserve of unrivaled "*un*diversity." Its institutional infrastructure was able to retain the Lutheran loyalties and identities of many of the five million German and two million Scandinavian immigrants who poured into the United States between the Civil War and World War I.[48]

Although this surge of immigration trailed off thereafter, Lutheran membership continued to expand. From 1916 to 1960, baptized Lutheran membership grew from 2.5 million to 8 million, pushing it to third place among Protestants, behind only the Baptists (21 million) and Methodists (13.2 million).[49] In this surge, even as late as 1982, Lutherans in America were 85 percent German and Scandinavian (58 percent and 27–28 percent, respectively), and only 11 percent "English."[50] Minorities could hardly be counted. When most other Lutheran churches, other than the two-million-member Lutheran Church–Missouri Synod, collected themselves into the Evangelical Lutheran Church in American (ELCA) in 1988, they lamented that their membership was only 1.85 percent minority (defined as African American, Hispanic, Asian, Middle Eastern, and Native American) and proclaimed a goal of achieving 10 percent minority membership in the new church. The only thing it succeeded in doing was to engender a twelve-year slide in membership, while reaching a paltry 2.1 percent minority membership by 2001.[51] No other Christian group in America has preserved its original ethnic identities so well.

Finally, the peculiar American Lutheran political goals—of serving society through its own institutions and viewing a separation of church and state as a way to limit the secular and alien government's encroachments into these activities—have led Lutherans to embrace political philosophies of limited government. It should come as no surprise, then, that American Lutherans are overwhelmingly Republican. With voter turnout rates above 80 percent in presidential elections (as opposed to a national average that hovers around 50 percent), Lutherans are exceeded in voting only by Presbyterians among religious groups. And Lutherans and Presbyterians vote for Republicans above 60 percent thresholds. Lutherans in particular contribute to the splash of red state color to U.S. maps by county by forming the largest religious bodies in 259 counties, 60 percent of them in Minnesota and North Dakota; they are also numerically strong in critical electoral states like Illinois, Michigan, Ohio, and Pennsylvania.[52]

Because of their paradoxical theological and political beliefs, Lutherans were among the strongest supporters of President George W. Bush's "faith-based initiative" to provide federal funds in support of the social service activities of church bodies. In a sense, this support is emblematic of a coming of age for a Lutheranism that is now prepared to accept government assistance as it is finally serious about coming out of its sheltered ethnic enclaves.

On this presidential initiative, Lutherans find themselves on common ground with the evangelicals of the Christian Right. But Lutherans, of all stripes, remain quite distinct from evangelicals, both theologically and politically. Modern evangelicals of the Pat Robertson and Jerry Falwell varieties have some focal characteristics. Prominent among them is a fundamentalist, or literal, interpretation of the scriptures. They also insist on personal religious experiences and conversions as defining hallmarks and evidence of Christian faith. Moreover, their recent surge into the political arena stems from an abhorrence for the socially liberal values and secular humanism of mainstream American political culture and from their intensely apocalyptic views on international politics, particularly in the Middle East and the need to defend Israel. Although some Lutherans share some of these concerns, the persistent hold of Luther's core beliefs on contemporary Lutherans keeps the Lutheran denomination aloof from much of this agenda.

The Missouri Synod, to be sure, is more fundamentalist in its scriptural beliefs than the larger Evangelical Lutheran Church in America (ELCA). But the *sola scriptura* of all Lutherans makes them reject the centrality of religious experiences and "born again" conversions because such emotionalism carries the danger of challenging the primacy of Holy Scripture. Similarly, because of *sola scriptura*, Lutherans are deeply squeamish about both apocalyptic theology and politics because scripture is willfully silent on the timing of the Second Coming of Christ. Given this silence, to Lutherans, apocalyptic visions with specific timetables from charismatic preachers are not permissible supplements to scripture. Finally, on the social issues that so motivate evangelicals, Lutherans have generally shied away from explicit partisan positions and definitive collective statements in favor of relying on the "priesthood of all believers" to individually address these issues as their personal prayers and scriptural study dictate.[53]

Conclusion

In this modern age of the devil, as Martin Luther has called it,[54] Lutherans remain suspended in their many paradoxes: between two kingdoms separate and inseparable across four dimensions, between contradictory beliefs that men are righteous yet "none is righteous," between a Eucharist that dispenses Christ's body and spirit "consubstantiated" together,[55] between a liberal Lutheran Europe and a conservative Lutheran America, and with a politics caught between a passion for divine justice and a fear of provoking the disorders riled up by the devil. It is these paradoxes that keep all Lutherans—medieval and modern, European and American—fused in the muddled middle of Martin Luther's still clear voice.[56]

NOTES

1. Ernst Troeltsch, *The Social Teachings of the Christian Church*, trans. Olive Wyon, vol. 2 (London: Allen and Unwin, 1950), 577. I would like to thank Dan Hofrenning, chair of the department of political science at St. Olaf College, for suggesting that I take up this assignment and Edmund Santurri, of the religion department of St. Olaf College, for bringing to my attention the basic political writings of Martin Luther. I am also grateful to my Saint Louis University colleagues Eloise Buker and Robert Cahill for their helpful comments.

2. Reinhold Niebuhr, *The Nature and Destiny of Man*, vol. 2 (New York: Scribner's, 1943), 194–195.

3. Martin Luther, *Schmalkald Articles*, trans. William R. Russell (Minneapolis, MN: Fortress Press, 1995), viii.

4. J. M. Porter, *Luther: Selected Political Writings* (Philadelphia: Fortress Press, 1974), 6.

5. Ibid., 4–7.

6. Ibid., 51.

7. Ibid., 41.

8. Ibid., 39.

9. Ibid., 104.

10. Heinrich Bornkamm, *Luther's Doctrine of the Two Kingdoms*, trans. Karl H. Hertz (Philadelphia: Fortress Press, 1966), 20.

11. The Greeks, particularly Plato, certainly saw these authorities as part of a rationally ordered cosmos but not something explicitly sanctioned by a personal

God, as was the view of both St. Augustine and Luther. Order to Plato was "divinely regenerative," but this was an order emanating from *dike* (the ordering principle of the cosmos) that was communicated by *logos,* the "word" that reflects this principle largely in philosophical writings. To both St. Augustine and Luther, *logos,* the communicative arm of God, was made human in the person and sacrifice of Jesus Christ. For a definitive work on Plato's views on this subject, see Eric Voegelin, *Plato* (Baton Rouge: Louisiana State University Press, 1966), esp. 7–23.

12. Luther Hess Waring, *The Political Theories of Martin Luther* (Port Washington, NY: Kennikat Press, 1968 [1910]), 73–74.

13. Bornkamm, 2, 6, and 34.

14. Ibid., 16.

15. Ibid., 6–10.

16. Ibid., 15.

17. Ibid., 10.

18. Waring, 198.

19. Theodore G. Tappert, ed., *Selected Writings of Martin Luther* (Philadelphia: Fortress Press, 1967), 48–49.

20. Waring, 196.

21. Tappert, 48–49; Waring, 200.

22. Waring, 203.

23. Tappert, 31–71. Luther was a great lover of music, and music has become a specialty of Lutheran higher education.

24. Lutherans in the United States have a rich history of sectarian division, with Germans and Norwegians having formed several synods apiece. Most of these joined together in 1988 to form the Evangelical Lutheran Church in America as a counterpoise to the Lutheran Church–Missouri Synod. But in 1900, there were still twenty-four separate Lutheran "denominations." See Winthrop S. Hudson, *Religion in America,* 2nd ed. (New York: Charles Scribner's Sons, 1973), 260.

25. So designated by Winthrop S. Hudson. See ibid., 32–48.

26. For example, Luther did invoke the just war formulary in calling on German princes to resist a contemplated suppression of the Protestant movement by Charles V in 1531. See Porter, 17.

27. Ibid., 108.

28. Ibid., 115–116.

29. Porter, 113, 114, and 118; Tappert, 342. Quote is in Porter, 113.

30. Because of the diabolical nature of the attacks on the World Trade Center and on the Pentagon on "9/11," the criterion of a war being forced on us was clearly met, and Luther would probably have approved of the war in Afghanistan to smash al Qaeda and overthrow the Taliban regime. As a supporter of the subsequent war in Iraq, however, I can find no basis for support of this war in the writings of Martin Luther. On the other hand, I think a case can be made for this latter war in the less stringent criteria of Catholic just war doctrine. Although Catholics do talk about going to war as a "last resort," some provisions are made for offensive war to "defend the faith," and there is considerable ambiguity over the necessity of a purely defensive war when the cause has been determined to be just. Indeed, a Lutheran political scientist

has invoked just war theory to justify both the wars in Afghanistan and Iraq. See Jean Bethke Elshtain, *Just War against Terror: The Burden of American Power in a Violent World* (New York: Basic Books, 2003). Another political scientist with a long career of writing in the just war tradition has employed this same theory to oppose the Iraq War. See Michael Walzer, *Arguing about War* (New Haven, CT: Yale University Press, 2004).

31. Both quotes are taken from Porter, 117.

32. See, for example, Richard J. Niebanck, "Conscience, War, and the Selective Objector," in *Studies in Justice, Peace and Freedom* 11, 2nd ed. (New York: Board of Social Ministry, Lutheran Church in America, 1972).

33. Ibid., 122–129. Quotes from 123, 129.

34. W. D. J. Cargill Thompson, *The Political Thought of Martin Luther* (Brighton, UK: Harvester Press, 1984), 20.

35. Porter, 25.

36. Luther, who wrote the "Schmalkald Articles" at a point in his life when he thought he was dying, intended them as a theological last will and testament. See Luther, 26.

37. Cited in Porter, 18.

38. Carter Lindberg, "Luther's Struggle with Social-Ethical Issues," in Donald R. McKim, *The Cambridge Companion to Martin Luther* (Cambridge: Cambridge University Press, 2003), 161, 171.

39. Porter, 12–14. Quote is from 14.

40. Ibid., 134–141. Here Luther came close to a demand for democratic safeguards in war making. Since it was morally the lesser of the two realms, Luther did not require the princes to be democratic. But he did levy an ecclesiastical democracy on the church. Because the "government" of religious ministers and bishops was one of service and merely of office, not one of authority and power, "they should impose no law or decree on others without their will and consent." See ibid., 64.

41. Thompson, 105.

42. Porter, 112.

43. Regarding the other traditions in this book, because of this age of the devil, Luther sees no possibility in any "perfectionism" through governments of "Christian exceptionalism," as some Calvinists do. On the other hand, he was not against the state, as Pentacostalists proclaim, because the state forms a pivotal bulwark against the devil. It is also the arena in which the struggle for justice must be waged. Finally, for Luther the "heavenly citizen" of the Anabaptists was not possible in this age of the devil. He also feared that, like Roman Catholic monasticism, such a posture could lead to a withdrawal from the world that would only hasten the victory of the devil.

44. Opinion polls show a differing impact of modernity on beliefs in God versus the devil. Polls consistently report that more than 90 percent of the American population believes in God; belief in a personal devil hovers at less than 30 percent. At the margins, Lutherans do a better job in believing in a personal devil than Methodists or Catholics, for example: 21 percent versus 18 percent and 17 percent, respectively. See Uwe Siemon-Netto, "Barna Poll on U.S. Religious Belief—2001," United Press International, 1. http://www.adherents.com/misc/BarnaPoll.html, accessed January 25, 2006. Modern Lutheran theologians, for the most part, still emphasize the perils of a

personal, pernicious devil. Carl Braaten, for example, insists that a belief in a personal God requires a belief in a personal devil as well. See Carl E. Braaten, "Powers in Conflict: Christ and the Devil," in Carl E. Braaten and Robert W. Jenson, eds., *Sin, Death, and the Devil* (Grand Rapids, MI: William B. Eerdmans, 2000), 94–108.

45. Hudson, 260, 436–438.

46. Samuel Schmucker (1799–1873), a professor at Gettysburg Seminary, tried to integrate Lutheranism into the liberal Protestantism of the day by revising the Augsburg Confession into more mainline beliefs on Communion and baptism. This was stoutly resisted by Charles Krauth (1823–1883), a professor at rival seminary Mount Airy in Philadelphia, and by C. F. W. Walther (1811–1887), the founder of the Missouri Synod, and the flirtation ended. See ibid., 151–152; and Mark A. Noll, "The Lutheran Difference," *First Things* 20 (February 1992): 3–21. http://firstthings.com/ftissues/ft9202/articles/noll.html, 5–6, accessed January 24, 2006.

47. Edgar R. Trexler, *High Expectations: Understanding the ELCA's Early Years, 1988–2002* (Minneapolis, MN: Augsburg Fortress Press, 2003), 165–166.

48. Noll, 2.

49. Hudson, 354.

50. Carl F. Reuss, *Profiles of Lutherans in the U.S.* (Minneapolis, MN: Augsburg, 1982), 95–96.

51. Unlike other mainline Protestant denominations whose membership slides began in the 1960s, Lutherans held their own until the mid-1980s. At its founding in 1988, ELCA membership stood at 5.25 million. In 2001, the slide was down to 5.1 million. See Trexler, 177, 188, 196, and 197.

52. Noll, 2.

53. In this discussion of Lutherans and evangelicals, I am indebted to e-mail comments from my fellow Lutheran Mary Todd of Ohio Dominican University.

54. Somewhat more gently, Roman Catholics refer to the present time as the age of mystery. Perhaps this is a concession to Luther's paradoxes.

55. Ever the one to claim the middle ground, in the complex theological debates over Holy Communion, Luther claimed a middle position between the orthodox Catholic position and the reformed Calvinist position. To Calvinists, Holy Communion was not a special means of divine grace, but rather a traditional celebration of remembrance of the sacrifice of Jesus on the cross. To Catholics, on the other hand, the bread and the wine underwent a mysterious transubstantiation through which these material elements were transformed into the "true Body and Blood of Christ." Luther fell short of this mystery by acknowledging that the bread and the wine retained their materiality, but he did still insist that in the service of the Eucharist "the real presence of Christ" came into these material elements through what he called "consubstantiation." Consubstantiation, then, was a theological extension (or foundation) of the fused paradox of Luther's two kingdoms, the material and the spiritual.

56. Indeed, Mark A. Noll, a Calvinist church historian, contends that the best contribution Lutherans can make to Christianity today and to the politics of the twenty-first century is the profound thought of Martin Luther in his unvarnished "theology of the cross," that is, that human salvation can come only from Christ's suffering on the cross, for which Christians should respond with loving vocations in the world. See Noll, 11–13.

4

Reformed . . . and Always Reforming?

James W. Skillen

When Calvinism—the Reformed tradition of Protestant Christianity—comes up for discussion today, one will probably hear reference to sin (total depravity) and/or God's sovereignty (predestination). For example, part of the explanation offered for America's constitutionally limited, checked, and balanced government is the need to restrain human wickedness that is so easily and frequently expressed when power is concentrated and not held to account. And one influential explanation of the work ethic and the remarkable economic achievements of people in countries influenced by Calvinism is the doctrine of predestination (God's foreordination of the elect to salvation). Max Weber (1864–1920) made the latter argument as follows: Calvinism is chiefly responsible for producing the modern entrepreneur—the "worldly ascetic." How so? "The Calvinist had no priest to stand between him and God or to give him the sacraments that would ensure his salvation," writes W. Fred Graham, summarizing Weber's thesis. Thus, the Calvinist could "either assume that he was predestined to glory and battle subsequent doubts to the contrary. Or, says Weber, he could look for evidences of God's blessing in his worldly calling to prove that God's attitude toward him was gracious. The result was a human being who strove unremittingly to glorify God in his daily toil."[1]

Do these ideas of sin and divine predestination represent the essence of Calvinism? Is there anything more to it than that? And what about John Calvin himself? Most important for our purposes, what, if anything, has the Reformed tradition contributed to government and politics, and particularly to international relations and foreign policy?

Historical Background

John Calvin (1509–1564), like Martin Luther (1483–1546) and a number of less well-known figures, including Balthasar Hubmaier (ca. 1480–1528), Ulrich Zwingli (1484–1531), Martin Bucer (1491–1551), Menno Simons (1492–1559), Philipp Melanchthon (1497–1560), Heinrich Bullinger (1504–1575), John Knox (ca. 1505–1572), and Theodore Beza (1519–1605), was a leading shaper of the Protestant Reformation. It is largely Calvin's legacy that is under consideration in this chapter. For some reason, the wing of the Reformation most influenced by Calvin was tagged "Reformed," while other Protestants became identified as "Lutheran" or "Anabaptist" (or "Radical Reformers"). However, the adjective "Calvinist" is often used interchangeably with the word "Reformed" when referring to churches or the social influences of churches identified as Reformed or Presbyterian. Two contemporary international organizations of such churches are the World Alliance of Reformed Churches and the Reformed Ecumenical Council.

This is not the place to try to detail the many theological and ecclesiastical similarities and differences in the diverse wings of Protestantism. Nor is it my purpose to try to show the extent to which the Reformers either broke with or maintained continuity with Roman Catholicism. All wings of the Reformation aimed to reform or purify the universal church or to recover the experiential reality of the true church that they believed had been deformed or obscured by the Roman Catholic Church. Calvin and early Calvinists were not trying to start something new. They were not revolutionaries.[2] We should not be surprised, therefore, to find continuity with the past in many theological doctrines, ecclesiastical practices, and approaches to government and political life.

The influence of John Calvin's work as pastor, theologian, educator, and social reformer spread outward from Geneva, where Calvin did most of his life's work, to other Swiss, French, and German cities or princely realms, and most influentially to the Netherlands, Hungary, Scotland, England, North America, and South Africa. Menna Prestwich emphasizes that the internationally networked character of Calvinism is due in no small measure to Calvinist academies and universities that were established almost from the beginning. These centers of learning attracted students from throughout Europe and eventually from around the world.[3] Some of the world's most influential colleges and universities, including those in Geneva, Leiden, Basel, and Debrecen, as well as

Harvard, Yale, and Princeton, began as Reformed institutions. And some of the most influential Christian theologians in the last two centuries have been Reformed: Charles Hodge at Princeton, Abraham Kuyper and Herman Bavinck in the Netherlands, Karl Barth in Switzerland, and Thomas F. Torrance in Scotland. And the influence has been significant not only in ecclesiastical and theological realms but also in social, scientific, economic, and political arenas.

According to Prestwich, there is quite a difference between the Calvinism of John Calvin, on the one hand, and the caricature of Calvinism that gained popularity within a century after Calvin, on the other hand. If, says Prestwich,

> we adopt the strict definitions [of Calvinism] given by the Synod of
> Dort in 1618 [called chiefly to oppose the Arminians] and the *Consensus
> Helveticus* of 1675 [which consolidated Reformed doctrine at the time],
> Calvinism can be, and has been, represented as a harsh, austere, and
> intolerant creed. Its theology centred on the forbidding and divisive
> dogma of double predestination, degenerating into arid scholastic
> disputes; its requirement of conformity to an unnaturally stiff code
> of conduct was productive of bigotry or hypocrisy; and its structure of
> consistories, colloquies, and synods formed an unyielding straitjacket.[4]

But this characterization, says Prestwich, is inaccurate and yields the "awkward consequence" that Calvin was not a very good Calvinist. After all, it was Theodore Beza, not Calvin, "who emphasized the doctrine of double predestination [namely, that prior to any human decisions, God determined who would be saved and who would be damned for eternity] and made it the core of reformed orthodoxy," and the Company of Pastors of Geneva eventually discarded the *Consensus Helveticus* as "distasteful."[5] Even to understand the doctrines of total depravity and predestination, therefore, we will have to approach Calvin and the Reformed tradition with a broader outlook and range of questions.

Consider, for example, one of the important similarities between Calvin and the Anabaptists in contrast to Luther and the Roman Catholics. As Graham explains, "The marks of the church for Luther were the right preaching of the Word and the administration of the dominical sacraments (Baptism and the Supper). To these marks the radical reformers [Anabaptists] added a third, that of godly discipline within the redeemed community."[6] According to Graham, Calvin was closer to the Anabaptists at this point. His understanding of God's judging and redeeming work in Jesus Christ was that all things—the whole creation—is being reconciled to God and therefore the believing community should demonstrate in its life the righteous fruits of that reconciliation. Thus, Calvin was like the Anabaptists in wanting serious discipline of the Christian community, emphasizing the radical difference between the way of life in

Christ Jesus and the way of death from which believers are being redeemed. The distance that remained between Calvin and the Anabaptists, however, was that Calvin, while emphasizing the distinction between ecclesiastical and civil authorities, did not want to separate the community of believers from society and government the way the Anabaptists did. Calvin saw the political community as one of the arenas of human responsibility that falls under Christ's lordship. The 1527 Schleitheim confession of the Anabaptists, by contrast, described the responsibility of government as falling "outside the perfection of Christ." (Political implications of Anabaptist beliefs are discussed in chapter 5.) Also in contrast to Calvin, Luther thought that government's responsibility should not be judged by the high standard of Christian love but by a lower standard of justice. Calvin, like both Luther and the Anabaptists, agreed that the church should not have direct authority *over* the magistrate or prince, but he believed strongly that church authorities and magistrates were both accountable to the same sovereign God who is judging and redeeming the creation in Jesus Christ.[7]

The Reformed tradition, consequently, must be tracked through its social, cultural, scientific, and political impact as much as through its ecclesiastical and theological development. And in the political realm, there is particular evidence of Reformed influence in several countries already mentioned—Switzerland, the Netherlands, England, Scotland, South Africa, the United States, and Canada.[8]

One reason for Calvin's comprehensive outlook was his attention to creation—to the world as God's handiwork. Calvin's reading of the scriptures put him in awe of God's sovereignty and therefore of all that God created. From biblical history, according to Calvin, we learn:

> that God by the power of his Word and Spirit created heaven and earth out of nothing; that thereupon he brought forth living beings and inanimate things of every kind, that in a wonderful series he distinguished an innumerable variety of things, that he endowed each kind with its own nature, assigned functions, appointed places and stations; and that, although all were subject to corruption, he nevertheless provided for the preservation of each species until the Last Day. We shall likewise learn . . . that he has so wonderfully adorned heaven and earth with as unlimited abundance, variety, and beauty of all things as could possibly be, quite like a spacious and splendid house, provided and filled with the most exquisite and at the same time most abundant furnishings. Finally, we shall learn that in forming man and in adorning him with such goodly beauty, and with such great and numerous gifts, he put him forth as the most excellent example of his works.[9]

To be sure, Calvin, following Augustine, affirmed the total depravity of sinners and taught that only through God's grace in Christ was redemption possible. Nevertheless, sinners are human beings whom God originally made good and righteous—the very image of God—as part of the Creator's marvelous handiwork. Therefore, the whole of creation, with all of the talents and responsibilities that belong to human beings, must be kept in view when Calvin talks about God's sovereignty. "I retain the principle," writes Calvin, "that the likeness of God extends to the whole excellence by which man's nature towers over all the kinds of living creatures."[10]

Marilynne Robinson writes that's Calvin's sense of things was "overwhelmingly visual and cerebral," and the dominant metaphor he used in speaking about the creation's relation to God was a mirror.[11] The creation, and particularly humans (the image of God), mirror God. When Calvin used the word *depravity* to describe the condition of disobedient, sinful humanity, he used the French *depraver*. The meaning of that word was, at the time, very close to its Latin root, which means "to warp" or "to distort," as the image in a mirror is distorted if there is something wrong with the mirror.[12] This does not weaken Calvin's emphasis on human sinfulness, but it does place sin where it belongs, as a warping of what God made good. Creation comes first; sin comes second. God's first and ultimate purpose was not to save sinners from sin, but to create a world that would mirror and glorify God. Thus, God's gracious redemption of fallen humanity through Jesus Christ is first and foremost a recovery and rectifying of God's creational purposes.

Consequently, everything in the entire range of human responsibilities should be renewed, rectified, and cleared of distortion so that humans can glorify God and exhibit God's righteousness imputed to them through Christ. For it is Jesus Christ, true man and true God, who reveals the perfect image of God, and his righteousness becomes our righteousness by God's grace through faith, setting us free to be what God created us to be. The Christ who reveals God without distortion does so as prophet, priest, and king, embracing all dimensions of human existence in relation to God.[13] Although the redeemed in Christ may be proportionately small in number among the whole of humanity, the church should be "that community where the original solidarity of men is restored"[14] and the full meaning of their humanity is renewed and developed. William Stevenson, commenting on Calvin's teaching of divine providence and human freedom, says,

> [T]he ends of providence and the ends of freedom are the same. On
> the one hand, in presenting believers with newfound security in
> God's salvation choices, Christian freedom unleashes a new gratitude

and a new excitement about the possibilities of Christian service. Yet on the other hand, in presenting believers with their complete emptiness in the face of Christ's redemptive work, Christian freedom lashes them ever more tightly to his loving and often mysterious guidance. . . . Freedom arises *from* God's sovereign choice, *out of* his forgiving temper, *for* thankful service, *under* his discerning eye, and *through* his parental foresight. Once God sets believers free from their own self-enslavement, he announces to them their new status and then nourishes and sustains their freedom as they move about in the world.[15]

In the historical development of the Reformed tradition, it is the Calvinists' attention to all spheres of life in this world that will often be noticed. Early in the twentieth century, Karl Barth emphasized Calvin's point that we can know ourselves only by knowing God and know God only by knowing ourselves. Moreover, "the only true knowledge of God is born of obedience. . . . Knowledge of God engenders a desire to act. A desire to act engenders a new seeking of God. A new quest for God engenders new knowledge of God. That is the way Reformed thinking goes."[16] And Reformed thinking in this sense is not narrowly about inner piety, worship, and spiritual discipline, and it is certainly not only about the callings of pastors and those in religious orders. The seeking of God and of self-knowledge has to do with human obedience in all spheres of life; it has to do with the priesthood of all believers.

Calvinism most emphatically then gives impetus to the desire for a Christian worldview—a view of the whole of life under the sovereignty of the God who created and is reconciling all things through the Son. This was certainly the argument made by the nineteenth-century neo-Calvinist Abraham Kuyper in his 1898 Stone Lectures at Princeton, against the backdrop of his efforts in the Netherlands to establish a Christian university, a Christian political party, and Christian newspapers, as well as to reform the church.[17] This is not to suggest that the Reformed tradition in all parts of the world developed as it did in the Netherlands, but Kuyper's neo-Calvinism is readily recognizable as an extension of the Reformed tradition.[18]

We might say, then, that compared with Lutherans and Anabaptists, Calvin was a social reformer and not just a church reformer. He wanted men and women in society to mirror God again, and that would require the ongoing reformation of every sphere of life in the power of the Holy Spirit. In this respect, perhaps a big difference between Luther and Calvin was that Luther emphasized the devil's control over this world in contrast to Calvin's emphasis on God's sovereignty over all, including the world of human depravity. (On Luther, see

Timothy Lomperis's chapter 3 in this book.) Unlike Luther and the Anabaptists, Calvin did not think about church and world in terms of paradox and dualism. He thought in terms of the integrity of God's entire creation and of God's sovereignty over all, sealed now in the Lordship of Christ. Sin leads to the darkness and distortion of all of life because of human disobedience to God, but the devil does not, through human sin, have the power to establish or control particular spheres or institutions over against Christ and the church. In Calvin's view, sin runs throughout all of human life and society; it is not located particularly in the political realm in contrast to the realm of the church. Calvin, like Luther and the Anabaptists, certainly wanted radical reform of the Catholic Church, yet for Calvin such reform meant, by extension, that Christians should reach out to seek the reform of the whole of society.

A Reformed Perspective on the State

Most Christians today, we can probably say, are Anabaptists in the sense that they contend for free churches in open societies with governments that give equal treatment to all citizens regardless of their faith. Calvin's traditional view that the state bears responsibility for enforcing Christian discipline throughout society[19] has been rejected. Yet our rejection of Calvin and Luther's position on that point should not lead us to overlook Calvin's contribution to *semper reformanda*—always reforming life and society. Christians, as the redeemed of God, bear responsibilities throughout God's creation, in education, the arts and sciences, medicine and law, politics and family life. Calvin was certainly more than a traditionalist in his approach to economic life and in his call for lower government authorities to hold monarchs and princes accountable, even challenging their right to rule if they did so in violation of God's commandments. These are areas in which Calvin and Calvinists are often recognized as important contributors to modern constitutionalism and representative government and to the advancement of commerce and capitalism.[20]

Those who stand in the Reformed tradition must, therefore, decide how and on what basis to take distance from Calvin's conviction that the state should enforce true religion. The fact is that almost every circle of Reformed Protestants has rejected that position. Kuyper, for example, was emphatic about Calvin's error in this regard, symbolized by Calvin's support of the Genevan government's burning of the heretic Servetus. What lies at the core of Calvinism, says Kuyper, is bowing before the sovereignty of God, not conservatively holding onto past social systems as if they were without sin and should not change. One of the consequences of this conviction that took time to work out historically was the growth of the idea of a more limited role for government and the civil protection of religious freedom. The Anabaptists had led the way on this front in seeking freedom for the church as community of faith, although they did not develop much of a political theory beyond that. By contrast, the restriction of such religious liberty remained strong for some time in countries where Calvinism had become dominant. But that should not have been the case, argued Kuyper. "The duty of the government to extirpate every form of false religion and idolatry," Kuyper said at Princeton, "was not a find of Calvinism, but dates from Constantine the Great, and was the reaction against the horrible persecutions which his pagan predecessors on the imperial throne had inflicted upon the sect of the Nazarene."[21] After Constantine, that system continued to be defended by the Roman Catholic Church, by Lutheran and Reformed churches, and by political rulers, all of whom fought with one another and oppressed the Anabaptists. "Notwithstanding all this," Kuyper concludes, "I not only deplore that one stake [at which Servetus was burned], but I unconditionally disapprove of it; yet not as if it were the expression of a special characteristic of Calvinism, but on the contrary as the fatal after-effect of a system, grey with age, which Calvinism found in existence, under which it had grown up, and from which it had not yet been able entirely to liberate itself."[22]

Reformed Christians in many countries, including the United States, have acquiesced in, or actively promoted, the secularization of state and society as a consequence of their discomfort with state-established churches. In doing so, however, Reformed and Presbyterian Christians have too easily bought into the Enlightenment's arguments for the privatization of religion in order to develop a tolerant, secular, rational public square. But that kind of Christian accommodation to secularizing humanism does not exhibit a Christian reforming impulse, as Kuyper saw it. One implication of Kuyper's renewal of Calvinism was drawing a distinction between two meanings of "secularization." On the one hand, the liberation of society, including the state, from direct ecclesiastical control was a legitimate type of secularization (or "deecclesiasticization"), because people ought to be free to respond to God's sovereignty *directly* in every sphere of life and not only indirectly through the subordination of other spheres to church authorities. On the other hand, the liberation of diverse spheres of society should not be driven by the kind of secularizing motivation that aims to disconnect life outside the church from any relation to God. Instead, Christians should recognize and serve the sovereign God directly in every sphere of life, recognizing that all spheres of nonecclesiastical or "secular" life, are religious, that is, thoroughly dependent on God. The state, therefore, can fulfill its limited responsibility before God to uphold public justice without having to impose Christian discipline on all citizens and without having to subordinate itself to an ecclesiastical authority.

If Kuyper's reforming efforts in nineteenth- and twentieth-century Holland appear to be unusual even in the Reformed tradition, one reason is that members of Reformed churches throughout the world have more often adopted a different pattern of engagement in life outside the institutional church. The pattern is to engage as individuals, not through Christian organizations, in business, politics, science, education, and the arts. Whether one attributes this development to the influence of the Enlightenment, to a particular interpretation of God's common grace, or to a gradual process of acculturation, the outcome is the same. Most of those associated with Reformed churches, whether theologically liberal, moderate, or conservative, can be found engaged in business, government, the media, and the academic world in ways that are indistinguishable from the ways other Christians and non-Christians are engaged. Many Reformed Christians vote for conservative or libertarian political candidates, many others for liberal or social democratic candidates. Many are ardent capitalists, others quite anticapitalist. Many continue to place confidence in scientific and technological progress, while many others have become serious critics of the reductive, instrumental reasoning associated with such confidence. Why is this so?

One cause of this accommodating pattern of life among Reformed Christians is their close attachment to the new states their predecessors helped to create and the prosperity and technological advances from which they have benefited. Are not all of these—constitutional democracy, capitalist-driven economic growth, and technological inventiveness—the fruits of a Reformed understanding of vocations, the goodness of creation, and precautionary efforts to restrain sin by restraining the concentration of power and promoting liberty? Indeed, one can find many connections between the Reformed tradition and modern institutions and ways of life. But what about the ongoing nurturing of discernment and critical judgment within Reformed circles about what is good and what is bad in modern institutions and ways of life outside the vocations of the institutional church? What about *semper reformanda*, the continuation of critical, Christian reflection and cooperative efforts in economic, political, and cultural affairs? Is all such learning, critical reflection, and development of disciplined Christian practices to be left to Sunday sermons, Sunday school, and a social ethics course or two in seminaries?

Return with me to Calvin for a moment. Calvin's concern with the right ordering of all of life was, in part, the fruit of a straightforward, historical, non-allegorical, nonspiritualizing reading of the Old Testament, a reading influenced by Jewish scholars whom Calvin sought out. He was not a legalist, and his preaching of salvation by God's grace alone is well known. What interested Calvin was the whole life of Israel, God's covenant people, as model or at least pedagogue for God's new covenant people in Christ.[23] Calvin, according to Robinson, considered that the covenant of God with Israel was, in effect, "identical with the covenant of Christ, and the Old and New Testaments one continuous revelation."[24] In our day, there is a renewed effort among Christians of many different stripes to read the New Testament as rooted in the Old and therefore deeply continuous with and connected to it.[25] In this we can see the impact of Calvin and the Reformed tradition.

There was, however, a negative consequence of Calvin's attention to Israel as covenant community, a consequence that must be noted if we are to understand domestic and international politics today. In almost all of the countries most influenced by Calvinism, new political regimes were being formed at the time. As a result, there was a considerable influence of "new Israelite" imagination and biblical interpretation in the way Reformers conceived of those new, mostly national, polities. The Puritan settlement in the United States, for example, was modeled in many ways on the biblical stories of the Exodus, the settlement in the promised land, and the purification of a people who would be an exhibit to all the world of God's glory and love in establishing the new covenant nation.[26] "John Winthrop could start from scratch in the 'wilderness' of America and on the deck of the Arbella he preached that the future settlement would be a new Jerusalem, a city set upon a hill."[27] But the New England Puritans were not unique in this respect, Prestwich explains. "The doctrine of predestination, which came into the forefront when Beza succeeded Calvin, led Calvinists to identify themselves with the Elect and with the children of Israel. The Old Testament was for them both a mirror and a guide, in which they found inspiration for their victories over the forces of Babylon and consolation for their tribulations in the desert or the wilderness on their way to the Promised Land."[28] Some of the same ideas guided Knox in Scotland and the Afrikaners who settled in South Africa. The problem was not in considering Israel as a pedagogue for the new Israel in Christ but in imagining that a modern state (rather than the international and transtemporal body of Christ) could be the new Israel.

Because the United States eventually became a major power and is now the world's lone superpower, its self-chosen nationalized and now secularized identity as "exceptional nation"—a people specially blessed by God for a global mission—has had a huge impact on international affairs. This has been especially true since the presidency of Woodrow Wilson and runs right up to the presidency of George W. Bush. One cannot, of course, blame Calvin for either the successes or the failures of American democracy and foreign policy, but note that Wilson, a Presbyterian who had been president of Princeton University, wanted the League of Nations to be headquartered in Calvin's Geneva and wanted the league's constitution to be called a "covenant," all as a witness to his American view of the world.[29]

This is precisely the point at which a concern about the distinction between church and state must continue to be aired and debated today, especially in regard to the new kinds of Christian political engagement emerging in Asia, Africa, and Latin America.[30] Although much of that growth is inspired and nurtured by indigenous churches and evangelists, much of it is and has been inspired by evangelical and Pentecostal missionaries from the United States and elsewhere. One consequence is that American ideas of church, state, and nation have been transmitted, along with the preaching (both in person and by radio and television) and church planting by missionaries. In a number of countries, consequently, there are growing movements of a Christian-nationalist or civil-religious type, such as we find among many politically conservative American Christians. The emergence of a pattern of civil-religious nationalism, as a secularized version of new-Israelitism, in countries influenced by the Reformed tradition, should lead Calvinists, and Christians generally, to take a more critical look at a development that is closer to idolatry than to Christian reformation. The New Testament certainly does not support the idea that a political entity can be God's new Israel, modeled after God's chosen people of the old covenant. Nevertheless, many Americans who are members of Reformed churches are conservative nationalists of this kind, and others, who may be very critical of political conservatives, are ardent in their conviction that liberal political reforms could make the nation great again as the lead nation in history.

Creation, Sin, and Civil Religion

Consider again, for a moment, the doctrines of creation, sin, and redemption. One of the big historical questions that is still very much alive in our day is whether government and the political community belong to human beings by creation or only as a result of the fall into sin. And from that question follows the next: is political life part of our humanity that God is redeeming in Christ, or is it something that will fall away with God's final victory over sin and death in Christ's triumph?[31] There is no unanimity in Reformed circles about the answers to these questions.

Calvinists have been far more influenced by Augustine than by Thomas Aquinas, and they have typically viewed government and political community as a response to sin rather than as original with creation. Yet if that view is correct, then any connection between creation and government appears to disappear. In that case, government's purpose is chiefly, if not only, to restrain sin and exercise retributive justice, not to express and develop part of the positive meaning of human creatureliness. However, at least a minority stream of thought within the Reformed tradition contends that the basis for political community is to be found in creation rather than in the Fall. This view is somewhat different, however, than the view held by Aquinas, who argued that humans are *naturally* political. Aquinas's understanding of the political community was more influenced by Aristotle than by the biblical teaching about creation.

An argument for the positive, revelatory character of government and political community as grounded in creation can be summarized in the following way.[32] Humans, fashioned in the image of God, have been created, in part, to reveal (mirror) something of the ruling, governing character of God, as the Bible articulates that from Genesis 1 on through to John's culminating vision of Christ's enthronement in the new Jerusalem.[33] Just as God is shown biblically to be like a friend, a bridegroom, a parent, a shepherd, a vineyard keeper, and an elder brother, so also the Bible portrays God to be like a righteous judge, a generous lord, a just king, and a wise public administrator. Christ as king in the trio of "prophet, priest, and king" has a positive meaning and not only a retributive meaning. To be sure, if it had not been for sin, there would be no need for the retributive functions of government, just as there would be no need for parental punishment of children. But the retributive and sin-restraining functions of government do not constitute the original or core purpose of government in a political community; rather, those functions arise from and depend on the positive constitution of political order as a public-legal community of distributive justice for the common good. The primary meaning of political community, in other words, is not to be found in retribution against injustice but in a well-administered public order that upholds justice for all as measured by a well-balanced harmony of all human interests, responsibilities, and institutions in a public commons. States, of course, did not exist in the Garden of Eden, but neither did extended families, agricultural cooperatives, universities, and art clubs. Yet most of us recognize the development of agriculture, family life, art, and science to be expressions of our creatureliness—in the image of God. The same should be said, I would argue, for political community.

If the reader will grant this hypothesis, at least for the sake of argument, then the meaning of God's sovereignty comes into view not first of all as an overwhelming power to predestine some sinners to heaven and some to hell. Rather God's sovereignty comes into view as the origin of human creatures, made in the image of God and called to love and serve God with everything we are and have, including our stewardship of political community for the good of all fellow creatures. To be sure, sin is totally debilitating—totally depraving—and leads only to injustice, disgrace, and justifiable condemnation. Apart from the grace of

God in Christ, we would all be lost and without hope, utterly without any good left in us and without the possibility of public justice. Yet God's grace in Christ is revealed not first of all as the antithesis of sin, though it is that, but as the power to reconcile the creation to God, the creation that God has loved from the beginning. This is the creation that holds together from beginning to end in the Son of God who took on flesh in Jesus (John 1: 1–3; Colossians 1: 16; Hebrews 1: 1–3). And if God, by his sovereign grace, has come in Christ to reconcile all things to himself, then political life, too, is being called back to its rightful place in creation to the glory of God. God's redeeming grace in Christ spills over into the blessings of common grace for everyone in this age, but common grace does not absolve Christians from responsibility to maintain a constantly reforming approach in all spheres of life in order to advance justice and oppose injustice. And from what source should Christians be drawing their understanding of justice?

The Reformed Tradition and Contemporary Politics

If we take seriously the biblical view of God's sovereignty over creation, it leads to an understanding of nations and international relations that demands the rejection of every form of civil religion, idolatrous nationalism, and messianic new-Israelitism. God established Israel, for example, in fulfillment of his promise to Abraham that through his seed all the nations of the earth would be blessed. Israel's calling was to be God's exemplar to the world of what human faithfulness to God should be. The existence of Israel was not an end in itself but an anticipatory revelation of God's fulfillment of his purposes for the whole of creation. And when the Messiah of the Jews appeared, he called all people to himself, reconciling through his death on the cross the divisions between Jew and Gentile, male and female, and poor and rich, as well as between humans and God. Israel, fulfilled in Christ Jesus through whom the Gentiles are grafted in, is the community of faithfulness to God composed of people from all nations. Consequently, nation and nationalism cannot be the widest, deepest, strongest communal bond for human beings in this world. The fact of being created in the image of God and being called back to God through Jesus Christ into one community of faithfulness should be the deepest bond of human identity and unity.

One of the great idolatries of American self-identity as a new Israel is a kind of civil-religious nationalism, rooted not in a common bloodline but in the adoption of a secularized idea of our nation as God's new covenant people, God's lead nation in history.[34] This idea also happens to be tied so intimately to the European experience that American self-identity was not able to include native

Americans or African slaves. Today, Americans (including many Reformed Christians) tend to view history and the place of Christians in it through the glasses of the history of the United States—the lead nation of freedom, prosperity, and democracy—rather than through the glasses of the coming of God's creation-wide kingdom in Jesus Christ. The United States, in other words, is thought to be the key to secular history as the exceptional nation, the nation most blessed by God, the nation called to bring freedom and democracy to the world.

Christians, particularly those in the Reformed tradition, should recognize this as an idolatry of the nation and should repent of this new-Israelite political ideology that controls so much of our thinking about American sovereignty and international relations. If we were to take our point of departure from the biblical view of creation, fall, and redemption, then American Christian thinking about war and peace and international relations would also have to change.

Calvinists have not been the only Christians to emphasize the doctrine of creation, nor have they always done much with the doctrine. But the potential for distinctiveness here is considerable, particularly when we turn our attention to politics and international relations today. First, if everything that exists *is* God's creation, then there is only one world in which a single humanity bears a wide variety of earthly responsibilities before the face of the one Creator God. The simplicity and unity of God's creational purposes fall from view, however, if one assumes that reality is constituted most fundamentally by a dualism between this creation and another world, between the damned and the saved, or between Christian nations and non-Christian nations. Distinctions and divisions do exist, to be sure, but to recognize that this world is God's one creation is to realize that the purpose of human history in its entirety is not, for example, to reach the goal of democracy, freedom, and free trade among sovereign states, embracing everyone throughout the globe. The key battles of history are not those between America and its enemies, between the free world and the communist world, or between Western freedom and radical Islamism. Rather, God's original end in view is the divine glory to be celebrated by all peoples and all nations everywhere—with every knee bowing before, and every tongue confessing, the lordship of Jesus Christ, who has ascended on high in resurrection power to rule God's kingdom.

From this point of view, the meaning of nations in the Bible is to be found not in the permanence of nation-states as sovereign, separated entities but in the fact that the many different language and cultural groups that have spread across the globe share a common calling, a single cultural mandate, to serve God by revealing manifold dimensions of the image of God and exercising stewardly dominion over the earth. To be sure, these human beings are often at odds in all kinds of ways because of their sinful alienation from God and one another. But sin is precisely what God condemns, and Christ's reconciling sacrifice for sin is the basis for the restoration of human community, for the reconciliation of nations at odds with one another, and for the fulfillment of God's one purpose for humanity.

The particular forms or modes of government and political community at any point in history, therefore, are of much less significance than the fact that God has called us at all times and in all places to do justice, to love mercy, to walk humbly with God, and in other words, to love God with all that we are and have and to love our neighbors as ourselves. Well-governed states may be very important at this point in history as a means of achieving a greater degree of just governance within particular geographical and cultural areas among billions of people in the world. But even the best modern constitutional state is not the goal or end of history. And if that is not history's goal, then the question that must be asked is whether it is possible for humans to do justice to one another in our rapidly shrinking world without building better and stronger international and even transnational institutions of government. If this question is asked from a traditional, state-centered, realist or idealist perspective, it does not meet with a very satisfactory answer. But if asked from a biblical point of view, then I think avenues of creative political thought and action open wide before us. While I believe that all Christians should be cooperating to work out the implications of a biblical, creation-order approach to politics today, this should certainly be the case for those who claim to stand in the Reformed tradition of *semper reformanda*.

One of the arenas of greatest contention over the responsibility of governments today is that of warfare. And in that arena, one of the longest standing and longest developing traditions of Christian moral engagement is represented by the so-called just war tradition. Calvin and most of those who followed in the Reformed tradition continued to support just war criteria because they recognized that the criteria put governments under the divinely mandated obligation to do justice and restrain the use of force. The more that governments go to war willfully, merely to achieve their own ambitions, the more anarchic and unjust the world becomes. Christians can have no part in contributing to such a chaotic world. This world is God's creation; all men and women have been created in the image of God; all are corrupted by sin. Yet God's mercy and patience have been extended to everyone, giving rain and sunshine to the just and unjust alike. And God's judgment will fall on all injustice and those who perpetrate it. Without the means of reaching agreements among states based on certain principles of justice, there can be no stability in international affairs. Without such stability, states will act with suspicion toward their neighbors and expect the worst from them. Most countries, however, have recognized that it is often in their own interest to comply with mutually agreed-upon standards that can serve every state's interest in stability, trade, diplomacy, and security. Such agreements, in themselves, will not keep states from war altogether, but Christians should be working in and through their governments to try to achieve such agreements and mutual trust to clarify and establish patterns of international behavior that reflect principles of justice.

One of the big questions today is whether the American-led war in Iraq has strengthened or weakened healthy global patterns of international relations.[35] Do countries around the world now look with more or less confidence to the United States as a contributor to just governance? At the moment of this writing, it appears that the United States has lost rather than gained standing and credibility among the nations since 2003. That could be a good thing, if it inspires nations throughout the world, including the United States in the future, to act with greater humility and in greater cooperation with other states. If, however, the diminishment of the United States leads other nations to try to emulate American unilateral arbitrariness in places where a power vacuum is emerging, then it could be a very bad thing indeed.

If just governance is the obligation that properly falls on governments, as the Reformed tradition has emphasized, and if the responsibility to reform is part of what God's reconciling work in Christ inspires, then Christians should be urging national governments to see themselves as having limited and mutual responsibility to contribute to a more just world order. Insofar as terrorism, economic globalism, and international ecological threats, to name only three challenges of our day, require international cooperation and even institution building, it is a clear sign of injustice when any state uses the means of warfare to try to achieve its goals in ways that weaken rather than strengthen cooperative international efforts to achieve greater justice and better governance within and among states. When actions that at best can serve the purpose of retributive justice are employed by one state as a means of trying to reorder the means of governance in other parts of the world, they represent that state's failure to understand the limits of the use of force for good governance.

Going hand in hand with the Reformed tradition's high regard for creation is its emphasis that government's calling is to do justice in humility and fear before God. There is no justification for governments to act aggressively out of a nationalistic, messianic, or totalitarian motivation to try to force the world into the shape they wish it to have. The opposite is what we need today, namely, governments acting as cooperatively as possible to uphold laws of distributive justice for the positive good of the commons—both the domestic commons within individual countries and the international commons of the world.

One of the greatest challenges facing Christians today is to learn how particular states and their governments should be acting to shape a more just international order. Most of that responsibility has to do with political, economic, environmental, health, and technological matters, not with war fighting. Nevertheless, the continuing development of military forces and weapons, as well as the continuing growth of terrorist and other violent movements, means that control of the use of force will remain one of the most important concerns of political responsibility. The Reformed tradition has something important to contribute to the development of Christian approaches to these most important challenges, and it should do so as part of a wider concern with the development of an always-reforming approach to life inspired by God's saving and reconciling work in Jesus Christ, the Alpha through whom all things were made and the Omega through whom God's kingdom will be fulfilled.

NOTES

1. W. Fred Graham, *The Constructive Revolutionary: John Calvin and His Socio-Economic Impact* (Richmond, VA: John Knox Press, 1971), 190–191. Max Weber develops his argument in *The Protestant Ethic and the Spirit of Capitalism* (New York: Scribner's, 1958, published in German in 1904–1905). Graham's book draws on and helps to represent the classic study of Calvin's social and economic influence by Andre Bieler, *La pensee economique et sociale de Calvin* (Geneva: Georg, 1959). For more on the relation of Calvin and Calvinism to modernity, see Ralph C. Hancock, *Calvin and the Foundations of Modern Politics* (Ithaca, NY: Cornell University Press, 1989), particularly 164–194; William R. Stevenson, *Sovereign Grace: The Place and Significance of Christian Freedom in John Calvin's Political Thought* (New York: Oxford University Press, 1999); James E. Block, *A Nation of Agents: The American Path to a Modern Self and Society* (Cambridge, MA: Belknap Press of Harvard University Press, 2002); and Mark A. Noll, *America's God: From Jonathan Edwards to Abraham Lincoln* (New York: Oxford University Press, 2002), particularly 31–92.

2. To speak of Calvin and Calvinists as reformers, not revolutionaries, is to disagree in part with Michael Walzer's argument in *The Revolution of the Saints: A Study in the Origins of Radical Politics* (Cambridge, MA: Harvard University Press, 1965). See Stevenson's discussion of Walzer and others on progress and/or revolution in Calvin's thought: *Sovereign Grace*, 109–130.

3. Menna Prestwich, ed., *International Calvinism: 1541–1715* (Oxford: Oxford University Press, 1985). "Calvinism was an international religion seeking not to adapt itself to society but to cast society into a new mould," writes Prestwich (7). It "was marked by a sense of international solidarity" (5). See also John T. McNeill, *The History and Character of Calvinism* (New York: Oxford University Press, 1967).

4. Prestwich, *International Calvinism*, 13.

5. Ibid., 13–14. Marilynne Robinson comments, for example, that Americans are indebted to Calvin for "relatively popular government, the relatively high status of

women, the separation of church and state, what remains of universal schooling, and, while it lasted, liberal higher education, education in 'the humanities.'" See *The Death of Adam: Essays on Modern Thought* (New York: Houghton Mifflin, 1998), 205–206. Robinson discusses Calvin's views of sin and predestination, to be sure, but her wider cultural perspective leads her to emphasize other themes in his work.

6. Graham, *Constructive Revolutionary*, 161. See John Calvin, *Institutes of the Christian Religion*, 2 vols., ed. John T. McNeill, trans. Ford Lewis Battles (Philadelphia: Westminster Press, 1960), book 4, chap. 1, 1024–1053.

7. Graham, *Constructive Revolutionary*, 160–161. See Calvin, *Institutes*, book 4, chap. 20, 1485–1493. On Luther and Calvin, see William A. Mueller, *Church and State in Luther and Calvin* (New York: Doubleday Anchor Books, 1954); and Oliver O'Donovan and Joan Lockwood O'Donovan, *From Irenaeus to Grotius: A Sourcebook in Christian Political Thought* (Grand Rapids, MI: William B. Eerdmans, 1999), 581–608, 662–684. On the Anabaptists and the Schleitheim Articles, see O'Donovan and O'Donovan, *Irenaeus to Grotius*, 631–646. On the impact of Luther and Calvin on the development of law in Germany and England, see Harold J. Berman, *Law and Revolution II: The Impact of the Protestant Reformations on the Western Legal Tradition* (Cambridge, MA: Belknap Press of Harvard University Press, 2003). On Calvin's and Calvinism's influence on the modern understanding of human rights, see John Witte Jr., *The Reformation of Rights: Law, Religion and Human Rights in Early Modern Calvinism* (Cambridge: Cambridge University Press, 2007).

8. In addition to the works of Prestwich and McNeill, see the following two volumes in Daniel J. Elazar's four-volume work on the covenant tradition in politics, published by Transaction, New Brunswick, New Jersey: *Covenant and Commonwealth* (1996) and *Covenant and Constitutionalism* (1998).

9. Calvin, *Institutes*, book 1, chap. 14, 179–180.

10. Ibid., chap. 15, 188. "We must now speak of the creation of man," writes Calvin, "not only because among all God's works here is the noblest and most remarkable example of his justice, wisdom, and goodness; but because, as we said at the beginning, we cannot have a clear and complete knowledge of God unless it is accompanied by a corresponding knowledge of ourselves. This knowledge of ourselves is twofold: namely, to know what we were like when we were first created and what our condition became after the fall of Adam" (183).

11. Robinson, *Death of Adam*, 221.

12. Ibid., 220.

13. See Calvin, *Institutes*, book 2, chap. 12–book 3, chap. 1, 464–542, esp. 494–503.

14. Graham, *Constructive Revolutionary*, 211.

15. Stevenson, *Sovereign Grace*, 149–150.

16. Quoted in Robinson, *Death of Adam*, 181.

17. Abraham Kuyper, *Lectures on Calvinism* (Grand Rapids, MI: William B. Eerdmans, 1961, 1931). Kuyper referred to Calvinism as a total "life system" parallel to "Paganism, Islamism, and Romanism" (17). Calvinism, he said, "is rooted in a form of religion which was peculiarly its own, and from this specific religious consciousness there was developed first a peculiar theology, then a special church-order, and then a given form for political and social life, for the interpretation of the moral world-order,

for the relation between nature and grace, between Christianity and the world, between church and state, and finally for art and science; and amid all these life-utterances it remained always the self-same Calvinism, in so far as simultaneously and spontaneously all these developments sprang from its deepest life-principle" (17). For more on Kuyper's Stone Lectures, see Peter S. Heslam, *Creating a Christian Worldview: Abraham Kuyper's Lectures on Calvinism* (Grand Rapids, MI: William B. Eerdmans, 1998), and for more on the meaning of "worldview" in Kuyper's thought, see David K. Naugle, *Worldview: The History of a Concept* (Grand Rapids, MI: William B. Eerdmans, 2002), esp. 16–25.

18. Creative contemporary development of the Reformed tradition as world-transformative Christianity is evident, for example, in Craig G. Bartholomew and Michael W. Goheen, *The Drama of Scripture: Finding Our Place in the Biblical Story* (Grand Rapids, MI: Baker Books, 2004); Paul Marshall, *God and the Constitution: Christianity and American Politics* (Lanham, MD: Rowman and Littlefield, 2002); Nicholas Wolterstorff, *Until Justice and Peace Embrace* (Grand Rapids, MI: William B. Eerdmans, 1983); and Luis E. Lugo, ed., *Religion, Pluralism, and Public Life: Abraham Kuyper's Legacy for the Twenty-First Century* (Grand Rapids, MI: William B. Eerdmans, 2000).

19. See Calvin, *Institutes*, book 4, chap. 20, 1495–1499.

20. On Calvin's impact on the development of capitalism and political economy, see, for example, Herbert Luthy, *From Calvin to Rousseau: Tradition and Modernity in Socio-Political Thought from the Reformation to the French Revolution*, trans. Salvator Attanasio (New York: Basic Books, 1970); and Graham, *The Constructive Revolutionary*. On Calvin's influence on the development of constitutionalism, the rule of law, and representative government, see, for example, Elazar, *Covenant and Constitutionalism*; in O'Donovan and O'Donovan, *Irenaeus to Grotius*, the chapters "Vindiciae, contra Tyrannos" (711–722) and "Johannes Althusius" (757–770); and Julian H. Franklin, ed., *Constitutionalism and Resistance in the Sixteenth Century* (New York: Pegasus, 1969).

21. Kuyper, *Lectures*, 100.

22. Ibid.

23. On Calvin's use of the Bible, including the Old Testament, to understand the task of government and lawmaking in the Christian era, see Guenther H. Haas, *The Concept of Equity in Calvin's Ethics* (Waterloo, ON: Wilfrid Laurier University Press, 1997); and Mueller, *Church and State*, 127–138, 157–165.

24. Robinson, *Death of Adam*, 192.

25. See, for example, the works of N. T. Wright, such as *The New Testament and the People of God* (Minneapolis, MN: Fortress Press, 1992) and *Jesus and the Victory of God* (Minneapolis, MN: Fortress Press, 1996); Bartholomew and Goheen, *The Drama of Scripture;* William J. Dumbrell, *The Search for Order: Biblical Eschatology in Focus* (Grand Rapids, MI: Baker Books, 1994); and Albert M. Wolters, *Creation Regained* (Grand Rapids, MI: William B. Eerdmans, 1985).

26. See Noll, *America's God*, 19–92; and James W. Skillen, *With or Against the World? America's Role among the Nations* (Lanham, MD: Rowman and Littlefield, 2005), 67–94.

27. Prestwich, *International Calvinism*, 7.

28. Ibid.

29. Lloyd E. Ambrosius, *Wilsonianism: Woodrow Wilson and His Legacy in American Foreign Relations* (New York: Palgrave McMillan, 2002), 36.

30. See, for example, Paul Freston, *Evangelicals and Politics in Asia, Africa, and Latin America* (New York: Cambridge University Press, 2001); and Paul Freston, *Protestant Political Parties: A Global Survey* (Aldershot, UK: Ashgate, 2004).

31. The importance of this question about the origin of government comes to the fore in the contemporary writings of Oliver O'Donovan, particularly *The Desire of the Nations* (Cambridge: Cambridge University Press, 1996) and, more recently, *The Ways of Judgment* (Grand Rapids, MI: William B. Eerdmans, 2005). See the review of the latter volume by Gilbert Meilaender, "Judging Politics," *First Things* (January 2006): 42–49; and James W. Skillen, "Acting Politically in Biblical Obedience" (with a response from O'Donovan), in Craig Bartholomew et al., *A Royal Priesthood? The Use of the Bible Ethically and Politically* (Grand Rapids, MI: Zondervan; Carlisle, UK: Paternoster Press, 2002), 398–417 and 418–420.

32. See the first chapter of James W. Skillen, *In Pursuit of Justice: Christian-Democratic Explorations* (Lanham, MD: Rowman and Littlefield, 2004), "What Distinguishes a Christian-Democratic Point of View," 1–17; and James W. Skillen, "The Common Good as Political Norm," in *In Search of the Common Good,* eds. Patrick D. Miller and Dennis P. McCann (New York: T. and T. Clark International, 2005), 256–278.

33. A clear overview of the biblical story of the realization of God's kingdom and of human responsibility in that kingdom is presented in Bartholomew and Goheen, *The Drama of Scripture.*

34. On "Christian" republicanism and new-Israelitism in America, see Mark A. Noll, *America's God: From Jonathan Edwards to Abraham Lincoln* (New York: Oxford University Press, 2002), 31–92.

35. My own attempt to assess American foreign and defense policy since 9/11, against the backdrop of American history, can be found in James W. Skillen, *With or Against the World?*

5

Anabaptists and the State: An Uneasy Coexistence

Sandra F. Joireman

In any compilation of Christian views of the state, the Anabaptist position stands out as unique or, if one wanted to be less compli-mentary, extreme. The Anabaptist view of the state is less focused on articulating the division between church and state responsibili-ties than the Reformed or Lutheran traditions. Indeed, Anabap-tists have no assigned role for government beyond the creation of order, emphasizing scriptural interpretations that give primacy to the church in the life of a Christian. As a result, political theology distances Anabaptists from both the Catholic Church and the main-stream of the Reformation.

There is no Anabaptist church; rather, Anabaptists are groups of Christians emphasizing similar faith positions. In the West, Anabap-tists are predominantly Mennonite, but Anabaptism encompasses groups such as the Brethren, Amish, and Hutterites, as well as numerous other denominations outside Europe and North America.[1] However, there are some who would call themselves Anabaptist (for example, some Baptists) who may not necessarily share a similar political theology. In this chapter, the term Anabaptist is used in discussing the historical progression of the movement and changes to Mennonite when describing contemporary beliefs regarding the church and citizenship. This is a necessary distinction because the Mennonite position on citizenship is certainly not that of all Ana-baptists. Anabaptism is a movement, and Mennonites are the largest church within that movement. Thus, to the extent that this chapter

addresses contemporary church positions, it must be from the slightly narrower Mennonite stance rather than from the Anabaptist perspective.

This chapter begins with a historical discussion of the roots of Anabaptism.
Although history is important for all religions, for Anabaptists the time of the
Reformation was not simply a chronological marker but a crucible that refined
the movement in terms of beliefs and greatly reduced its numbers through
martyrdom. It was during the institutional chaos and uncertainty of the Reformation that the political beliefs held by Anabaptists today were formed and
contextually articulated. The middle section of the chapter details the origin of
political beliefs that set Anabaptists apart from other denominations. The final
section of the chapter addresses the implications of Anabaptist political beliefs
put into practice within the contemporary state system.

Historical Background

The Anabaptist movement is often referred to as the radical fringe of the Reformation.[2] Some of the first Anabaptists, Felix Manz and Conrad Grebel, were
students of Ulrich Zwingli in Switzerland. They supported Zwingli's break with
the Catholic Church and his push for reform, but they were uncomfortable
with the way Zwingli used political power. Zwingli tried to work through the
Zurich council, the local political authority, to win the council over to his side.
His goal was to harness the power of the council and get it to establish policies
that supported the position of the reformers. Zwingli believed it was the role
and appropriate place of political authorities, such as the council, to oversee the
implementation of the Reformation. Manz and Grebel disagreed. They believed
that the progress and completion of the Reformation ought to be directed by
the churches and not by government; after all, one of the goals of the Reformation was to challenge the close alliance between the Catholic Church and political authority (Goertz 1996: 11). Manz and Grebel led a break with Zwingli and
the mainstream of the Swiss Reformation over the issues of political authority,
opposition to a state church, and believers' baptism.

The Anabaptist movement was founded on January 21, 1525, when Manz,
Grebel, and their followers acted on their differences with the mainline Swiss
Reformers by rebaptizing adults. These early Swiss Anabaptists believed that there
should be a free church patterned on the congregations of the New Testament
and peopled by adults who were baptized as believers.[3] This second or believers'
baptism earned them the derisive name of Anabaptists, literally rebaptizers.

There were three strands of early Anabaptists: (a) the Swiss Brethren, as just
mentioned; (b) Anabaptist groups in South Germany and Austria (Hutterites);

and (c) Dutch Mennonites. The Hutterite and the Dutch Anabaptist movements were more spiritualist and apocalyptic than the Swiss Anabaptists, and dialogues between leaders from these different Anabaptist movements demonstrated clear theological disagreements (Harder 1985). Balthasar Hubmaier, an Austrian Anabaptist reformer who had been part of the group who studied with Zwingli, commented regarding Hans Hut, a south German Anabaptist and the founder of the eponymous Hutterites, "[T]he baptism which I taught and the baptism which Hut purported to teach are as far apart as heaven and earth, east and west, Christ and Belial" (Goertz 1996: 7). Given this depth of feeling, it is not surprising that one "Anabaptist Church" never formed and that Anabaptism remained a movement, splitting into different sects based on locality of origin and beliefs, rather than a theologically unified group.

One of the first lasting articulations of Swiss Brethren theology was the Schleitheim Confession of 1527, which marked the beginning of the free church, meaning that its membership was not defined by political authorities.[4] The Schleitheim Confession expressed the Swiss Anabaptist positions of adult baptism based on professed belief, refusal to take oaths, the free election of church leaders, and Communion not as a sacrament or transubstantiation, but as an expression of Christian community. The rejection of violence or the "devilish weapons of force—such as sword, armor and the like, and all their use [either] for friends or against one's enemies—by virtue of the Word of Christ" (Swiss Brethren Conference 1527) was also present. Beliefs regarding the state were taken a step further than previously articulated, and members of the Brethren were encouraged to reject any service to the state, be it military or otherwise.

> Finally it will be observed that it is not appropriate for a Christian
> to serve as a magistrate because of these points: The government
> magistracy is according to the flesh, but the Christian's is according
> to the Spirit; their houses and dwelling remain in this world, but the
> Christian's are in heaven; their citizenship is in this world, but the
> Christian's citizenship is in heaven; the weapons of their conflict and
> war are carnal and against the flesh only, but the Christian's weapons
> are spiritual, against the fortification of the devil. The worldlings are
> armed with steel and iron, but the Christians are armed with the
> armor of God, with truth, righteousness, peace, faith, salvation and
> the Word of God. In brief, as in the mind of God toward us, so shall
> the mind of the members of the body of Christ be through Him in
> all things, that there may be no schism in the body through which it
> would be destroyed. For every kingdom divided against itself will be
> destroyed. (Swiss Brethren Conference 1527)

Anabaptism is clearly linked to the revolutionary changes in patterns of religious organization and belief that were happening during the Reformation. Yet because of the Anabaptist rejection of the organizational hierarchies of both Protestants and Catholics and their sharp break with the Protestant Reformation, both Catholics and Protestants persecuted Anabaptists.[5]

In the early 1600s, Dutch Anabaptists were vocal in their opposition to government efforts to cede authority of the state to the Dutch East Indies Company for law enforcement and the punishment of wrongdoers within territory controlled by the company. The Dutch Anabaptists believed that the state and no other must wield the powers attributed to it in Romans 12 and 13. While the Dutch Anabaptists supported the articulated responsibilities of the state, they did not think that vengeance belonged in the hands of the individual Christian or in the hands of a business venture with delegated state responsibilities (Brock 1972). Early Dutch Anabaptists rejected violence by believers but supported the right of the state to use violence in some circumstances, which was what they perceived to be the appropriate role for the state.[6]

Protestant, Catholic, or Evangelical?

The unique position of Anabaptists during and after the Reformation has led to the description of Anabaptists as "neither Catholic nor Protestant" or "both Catholic and Protestant."[7] Ambiguity regarding the categorization of Anabaptist beliefs has carried through in some form to the present day. Many Mennonites view themselves to be under the Protestant umbrella, albeit of a different persuasion than most, but others do not see themselves as Protestants and see Anabaptism as a third stream of Christianity.

To the extent that evangelicalism can be characterized by the three *solas*— *sola scriptura* (scripture alone), *solus Christus* (Christ alone), and *sola fides* (faith alone)—Anabaptists can find themselves both within and outside the evangelical tradition.[8] During the early 20th century, as North American Mennonites turned outward and began to engage the wider culture, they identified themselves with fundamentalist concerns. Craig Carter notes that Anabaptist leaders in the mid-20th century, such as Harold Bender, tried to make "evangelical Anabaptism" the focus of Mennonites in North America (Carter 2001: 37). In the contemporary era, the term *evangelical* does not have the same appeal. As the evangelical movement in America has come to be so closely identified with the state that there is no obvious separation between the two, the possibility of the church as witness to the world is eroded, and fewer Mennonites are willing to use the term *evangelical* without caveat.

The lack of a creedal tradition within Anabaptism and its low-sacramental nature are elements of evangelicalism that fit well with Anabaptist beliefs. However, among Anabaptists there would be a strong challenge to the idea of *sola fides*. Anabaptism has historically been characterized by a strong belief in the Jamesian statement that "faith without works is dead." Menno Simons, an early Mennonite leader, famously stated: "True evangelical faith cannot lie dormant. It clothes the naked, it feeds the hungry, it comforts the sorrowful, it shelters the destitute, it serves those that harm it, it binds up that which is wounded, it has become all things to all people" (Simons 1956: 246).

An Anabaptist Perspective on the State

Anabaptists, particularly Mennonites, are popularly known for their pacifism and conscientious objector status during times of war. Yet, this is but one manifestation of deeply held beliefs regarding the suitable role of government and the appropriate role of the church. Pacifism is epiphenomenal to the Anabaptist view of the appropriate roles of the state and the church.[9] The state has the function of ordering the social world, and the church should be the visible witness of believers, the primary affiliation of Christians, and separate from the state.

Some agreement regarding the role of government has developed among Mennonites in the contemporary era. Government exists within the world with a particular function—to provide order. This position is most strongly articulated in English through the works of Mennonite theologian John H. Yoder in the 1960s and 1970s (Yoder 1972, 2002).[10] Order created by the state allows the church to grow and the gospel to be spread. Yoder argued that the necessity of the government derives from its responsibility in providing a service to the church. This position with regard to the role of the state is a result of early theological positions that rejected political authority in determining people's religious beliefs. Moreover, in the early years of the Reformation, Anabaptists objected to forcible conversions of people from Catholicism to Protestantism or the determination of religion by geography; they argued that conversion should be an individual and not a political choice. It was this opposition to the role of state religions that led both to the persecution of Anabaptists and to their strong conception of the church as separate from and superior to political powers.[11]

Contemporary Mennonites view the church and the state as separate and unequal, with an elevation of the church over the state. The state is useful on earth for creating order so that the gospel can be spread, but the church is more important. This is very distinct from other theological approaches: "In contrast to the church, governing authorities of the world have been instituted by God for maintaining order in societies. Such governments and other human institutions as servants of God are called to act justly and provide order. But like all such institutions, nations tend to demand total allegiance. They then become idolatrous and rebellious against the will of God. Even at its best, government cannot act completely according to the justice of God because no nation, except the church, confesses Christ's rule as its foundation" (Inter-Mennonite Confession of Faith Committee 1995: 85).[12]

The belief in the order-providing role of the state derives from both historical experience and an interpretation of Romans 13 that assumes the state does not have the right to command a Christian to do what God has forbidden. Romans 13: 1–5 has been viewed by some Christian groups as a call to obey the state in all matters or as absolving the Christian of guilt for obeying the state.[13] Mennonites interpret the same passage differently, through the hermeneutical lens of the life of Christ. The text of Romans 13: 1–5 (Today's New International Version) is as follows:

> Let everyone be subject to the governing authorities, for there is no
> authority except that which God has established. The authorities that
> exist have been established by God. Consequently, whoever rebels
> against the authority is rebelling against what God has instituted,
> and those who do so will bring judgment on themselves. For rulers
> hold no terror for those who do right, but for those who do wrong.
> Do you want to be free from fear of the one in authority? Then do
> what is right and you will be commended. For the one in authority
> is God's servant for your good. But if you do wrong, be afraid, for
> rulers do not bear the sword for no reason. They are God's servants,
> agents of wrath to bring punishment on the wrongdoer. Therefore, it
> is necessary to submit to the authorities, not only because of possible
> punishment but also as a matter of conscience.

John Howard Yoder interprets Romans 13 as follows: "God is not said to create or institute or ordain the powers that be, but only to order them, to put them in order, sovereignly to tell them where they belong, what is their place. It is not as if there was a time when there was no government and then God made government through a new creative intervention; there has been hierarchy and authority and power since human society" (Yoder 1972: 203).[14] The appropriate roles of the church and the state have been debated throughout the history of the Mennonite tradition. The early Dutch Mennonites used Romans 13 to support their claim that only the government has the power to wield the sword, an argument against the authority of the Dutch East Indies

Company. Additionally, a related Mennonite hermeneutic interprets the Old Testament through the lens of the New Testament (Inter-Mennonite Confession of Faith Committee 1995).[15] The two Testaments are not given equality, as they might be in other Protestant denominations, but are viewed progressively.[16] The life of Christ, in particular, should enlighten the interpretation of all other scripture (Weaver 2005: 169–179). Thus the interpretation and understanding of New Testament verses on the role of the state are far more important than any of the examples of the Old Testament monarchies. From a Mennonite perspective, the state is not the Christian's fundamental allegiance. Mennonites are particularly suspicious of calls to engage in violence on behalf of the state. They believe that Christians live in a different reality than that faced by the state, as well as a different reality than that experienced by non-Christians.

The Mennonite view of the role of the state is complemented by a unique understanding of church. The role of the Christian community is essential, not only for reasons of discipleship and teaching but also because of the belief that it is within the church that one can see the presence of Christ.[17] The church stands as a visible witness to the world, distinct and different from it. This idea of church as witness makes strongly held and unpopular positions, such as pacifism, much easier for the church to bear because the church is understood to be an alternative polis. While Niebuhr (1951) goes too far in suggesting that the Anabaptist vision is that of the church against "culture,"[18] the church should be recognizably different than the world. When the distinction between the church and the world is no longer discernible, the church has lost its ability to bear witness to the good news of Christ.

Implications of the Church-State Hierarchy

The Mennonite beliefs regarding the role of the church and the state and its implications for military service are familiar to many Christians. Mennonites are conscientious objectors and have either negotiated with governments to engage in alternative service during times of conscription or been imprisoned. Pacifism is a manifestation of the early understandings of the Anabaptist movement regarding the proper relationship of political authority to the church and the correct interpretation of scripture. Although not present in all early strains of Anabaptism, the issue dates back to the Reformation era, even prior to the Schleitheim Confession. Conrad Grebel, the founder of the Swiss Brethren Church, wrote to Thomas Muntzer in 1524: "True believing Christians are sheep among wolves, sheep for the slaughter. They must be baptized in anguish and tribulation, persecution, suffering, and death, tried in fire, and must reach the fatherland of eternal rest not by slaying the physical but the spiritual. They use neither worldly sword nor war, since killing has ceased with them entirely, unless indeed we are still under the old law, and even there (as far as we can know) war was only a plague after they had once conquered the Promised Land. No more of this" (Harder 1985: 284). This quote is from one of the founding Anabaptists at a time when the various streams of Anabaptism were still present within the main flow of the Protestant Reformation. It illustrates quite well the Anabaptist position regarding the use of force by Christians.

Most present-day Mennonites still articulate a belief in nonviolence, particularly state violence in times of war. Some would accept that violence by the state is never appropriate, and others would argue that violence by the state is necessary for the state to keep order, but only against those who have done wrong. In either case, participation in the military is never understood to be a legitimate vocation of the Christian.[19] The position of the church regarding military service is the most visible evidence of the Mennonite belief regarding the responsibilities of the church and the state. Yet, the position of nonviolence is not limited to its collective denominational manifestations. Mennonites focus on nonviolence within congregations, and many try to make it a way of life, though there is certainly a great deal of variation in practice. There are four more implications of the Mennonite belief regarding the role of the state identified next. They move beyond the more traditional discussion of pacifism and tease out the contemporary meanings of the belief that the church ought to be above the state.

First, if the church holds a primary claim on Christian allegiance, then all state decisions and policies should be considered in relation to their effect on the church and its mission in reaching unbelievers and providing a witness to the love of Christ. Any state policy that might affect not just the domestic church but the church worldwide is a matter of concern for Mennonites. This perspective provides an unusual lens for examining foreign policy. For example, Mennonites in America and in other countries can be opposed to the war in Iraq because they are against violence.[20] However, theologically they also ought to be opposed to the war, and many are, because of its potential negative effects on Iraqi Christians, whose lives will be rendered more difficult, or even ended, because of the war in Iraq. Moreover, to the degree that American intervention in Iraq is perceived as a "Christian" action by others, and this action confers a negative image upon the church that impedes its growth and attractiveness, Mennonites ought to be opposed to it. The idea that the church holds the primary claim on Christian allegiance and that foreign policy should be examined in light of its effects on the church worldwide should also apply in other policy areas, such as trade and diplomatic relations with other countries. Any government action that is injurious to the worldwide body of believers in Christ should be rejected.

The second implication of the Mennonite prioritization of the church is that as the nature of the church changes, political issues of concern to Mennonites will change as well. The growth of Christianity worldwide is concentrated in the global South, in Africa, India, and South America. Such popular commentaries on this trend such as Jenkins's *The Next Christendom* (Jenkins 2002) note that this will change the nature of Christianity, including the concerns of the church. As the church grows in the global South, international issues of concern to Mennonites in North America and Europe should be more focused on foreign policy issues as they relate to the global South and the church there. Issues such as debt relief, poverty alleviation, and the HIV/AIDS epidemic have been and will continue to be major policy concerns for Mennonites because they directly affect the church.

In a somewhat circuitous manner, this Mennonite concern for the church worldwide places Mennonites in the same place politically as many Catholics, though via a different mechanism. Catholic social teaching articulates a "preferential option for the poor," meaning that when there is a trade-off between what is beneficial for the rich and what is beneficial for the poor, the correct choice is the option that is beneficial for the poor. As a result, the Catholic Church has been at the forefront of movements that are specifically concerned with Christians in the global South. An excellent example is Catholic leadership on the Jubilee debt relief campaign. Mennonites arrive at the same place via a different theological route and support issues such as debt relief, conflict resolution, and international development efforts because they help our brothers and sisters in the church in the developing world, promote primary justice worldwide, and demonstrate the concern that God has for the poor.[21] Both Mennonites and Catholics are extremely active in poverty reduction efforts around the globe, though with slightly different theological justifications.

The third implication of the Mennonite belief regarding the appropriate relative positions of the church and the state is that nationalism is viewed in a dubious manner by most Mennonites. Nationalism, the psychological or emotional attachment to a group, is acceptable only insofar as it does not become idolatrous.[22] Consistent with the earlier points, nationalism can be harmless up to the point at which it leads people to favor their allegiance to the state or other substate group over that of the church and the gospel. In practice, this means that cheering for your state in the Olympics would be fine, as might be standing for the national anthem.[23] However, any sort of nationalist sentiment that leads one to forget or degrade the primary role of the church is eschewed.

As noted previously, the war in Iraq was problematic for Mennonites because the potential killing of Iraqi Christians might impede the spread of the gospel. Arguments by politicians for the U.S. national interest in the Iraq war were widely labeled idolatrous within the Mennonite church because they elevated national interest above the church. These systemic concerns are in addition to individual practice: the avowed Anabaptist imperative is that Christians should not kill; therefore, they should not be involved in the armed forces in any capacity that would lead them to kill another human being.[24]

The fourth implication of the Mennonite belief regarding the role of the state and the church is its effect on political action. During the Reformation, early Anabaptists rejected the idea that they should play any role at all in governance. Many Mennonites follow this logic in the contemporary era and refuse any sort of government service (not just military). Other Anabaptist communities, such as the Hutterites and Old Order Mennonites, refuse to even vote. However, there is no explicit church position, and more Mennonites are taking political action within the governing structures than ever before, even going so far as to run for political office.[25] John Redekop has argued that the Schleitheim Confession has carried too much weight with Mennonites and is no longer useful in the North American context. He views the confession as too strong for present-day theological guidance, originating, as it did, during a time when Anabaptists were persecuted by the government and governments did not perform many positive roles for the population. For those of us living in democratic states with governments that are pursuing the welfare of their citizenry (albeit not always well), Redekop argues that the Schleitheim Confession leads us in the wrong direction, toward sins of omission, where the state could be used to pursue good and is neglected (Redekop 2007).

If Mennonites are cautious regarding political action, it is partially because of the belief of the primacy of the church over the state. Yet there is also a second impediment to Mennonite political action, and that is a unique understanding of citizenship. Elements of this unique understanding of citizenship are evidenced in the quote from the Schleitheim Confession. Mennonites, and many other Anabaptists, take seriously the idea of citizenship in heaven, an idea that, although it might be familiar to Christians, is quite alien to political scientists.

Citizenship

The apostle Paul discusses his place as a citizen of heaven in Philippians 3:20: "But our citizenship is in heaven. And we eagerly await a Savior from there, the Lord Jesus Christ" (NIV). Coming from another biblical figure, this statement would not have been as persuasive.[26] But Paul understood the benefits of Roman citizenship and demonstrated it through his actions. He used his citizenship as a tool to further the kingdom of God. When he was attacked or vulnerable to the caprice of authority, Paul frequently made use of the privileges of his Roman citizenship, understanding quite well the superiority of his status under Roman law compared with others around him who were not Roman citizens.[27] Did Paul do this in a purely self-interested way? No. Anyone reading through Paul's letters to the early church cannot escape noticing Paul's complete commitment to building the church and telling the good news to those who had not heard it. Paul's self-interest was to stay alive so that he could continue to serve the church. As he notably stated in Philippians 1: 21: "To live is Christ and to die is gain."[28] Following his goal of building the church and spreading the gospel, Paul was willing to use the resources of his Roman citizenship. Yet, after claiming all the rights of citizenship that could protect him against wrongful punishment and imprisonment, Paul says: "I am a citizen of heaven."

It is this model of heavenly citizenship that was adopted by the early Anabaptists and provides some of the justification for modern Mennonite approaches to the state. There is an understanding within the Mennonite and Anabaptist traditions that as Christians we have citizenship first in heaven and our citizenship in the state in which we live is subordinate. It is right and proper for Christians to hold a distinctly alternative understanding of citizenship than political scientists.

There is such a clear and contemporary understanding of citizenship in heaven as the Christian's fundamental affiliation that it caused problems in naming the recent merger of the Mennonite Church and the General Conference Mennonite Church. A debate occurred over whether the new body could be referred to as the Mennonite Church USA or whether this name would be unacceptable because of the implication of citizenship in the United States of America.[29] Mennonites present were not so out of touch with political realities that they did not understand that they were citizens of the United States; rather, they understood that putting the name of a state in the title of a denomination contradicts fundamental Mennonite beliefs regarding citizenship. It was debated at length and decided that the title Mennonite Church USA stands as an oxymoron. "The Mennonite Church" acknowledges our citizenship in heaven as followers of Jesus, and "USA" notes merely where these followers of Jesus are located. This understanding of the title of the church neatly avoids ever declaring citizenship in a state.

This example is fascinating because it denotes the seriousness with which the idea of citizenship in heaven is held by many Mennonites and the present nature of that understanding as something that exists apart from a historically limited scriptural interpretation. From a Mennonite perspective, it is insufficient to read Paul's discussion of his citizenship in heaven and understand it in a temporally delimited way, exclusively as his relation to the Roman Empire at that time.

The Anabaptist Tradition and Contemporary Politics

The unique understanding of citizenship held by Mennonites does not lend itself well to manipulation by political leaders. Cries to do something because it is "right for America" (or some other country) are likely to fall on the ears of those who are deaf to the message, or even condemning of it. Mennonites who avidly adhere to a theological tradition that encourages them to understand themselves as citizens of heaven can find themselves in tension with those who treasure their citizenship in a particular country.[30] These tensions can be difficult to negotiate among Christians, and almost impossible to explain to those who are not.[31]

In addition to these difficulties in communicating, there are more tangible issues that relate to academia and government. Mennonites remain ambivalent about participation in government and lack enthusiasm for studying politics, power, and policy. There are not many Mennonite political scientists. The Anabaptist tradition does not incline Mennonites, or other Anabaptist groups, to take the role of the state seriously. Mennonite colleges do not have political science departments, although they do have conflict resolution programs. The scarcity of teaching on political science in Mennonite institutions of higher learning sends a message to students that is implicit in its absence and occasionally made explicit in rhetoric, that the study of the state and political power is an unworthy or inappropriate pursuit. The neglect of teaching on the state and formal power relationships between states is understandable, given the dominance accorded to the church and the understanding of citizenship.

Mennonites have sacrificed the study of politics, and this has led to a lack of sophistication in efforts to advocate for the worldwide church and an ineffectiveness in efforts to promote development and the well-being of Christians around the globe. Ironically, many others with less theological motivation have been ahead of the Mennonites in encouraging political activism on issues of concern to the Christian church worldwide (Hertzke 2004). Mennonites are not completely absent from political lobbying. However, they are not as engaged across a wide spectrum of issues as they could be, nor is political activism given much emphasis. Mennonite advocacy in Washington, D.C., has been spearheaded by the Mennonite Central Committee's Washington Office, which focuses on informing policy makers about events and perspectives from around the globe and not necessarily those issues that are in the spotlight at any given time (Miller 1996).

In the United States, issues of political inaction or resistance by Mennonites are partly explained theologically, yet another piece of the explanation has to do with the uneasiness that many Mennonites have with living in an imperial state. Anxiety regarding U.S. military endeavors overseas and the role of the state makes it difficult to conceive of using U.S. political power in a positive way that might benefit the church. A more pragmatic approach would allow Mennonites to use the power of the empire while remaining opposed to the dangerous and theologically objectionable elements of U.S. foreign policy. For example, Mennonites could lobby the State Department to exert pressure on governments that oppress Anabaptists as a matter of policy, such as Eritrea and Vietnam. This kind of pragmatic approach to empire would be much like that of the Apostle Paul. Anabaptists would be following in Paul's footsteps by using earthly citizenship for the good of the church while acknowledging primary citizenship in heaven.

Conclusions

If the negative side of Mennonite political theology is that Mennonites often abdicate from a serious consideration of the role of the state, there is also a positive side to this "neglect of the state," which is that Mennonites take the role of the worldwide church very seriously. This means that Mennonites have historically been tremendously active in the areas of relief, development, and conflict resolution as areas that are clearly building the church and furthering the spread of the gospel. In any given Mennonite congregation in the United States, one can find a handful of people who have served overseas with the Mennonite Central Committee (MCC), the relief and development arm of the Mennonite Church. Moreover, MCC's work is given quite an elevated status within the denomination, with many congregations having a designated MCC representative to that congregation with the responsibility of keeping the congregation informed about MCC's efforts overseas and ensuring that MCC has a steady supply of school kits, hurricane relief containers, and other project-related donations. The work for the church worldwide is visible on a regular basis and not something discussed one Sunday a year. Moreover, MCC also works in the area of conflict resolution, doing grassroots justice facilitation in areas all around the world. This is seen as both evangelistic and palliative in conflict areas.

Not surprisingly, Mennonite scholarly contributions on the study of nations have been in areas of conflict resolution and development rather than in more conventional areas of international relations, such as security, grand strategy, or even trade. Perhaps in the future this trend will change, and more Mennonites will become engaged and be affirmed in the study of states while still maintaining the beliefs that the church is superior to the state and that believers are primarily citizens of heaven. This is not advocacy for replacing what is currently being done; rather, it is advocacy for augmenting Mennonite involvement with the state so that core goals of building the church and spreading the gospel would be advanced. In this the church should take the Apostle Paul as an example. Paul shared Mennonite beliefs regarding citizenship and the state. The church should emulate his tactics and use the state and citizenship wisely, without allowing Mennonite values or agendas to be co-opted.

NOTES

So many people were helpful in the preparation of this chapter. Not wanting to misrepresent the Anabaptist position, I distributed the manuscript quite widely for comment, and I owe a debt of gratitude to those who were willing to read through the various drafts and offer comments. Thanks go to Sarah Baggé, Daryl Byler, Victor Hinojosa, John Roth, David Peyton, Bill Swartzendruber, Kimberly Gilsdorf, Paul Joireman, Todd Friesen, Richard Kauffman, Derek Keefe, and Andrew Sprunger. All flaws are my own responsibility and not the responsibility of these generous readers.

1. The largest Anabaptist national conference in the world is that of the Meserete Kristos Church (MKC) in Ethiopia. Large Anabaptist churches also exist in Indonesia (Jemaat Kristen), the Democratic Republic of Congo, India, Zimbabwe, and Vietnam.

2. There are divergent opinions as to which groups are correctly included in the early Anabaptist movement. Snyder eludes the quagmire by categorizing early Anabaptist as "anyone in the sixteenth century who practiced the baptism of adult believers" (Snyder 2004: 16).

3. This narrative privileges the Swiss Anabaptist tradition over the Dutch Anabaptist or Hutterite movements for several reasons, the dominant one being that it is the Swiss Anabaptists that lend the most to the understanding of the political beliefs of Anabaptists in the current day. One could argue that by doing so I am articulating a less spiritualist or apocalyptic tradition. There is precedent for the emphasis on the

Swiss strand of Anabaptism in the work of Harold Bender, who views some of the more radical vestiges of the movement as aberrations (Bender 1944).

4. One of the problems in studying Anabaptist history is that so many people were killed for their beliefs during the Reformation era. People who die untimely deaths due to persecution are less likely to leave collections of letters and sermons or treatises on the evolution of their beliefs.

5. John Roth would argue that the rejection of the oath was even more politically troubling and revolutionary than the appropriate moment of baptism (Roth 2005b).

6. One can identify similar reasoning among some contemporary Anabaptists who would not personally engage in violence in service to the state but would not reject any use of violence by the state, particularly in defending the vulnerable and fighting oppression.

7. One of the interesting trends of Anabaptism in the past twenty years has been dialogues recognizing the history on Anabaptist persecution between Mennonites and the churches that persecuted them during the Reformation.

8. This shorthand definition is from Buckley's introduction to George Lindbeck's book (Buckley 2002: viii).

9. Craig Carter described this nicely in his articulation of the theology of John Howard Yoder. Carter argues that, for Yoder, "pacifism is not the point; Jesus is the point" (Carter 2001: 17).

10. Yoder was writing in English. Paul Peachey and Clarence Bauman, writing in German, also contributed to the articulation of a common understanding regarding the role of the state.

11. To my knowledge, no other Christian sect gives primacy to the church over the state. Most Christian denominations and groups choose between two models of church and state originally articulated at the council of Nicaea in 325, the first being the subservience of the church to the state, and the second being the two kingdoms conception of the church and the state occupying two separate spheres of power. See Kuyper (2002) for a Calvinistic view and Lomperis, chapter 3, for the Lutheran point of view. See Mark Noll for a succinct description of the political implications of the Council of Nicaea (Noll 2000: 59–62).

12. The confession unhelpfully confuses the two terms, *state* and *nation*, and used them interchangeably to refer to the state.

13. For example, Luther, raising the bar on the just war tradition regarding participation in war, argued that if a Christian knew the war to be wrong he should not fight in it, but if he was not certain, he should obey the ruler, and the responsibility of sin would fall on the ruler. Mennonites and early Anabaptists would disagree, arguing that "do not kill" means "do not kill" and that the state cannot order Christians to do that which God has forbidden.

14. One may find an earlier expression of a similar view in the 1632 Dortrecht Confession, adopted by the Mennonites in Dortrecht, Holland. Article 13 states:

> We also believe and confess, that God has institutes civil government, for the punishment of the wicked and the protection of the pious, and also further

for the purpose of governing the world—governing countries and cities; and also to preserve its subjects in good order and under good regulations. Wherefore we are not permitted to despise, blaspheme, or resist the same; but are to acknowledge it as a minister of God and be subject and obedient to it in all things that do not militate against the law, will and commandments of God; yea, "to be ready in every good work" also faithfully to pay it custom, tax and tribute; thus giving it what is its due; as Jesus Christ taught, did himself, and commanded his followers to do. That we are also to pray to the Lord earnestly for the government and its welfare, and on behalf of our country, so that we may live under its protection, maintain itself and "lead a quiet and peaceable life in all godliness and honesty." And further, that the Lord would recompense them (our rulers) here and in eternity, for all the benefits liberties and favors which we enjoy under their laudable administration. Rom 13:1–7; Titus 3:1, 2; 1 Pet 2:17; Matt 17:27; 22:21; 1 Tim 2: 1, 2. (Hershberger 1969: 319)

Clearly the difference between Mennonite and other positions with regard to the interpretation of the Romans passage is expressed in the Dortrecht Confession in the phrase "all things that do not militate against the law, will and commandments of God."

15. Another important verse to justify this position is Colossians 2: 15: "And having disarmed the powers and authorities, he made a public spectacle of them, triumphing over them by the cross" (NIV).

16. For a description of early Swiss-Anabaptist approaches to the Old Testament, see Roth (1999).

17. This is not because of the believed superiority of Christians in community but because of the view that, unlike the state and other institutions, the church is not less moral than its individual members. As Carter paraphrases Yoder, "Being a member of the church does not cause one to adopt a lower form of morality than that which is commanded by Jesus" (Carter 2001: 45).

18. Niebuhr is almost forced into this extreme position by his encompass-ing definition of *culture* as everything from the arts, to the state, to organizational life. Even the most extreme communities of Anabaptists, such as the Hutterites or Amish, would have trouble with the complete rejection of all that Niebuhr means by "culture." The more mainstream Anabaptist position would be similar to that of most Christians: some elements of the culture are to be appreciated; others are to be rejected. John Howard Yoder and Richard Niebuhr engaged in a discussion of this issue in print that is nicely summarized in Carter's *The Politics of the Cross* (2001: 215–223).

19. See Roth (2005a) for a discussion of the variety of Mennonite beliefs on the issue of the use of force.

20. The language here is chosen carefully. What is important from a Mennonite perspective is that one does not disobey God by killing for the state. Mennonites would hold other Christians to a similar standard and say that they are not in obedience

to God when they kill for the state. Christians who kill for the state have seriously confused allegiances. However, there is less judgment for nonbelievers who have no competing loyalty to that of the state.

21. I prefer Nicholas Wolterstorff's concept of primary justice to the more commonly used and often polemicized phrase "social justice."

22. This definition of nationalism is inclusive of patriotism, which would be an emotional or psychological attachment to a state, as well as substate ethnic identifications such as Xhosa, Hutu, Scottish, or Basque. See Joireman (2003) for a discussion of nationalism. Interestingly, there are Mennonites, called within the church "ethnic Mennonites," who may see their identity as Mennonite only as a "nationality," not as a religious position. These are people who may have been raised in Mennonite communities or come from Mennonite backgrounds, identifiable by certain names and traditions, who do not necessarily hold to Mennonite religious beliefs. Thus one could find non-Christian, agnostic, Reformed, and Catholic Mennonites, with Mennonite in this context indicating ethnicity.

23. Though certainly not pledging allegiance to the flag, which is a declaration of allegiance to something other than Christ and his church. There is a heated debate among Mennonites about what acceptable displays of nationalism might be, if in fact there are any. John Roth's book *Beliefs* gives examples of the spectrum of Mennonite/ Anabaptist opinion on this issue (Roth 2005a).

24. Again, John Roth (2005a) gives examples of Mennonite opinion on this issue. The theology of the denomination is not necessarily belief in the pews.

25. In my own congregation, one of the members announced that he was running for the U.S. House of Representatives and created a campaign committee that included church members.

26. This is not to suggest that I hold the writings of Paul above other scriptural texts. However, given the fact that the state as we know it did not come into being until the Treaty of Westphalia in 1648, and Paul lived as a citizen of the Roman Empire, which would have been the closest thing to a modern state at that time, his writings have a contextual validity for an understanding of citizenship in the current day that the writings of Peter, for example, would not.

27. Acts 22: 2–29.

28. The whole section of Philippians 1: 21–26 from the New International Version of the Bible is: "For to me, to live is Christ and to die is gain. If I am to go on living in the body, this will mean fruitful labor for me. Yet what shall I choose? I do not know! I am torn between the two: I desire to depart and be with Christ, which is better by far; but it is more necessary for you that I remain in the body. Convinced of this, I know that I will remain, and I will continue with all of you for your progress and joy in the faith, so that through my being with you again your joy in Christ Jesus will overflow on account of me."

29. For this example, I thank John Stolzfus, who used it in a sermon to illustrate another point entirely.

30. This is especially problematic in the United States and in other countries where the sense of patriotism (a form of nationalism that supports the state) is very

strong. In Canada and other countries where nationalism is less virulent, presumably there is less tension between Anabaptists and others.

31. Imagine the difficulty of telling a well-educated, secular, and professional person that your citizenship is in heaven, and you will understand the difficulty of explaining a political position that derives from that point of view.

BIBLIOGRAPHY

Bender, Harold S. 1944. *The Anabaptist Vision*. Scottdale, PA: Herald Press.
Brock, Peter. 1972. *Pacifism in Europe to 1914*. Princeton, NJ: Princeton University Press.
Buckley, James J. 2002. "Introduction." In *The Church in a Postliberal Age*, ed. G. A. Lindbeck. Grand Rapids, MI: William B. Eerdmans.
Carter, Craig A. 2001. *The Politics of the Cross*. Grand Rapids, MI: Brazos Press.
Goertz, Hans-Jurgen. 1996. *The Anabaptists*. New York: Routledge.
Harder, Leland, ed. 1985. *The Sources of Swiss Anabaptism: The Grebel Letters and Related Documents*. Scottdale, PA: Herald Press.
Hershberger, Guy Franklin. 1969. *War, Peace and Nonresistance*. Scottdale, PA: Herald Press.
Hertzke, Allen D. 2004. *Freeing God's Children: The Unlikely Alliance for Global Human Rights*. New York: Rowman and Littlefield.
Inter-Mennonite Confession of Faith Committee. 1995. *Confession of Faith in a Mennonite Perspective*. Scottdale, PA: Herald Press.
Jenkins, Philip. 2002. *The Next Christendom: The Rise of Global Christianity*. New York: Oxford University Press.
Joireman, Sandra F. 2003. *Nationalism and Political Identity*. New York: Continuum.
Kuyper, Abraham. 2002. *Lectures on Calvinism*. Grand Rapids, MI: William B. Eerdmans.
Miller, Keith Graber. 1996. *Wise as Serpents, Innocent as Doves*. Knoxville: University of Tennessee Press.
Niebuhr, H. Richard. 1951. *Christ and Culture*. New York: Harper and Row.
Noll, Mark. 2000. *Turning Points: Decisive Moments in the History of Christianity*. Grand Rapids, MI: Baker Academic.
Redekop, John H. 2007. *Politics under God*. Scottdale, PA: Herald Press.
Roth, John D. 1999. "Harmonizing the Scriptures: Swiss Brethren Understandings of the Relationship between the Old and New Testament during the Last Half of the Sixteenth Century." In *Radical Reformation Studies*, eds. W. O. Packull and G. L. Dipple. Brookfield, VT: Ashgate.
Roth, John D. 2005a. *Beliefs: Mennonite Faith and Practice*. Scottdale, PA: Herald Press.
Roth, John D. 2005b. Personal communication. Wheaton, IL, August 19.
Simons, Menno. 1956. "Why I Do Not Cease Teaching and Writing." In *The Complete Writings of Menno Simons*, ed. J. C. Wenger. Scottdale, PA: Herald Press.
Snyder, C. Arnold. 2004. *Following in the Footsteps of Christ: The Anabaptist Tradition*. Maryknoll, NY.

Swiss Brethren Conference. 2005. *The Schleitheim Confession.* http://www.anabaptists.
     org/history/schleith.html. Accessed June 20, 2005.
Weaver, J. Denny. 2005. *Becoming Anabaptist.* 2nd ed. Scottdale, PA: Herald Press.
Yoder, John H. 1972. *The Politics of Jesus.* Grand Rapids, MI: William B. Eerdmans.
Yoder, John H. 2002. *The Christian Witness to the State.* Scottdale, PA: Herald Press.

6

The Anglican Tradition: Building the State, Critiquing the State

Leah Seppanen Anderson

The seventy-seven million Anglicans[1] around the globe form the third largest Christian communion, smaller than only the Roman Catholic Church and the Eastern Orthodox Church. The tradition began in Europe with the creation of the Church of England in the early 1500s, but today, as a result of British colonization and the missionary efforts of the Church of England, there are thirty-eight provinces, or national branches, of Anglicanism in such varied locales as Sudan, South Korea, and Mexico. The Anglican Communion is the name for the loose denominational association that joins these national churches. The historical particularity of the Church of England and the contemporary diversity of the Anglican Communion create complicated implications for politics.

Unlike other traditions in this book, it was not a distinctive theology that generated Anglicanism's initial views of the state, but a unique political history. The Church of England established a distinct model of church-state relations where the church and state cooperated to promote good governance and sound religion, but the state reigned supreme, even on issues of doctrine and clerical leadership. In contrast to this clearly important historical experience, it is difficult to identify the theological commitments that are both unique to Anglicanism and shared by all Anglicans. This makes the connections between the theology of Anglicanism and its view of the state less influential.

The Church of England's historical experience yields at least two identifiable and transferable implications for politics: a high view of the state and an expectation that Christians should engage in politics. The state is respected and considered to be a God-ordained institution capable of executing justice and providing peace and order. This support for the state has often translated into church support for the political status quo, as churchgoers were encouraged to obey the government and contribute to its stability, rather than critique its actions. The second implication to follow from the Church of England's practice is the belief that Christians should participate in politics and the state. According to the tradition, politics is a legitimate vocation for an Anglican, and the church, as an institution, should engage political leaders and its congregation on political issues of the day.

Historically, the experience of the Church of England was normative for all Anglicans. Whether in theology, worship, or politics, the practice of the mother Church of England served as the model for Anglican churches everywhere. The increase in the number of autonomous provinces of the Anglican Communion, especially after the collapse of the British Empire, deteriorated the authority of the English model and stimulated a variety of localized practices. As the Church of England ventured into other countries, it had to adapt its church-state model to new political realities, from democracies with a separation of church and state, like the United States, to countries with large Muslim populations and a history of authoritarianism, such as Nigeria. In fact, no other Anglican church in the communion enjoys the same legal establishment as the Church of England. Despite the diversity in local context, the Church of England's treatment of the state still serves as the starting point for national Anglican reflection, whether in the United States, Nigeria, or other provinces.

Outside England, loyalty to the state often remains strong, but without establishment, these Anglican churches lack the Church of England's institutional platform from which to speak the gospel to the political powers. This could leave the historical Anglican position on politics crippled; the church might only support the state without the ability to challenge it. Or the tradition could be reinterpreted, and national churches could identify locally appropriate and effective ways to voice criticism. As the numbers of Anglicans outside England and the West increase, Anglicans could dismiss the Church of England's practice as outdated and craft a new vision grounded on something other than the political and historical experience of the Church of England. Anglicanism's character of comprehensiveness might be such a new foundation for an Anglican view of the state.

Historical Background

The Anglican tradition began after political acts created the Church of England, a church autonomous from the pope in Rome. Although this was to be the church for the entire English nation, the diversity of Christian practice within England challenged the notion of one unified, established church. As the Church of England expanded around the globe with the British Empire, its original Anglican model of church-state relations had to adapt to new political contexts.

A conflict between King Henry VIII and Pope Clement VII in the mid-1500s produced the Church of England. The English King Henry requested the pope's approval to divorce his wife, Catherine of Aragon, so that he could marry Anne Boleyn. Henry loved Anne and hoped she might provide the legitimate male heir he desired to succeed him to the throne and secure England's political stability. When the pope refused to act on Henry's request,[2] Henry turned to domestic politics to achieve his goal. Over the course of several years, Henry drew on existing antipapist and nationalist sentiment in England to convince Parliament to name him the supreme head of the church and to deny explicitly the authority of the pope in England. By 1534, authority over the church in England and its wealth was vested solely in the king and, under the king, Parliament. The new ecclesial leader, the archbishop of the Church of England, possessed autonomy from the pope in Rome but served the church under the authority of the English monarch. The church *in* England and been transformed into a church *of* England.

Despite this relocation of church authority to the English monarch, the theology and practice of the Church of England remained largely untouched under Henry's leadership.[3] When Henry's Catholic daughter, Queen Mary, took the throne in 1553, she quickly undid her father's work and pursued communion with the church in Rome. By the time that Queen Elizabeth I ascended to power in 1558, twenty-four years after Henry's split from Rome, the monarch was no longer the supreme head of the Church of England (Moorman 1980: 161–179, 191–192; Thomas 1930: xxxii–xl). Henry's new church and the English monarch's new ecclesial powers had been short-lived.

Queen Elizabeth I oversaw the lasting establishment of the Church of England in 1559 through two acts of Parliament. The first, the Act of Supremacy, restored "to the crown the ancient jurisdiction over the state ecclesiastical and spiritual and abolish[ed] all foreign power repugnant to the same" (Elizabeth's Supremacy Act 1921: 442). It compelled all clergy to testify "that the queen's highness is the only supreme governor of this realm . . . in all spiritual or ecclesiastical things . . . and that no foreign prince, person, prelate, state or potentate hath or ought to have any jurisdiction, power, superiority, pre-eminence, or authority, ecclesiastical or spiritual, within this realm" (Elizabeth's Supremacy Act 1921: 449). Elizabeth's title of supreme governor was slightly more restricted in language and practice than Henry's designation as supreme head of the church. Elizabeth needed, for example, the clergy's approval to define church doctrine (Hylson-Smith 1996: 34–35), but she still possessed the highest human authority in the church.

The second piece of legislation, the Act of Uniformity, established the state-led Church of England as *the* church of the English state and nation. The act required that "all and singular ministers in any cathedral or parish church, or other place within this realm of England [or] Wales . . . or other the queen's dominions, shall . . . be bounden to say and use the Matins, Evensong, celebration of the Lord's Supper and administration of each of the sacraments, and all their common and open prayer, in such order and form as is mentioned in [The Book of Common Prayer], so authorized by Parliament in the said fifth and sixth years of the reign of King Edward VI" (Elizabeth's Act of Uniformity 1921: 459). This act mandated one form of public worship found in the 1552 prayer book and proscribed other liturgies, including Catholic or Puritan services, with threat of fines or imprisonment (Hylson-Smith 1996: 35). All English citizens were expected to be members of *the* Church of England, and civil officials could legally remove Dissenters, those who worshipped outside the Church of England, from their territory (Nockles 1994: 54).

Politics conceived the Church of England, and politics was the rationale for the church's union with the state. Devout church members soon developed more sophisticated, theological justifications for the new ecclesial and political reality. Richard Hooker, an Oxford theologian, wrote the most famous early defense of the Elizabethan Settlement almost forty years after church establishment. The foundation of Hooker's argument in *Of the Laws of Ecclesiastical Polity*, published in 1594, was the assertion that in England, church and national membership overlapped. He believed that "there is not any man of the church of England, but the same man is also a member of the commonwealth; nor any man a member of the commonwealth which is not also of the church of England" (as quoted in Lake 1988: 207). The political institutions of England even incorporated church leaders and laity: bishops received representation in the House of Lords and Church of England parishioners in the House of Commons. This meant that the state institutions were also church institutions and could thus make decisions for the church.

Hooker's theological reasoning drew primarily from Old Testament texts and compared the situation of the English nation with that of the nation of Israel: "God's own ancient elect people, which people was not part of them the commonwealth and part of them the church of God, but the self same people whole and entire were both under one chief governor on whose supreme authority they did depend" (as quoted in Lake 1988: 208). This led to Hooker's idea that kings had a divine, God-given right to rule the nation, state, and church. In practice, this royal supremacy shifted the location of the church's authority and legitimacy from God and the foreign pope to the English monarch and the English state.

Establishment led to laws that privileged the Church of England and excluded Dissenters from civic life. For example, the Clarendon Code of the 1660s required all political officers to take Communion in a Church of England parish (Moorman 1980: 252–253; Sachs 1993: 12–13). Allegiance to the state meant participation in the Church of England, and membership in the church demanded loyalty to the state. The English state possessed extensive authority over church affairs, including the appointment of church bishops, the determination of its liturgy, and interpretation of its theological stance. The state's unconstrained control over the Church of England reached its apex in the 1700s, when the church operated much like another branch of the government rather than an entity coequal with the state (Cornwell 1985: 45). But changes in England's religious landscape and frustration with what many perceived as the perversion of England's church-state framework challenged Hooker's idea of a coterminous religious and political community.

Challenges to Establishment: Evangelicals and Anglo-Catholics

The Church of England is one church, but it is a broad church. As Anglicans developed different theological emphases and worship practices, they divided into distinct parties within the church. In the past and present, two of the major parties within Anglicanism have been the evangelicals and the Anglo-Catholics.[4] True to the nature of these groups, the evangelicals challenged establishment through force of numbers and religious activity. Anglo-Catholics mounted a theological and historical critique of establishment as practiced in England.

The pretense of one united Church of England had already dissolved by the time the evangelical movement started in the 1730s. The Toleration Act of 1689 allowed dissenting churches to exist legally and worship without state interference, but nonconformists still faced discrimination in civil affairs (Moorman 1980: 266). Forty years later, the evangelicals refocused the religious life of many English, placing stress on conversion from sin to a life in Christ, active service to others as an expression of God's love, scripture as the single authority for the faith, and Christ's death and resurrection as the pinnacle event for

Christian doctrine and practice. This movement brought many to faith and active service in the church. Although English Protestantism had been in rapid decline in the early 1700s, as a result of the evangelical movement, the number of Independents and Baptists more than doubled from 1750 to 1800, and Methodist membership more than quadrupled in roughly the same time period (Bebbington 1992: 1–17, 21).

Evangelicalism is a Christian movement that runs through rather than along denominational lines, so that evangelicals could also be found in the Church of England. Anglican evangelicals often gathered outside regular liturgical services for meetings sponsored by the Methodists, who at the time operated more like a parachurch organization within the Church of England than like a distinct denomination. John Wesley, an Anglican, a prominent revival preacher, and the leader of the Methodists, initially resisted separation from the Church of England, but eventually Wesley ordained Methodist priests, and a new, distinct denomination was born, pulling even more Christians outside the orbit of the established church (Moorman 1980: 315).

Despite Wesley's move toward a new sect, many evangelicals remained within the Church of England, but they were in the minority and remained on the margins of church leadership and power until the late 1800s (Hylson-Smith 1988: 50).[5] In fact, while the dissenting churches experienced explosive growth in membership in the late 18th century, the number of baptized and confirmed communicants in the Church of England declined relative to population growth until the 1830s (Bebbington 1992: 21). The evangelical dynamism of the dissenting Protestant sects defeated the notion of a nation unified through participation in one church.

In contrast to Anglican evangelicals, who were firmly rooted in the Protestant tradition, Anglo-Catholics emphasized the Church of England's catholicity and considered their church a "via media" between the corruption of the Roman Catholic Church and the schisms of Protestant churches (Moorman 1980: 338–360). About a century after the evangelical revivals, Anglo-Catholic activity formed the Oxford Movement of the 1830s. The Tractarians, as they were called in reference to their publication of twenty-five tracts that detailed their theological positions, were concerned, among other things, with state interference in Church of England affairs.

In fact, the proximate cause of the movement was a response to the Irish Church Bill, in which Parliament removed a number of bishoprics in the Irish Church. This infuriated the leaders of the Oxford Movement because they rooted the church's authority in apostolic succession, that is, the passing of leadership from one generation of bishops to another. How could the state, they asked, presume to dissolve bishoprics, which were part of this holy line of succession? This was a radical departure from the church's past under-standing of its authority over the nation being attached to its position under the state. The Tractarians "proclaimed the church to be a spiritual entity, not created by the state, and with a life independent of the state. In 1833 this was a new idea" (Hylson-Smith 1988: 113). Not all participants in the Oxford Move-ment called for an end to establishment, but their ideas challenged the status quo of state over church.

In response to these and other challenges to establishment, the exclu-sivity of the Church of England's privileges and state control over its affairs declined. In the 1820s, independent Protestants and Roman Catholics were allowed to hold political office, and in 1858 Jews were allowed to be members of Parliament. In the 1830s, births, deaths, and marriages were registered by civil authorities and no longer just by the Church of England. The church also lost state access to funds through taxes in 1869 (Morris 2005: 166), and reli-gious tests for university entry were eliminated in 1871. These changes were not initiated by the Church of England leadership; instead, "it was the blunt realization by the state that it could not effectively force religious conformity on a recalcitrant nation [that] led by necessity to the more liberal church-state policy" (Monsma and Soper 1997: 124–125). As the state reduced the privileges of the Church of England, it also granted Anglicans greater self-governance, as the Anglo-Catholics had demanded. For example, a number of clergy and lay church bodies were established in the early 1900s to take over from Parliament the governing of the Church of England's affairs (Cornwell 1983: 19).

Establishment was eroded by the plurality of Christian practices within England and by the Anglo-Catholics' articulation of a different vision of church establishment, one in which the church no longer served as a department of the state and was free to govern the spiritual matters at the core of the church's mission. The church had moved to a position of partial establishment.

Establishment Fails Abroad: Missions and the Church of England

As the Church of England expanded beyond the confines of the British Isles, the belief that the state ruled over a unified political and religious nation faced even greater challenges. The evangelical revival created a new missionary con-cern among the English in the late 1700s and early 1800s, including within the Church of England. In 1786, Parliament passed a law that enabled the Church of England to extend the episcopate to the country's colonial territories, and the Church Missionary Society was formed thirteen years later in 1799. Initial efforts were slow; the idea of missions was new to the church, and the supply of missionaries sparse (Hylson-Smith 1988: 211–216). Initially, the missionary dioceses of the Church of England were under the authority of the Archbishop of Canterbury, but gradually these dioceses gained autonomy from England and were established as independent provinces (Buchanan 2006: 231). As Anglicanism spread around the world, the Church of England had to rethink its understanding of the relationship of the state to society. The tradition moved "away from an understanding of the church as coterminous with a settled Christendom, towards an understanding of the church as engaged in mission to a world of many cultures" (Hefling 2006: 5). The experience of American Anglicans illustrates this point.

Anglicanism arrived in the United States with the earliest colonial missions and was soon the established church of the Virginia Colony. Following the practice in England, there was an underlying assumption that the political unity of the state required the religious unity of the nation (Monsma and Soper 1997: 18). In the Southern colonies, established Anglican churches controlled the religious landscape, but in the North, Puritans, critical of the British monarchy and Anglicanism's links to it, opposed Anglican establishment there and instead supported the establishment of the Congregational Church. Anglican churches still operated there, but with far fewer privileges and less access to civil power (Hein and Shattuck 2004: 15–18).

In the mid-1700s, some American Anglicans pressed the Church of England to ordain bishops for America so that the church might have leadership closer to its parishes. This was a politically controversial issue because many non-Anglicans in the United States viewed attempts to appoint a bishop as another example of the Crown's efforts to control the political life of the colonies. Anglicans and non-Anglicans alike expected that these bishops would not only govern spiritual life but also have authority in civil matters, just as they did in England (Hein and Shattuck 2004: 35–38). Anglican clergy in America had, upon taking office, sworn an oath to remain loyal to the king and to use the official church liturgy without changes, including prayers for the king. For this reason, the majority of Anglican clergy remained loyal to the monarchy, even as the winds of revolution swept through the colonies.[6]

When the Declaration of Independence broke political ties with Great Britain and explicitly prohibited prayers for the king and the British Parliament, these clergy were placed in a difficult position. Many fled the colonies or stopped holding services rather than go back on their oaths. Those who continued to offer services and support the monarchy were harassed by the revolutionaries (Hein and Shattuck 2004: 39). American independence forced the Anglican Church to reconstitute itself. The Protestant Episcopal Church in the United States of America declared its independence from the Church of England in 1785. The practice of established churches in the United States ended when the First Amendment to the U.S. Constitution passed in 1791. All mention of the king and Parliament were removed from the American version of the Book of Common Prayer (Hein and Shattuck 2004: 44–46, 55), although the Episcopal Church continued to take seriously its role in praying for the state and the nation, and prayers for those governing the country remain part of the church's liturgy today.

The Anglican tradition's history heavily influences its approach to politics. In England, state dominance over the church was the rule until increased religious diversity within England and the success of Anglicanism abroad forced the state-church framework to adapt to new social and political contexts. The Church of England is still the established church in England, but its benefits and responsibilities have declined considerably, as has, most significantly, Parliament's control over the internal affairs of the church. The provinces of the Anglican communion have altogether abandoned the legal integration of state and church authority. In this new, diverse context, how does Anglicanism understand politics and the state? If the history of the church no longer provides a unified view of politics, then a consideration of the tradition's theological distinctives offers another possible source of guidance.

Theological commitments inform most Christian traditions' perspectives on the state. It is difficult, however, to identify common theological positions that unite all Anglicans. For this reason, the historical development and practice of the Church of England has often played a more significant role than church doctrine in shaping the Anglican perspective on the state.

Theological Distinctives of Anglicanism

Unlike Calvinism and Lutheranism, Anglicanism does not have one preeminent theological originator whose writings serve as the base of arguments about the "true" form of the tradition. In contrast to the centralized hierarchy of Catholicism, in which the ex cathedra statements of the papacy can serve as the official view of the church, the Anglican communion does not recognize one person or office as the final authority for the entire fellowship. Anglicans disagree among themselves about what makes them distinct from other Christian traditions and what holds them together in the Anglican communion. Efforts to demonstrate unity among Anglicans usually point to its common theology rooted in the Thirty-Nine Articles or similar worship patterns based on the Book of Common Prayer.[7] But diversity of beliefs and practices within each national Anglican church and across the Anglican communion challenge these efforts. Anglicanism's ability to hold a variety of practices in tension and in unity, often referred to as its comprehensiveness, is its strongest unique and unifying characteristic.

The English Parliament approved the church's confessional statement, the Thirty-Nine Articles, in 1571 "[f]or the avoiding of the diversities of opinions, and for the establishing of consent touching true religion" (as quoted in Thomas 1930: liv). Because the statement sought to appease various groups of Puritans who disagreed on finer points of theology and to encompass those members of the national church with more Catholic leanings,[8] the statement leaves considerable room for diverse interpretation and application. In addition, a Lambeth Conference, a gathering of bishops from all the provinces held every ten years to discuss and coordinate the work of the churches in the Anglican Communion, recommended that the provinces honor the Thirty-Nine Articles "for their historical significance but [discard] any attempt to utilize them as a contemporary confession of faith" (Thomas 1998: 259). The Thirty-Nine Articles bind the doctrinal beliefs of the Church of England and the wider Anglican Communion, but they do so loosely.

Worship guided by the Book of Common Prayer is, for some Anglicans, the essential, distinct characteristic of Anglicanism. The Church of England's Book of Common Prayer, which includes the format for services, prayers, and personal devotions, was composed initially in 1549, with revisions in 1552 and again in 1662. The 1662 version is still the only version of the prayer book to be approved by Parliament, but a number of alternative liturgies have been published and sanctioned by the church as contemporary supplements to the official prayer book, which leads to a diversity of worship practices across Church of England parishes.

There is also a multiplicity of worship and liturgical patterns in the national churches of the Anglican Communion. The Book of Common Prayer is no longer translated directly from the English, but each national church develops its own liturgical books that bear a "family resemblance" to the prayer book.[9] At the 1958 Lambeth Conference, church leaders tried to manage and coordinate liturgical revisions across the communion, but these efforts produced conversations rather than strict guidelines or lists of essential qualities that must be contained in the revised prayer books (Buchanan 2006: 235; Sykes 1995: xviii; Whalon 2006: 552–555). As Charles Hefling comments, "The Prayer Books currently authorized are not cast from the same mould, but they are cut from the same cloth. They are Prayer Books, not something else" (Hefling 2006: 5). But that would be a rather thin conception of what makes Anglicanism unique and binds all Anglicans together. As the movement for enculturation of worship practices continues and the

Anglican church outside England and other English-speaking, Western countries grows, unity through the prayer book will be stretched even further. Its ability to serve as the key, substantive unifying characteristic of Anglicans is questionable.

This leads Paul Avis to ask if "the faith, practice and spirit of the churches of the Anglican Communion [is] merely a product of the accidents of history, a legitimization, for reasons of expediency, of the way things have happened to turn out? . . . [I]s [it] merely the decadent legacy of unprincipled Anglo-Saxon imperialism?" (Avis 1998: 459). Anglicans would perhaps reject (as Avis does) this cynical view of their tradition's identity and, instead, turn diversity into Anglicanism's great and most distinct asset. Rather than regret the variety within the church, Anglicans can celebrate the tradition's comprehensiveness. According to this perspective, the genius of the church has been its ability to hold in tension but also in unity a broad, but limited, range of beliefs and practices.

This approach to theology attempts "to reconcile opposed systems, rejecting them as exclusive systems . . . showing that the principle for which each stands has its place within the total orbit of Christian truth, and in the long run is secure only within that orbit or . . . when it is held in tension with other apparently opposed, but really complementary principles" (as quoted in Avis 1998: 469). This "comprehensiveness, that is, the ability to absorb extremes and at the same time be the milieu for debate without giving rise to disunity, is the overriding virtue of Anglicanism" (Pickering et al. 1998: 412). Living in the tension that comes as a result of comprehensiveness is, according to this account, the genius and unique character of Anglicanism.

Bitter internal disputes and mistrust have plagued Anglicanism in the past, but enough leaders exemplified long-suffering patience and held the communion together. The latest threat to Anglican comprehensiveness is the current row over homosexuality, the authority of scripture and discipline within the church. The 2003 ordination of Gene Robinson, a practicing homosexual, as a bishop in the Episcopal Church USA provoked a strong reaction from the larger Anglican Communion, especially from conservative, evangelical churches in the global South. Differences over how scripture guides theology and practice and the church's response to homosexuality press the boundaries of Anglican comprehensiveness.[10] The tension plays out at the national level, among members of the U.S. Episcopal Church who disagree about the decision to appoint Robinson, and at an international level between, for example, liberal bishops from the United States and Canada, where the Anglican church sanctioned same-sex marriage in 2002, and evangelical bishops in provinces like Nigeria and Rwanda.

This debate causes so much worry about the future of the Anglicanism because it has already compromised the traditional structure of the Communion. In the United States and Canada, many local churches and individual Anglicans left the Episcopal Church and the Anglican Church of Canada to form alternate Anglican groups, many of which were under the leadership of bishops from provinces outside of North America, such as the bishops of Nigeria, Rwanda, and the Southern Cone. In December 2008 a federation of these groups claiming to speak for more than 100,000 Anglicans established its own province: the Anglican Church in North America. While conservative bishops around the globe voiced support for this new province, many others were critical. It is not yet clear whether the Archbishop of Canterbury will recognize the Anglican Church in North America as an official new province and member of the Anglican Communion. Meanwhile, the Communion has its own internal process underway to craft a new Anglican Covenant, a document that would provide specific procedures for managing and resolving doctrinal disagreements among provinces in the Communion. The draft Covenant received mixed feedback from global Anglican leaders and the future of the document as a mechanism to successfully resolve disputes is uncertain. If the Communion can not overcome these divisions through the new North American province, the Covenant, or some other means, it could lead to irreparable schism within Anglicanism, and would necessarily narrow the comprehensiveness of the tradition.

Given the limits of Anglican unity in theology and worship, comprehensiveness, the tradition of a broad church in prayerful dialogue with its many branches, may be the most accurate description of what unites Anglicans and distinguishes Anglicanism from other major Christian traditions. This distinctive of the tradition is not directly related to politics, but it, along with the influence of the history of Anglicanism, offers some general guidelines to an Anglican view of the state.

An Anglican Perspective on the State

The Church of England's historical legacy colors contemporary Anglican approaches to politics, but it does so in two potentially rival ways. First, there is the church's inheritance of a strong loyalty to the state and a conservatism that has led the church to promote the status quo more often than it agitates for reform. Simultaneously, however, the established Church of England is expected to engage in politics and speak on political issues from an explicitly Christian perspective. The history of the Church of England offers the broader Anglican movement a model of both political conservatism and political activism.

Since the Church of England was a legal creation of the state, brought into existence through acts of Parliament, it is not surprising that the church holds the state in high regard and expects close ties between the state and the church. No higher respect could be granted than allowing the state to hold authority over the church, as is still technically the situation in the United Kingdom. Although the queen no longer exercises real power over the church, esteem for the monarchy and its position as head of the church remains among many in the Church of England.[11] Anglicanism expects the national church as an institution to participate in the state and its work.

Since the Church of England played a role in England's state development and because the monarch officially heads the church, it is not surprising that Anglicanism has often been a force for conservatism, an acceptance and even promotion of the political status quo. Early supporters of church establishment considered "the mission of the church to consecrate or sanctify the state in a spirit of service" (Nockles 1994: 54). This contrasts with other traditions' vision of the church as a community outside the state, and one that might speak prophetically and critically to the powers that be. The link to conservatism was so strong that for many years, the Church of England was described sardonically as the "Conservative Party at prayer." While this was an empirically accurate statement because of the high percentage of Conservative Party members who worshipped in the Church of England and the large numbers of church clergy who supported the Tories, this close alliance has declined in recent decades (Monsma and Soper 1997: 123). The Church of England's role in state formation created a legacy of loyalty to the state.

This posture, critics argue, makes it impossible for the church to criticize the excess or errors of the state because to do so would jeopardize its own comfortable status as an established church. But there are examples of the Church of England dissenting vocally from the state's policy. The church is able and, indeed, expected to do this precisely because of its legal position within the state. The church expresses its views on political issues through its bishops who hold seats in the House of Lords and through statements made by the Archbishop of Canterbury. Although in the United Kingdom's modern, pluralistic society, not everyone will agree with or follow the church's guidance, there is an expectation from the public and the media that the church will be present and vocal in the public political arena.

Anglicanism also promotes the participation of individual Christians in political movements and state offices. In the Church of England, there's no confusion about whether Christians can be involved in the state because the supreme governor, the queen, is also the head of state. Also, the bishops sitting in the House of Lords model devout faith matched with official political positions. Anglicanism considers Christian participation in official state activities as not only permitted but also encouraged. Christians are there to bring religious considerations of justice to legislation and the activities of the state.

Anglicanism has not encouraged pacifism or criticism of Christians serving in the military. The Anglican tradition has historically read scripture as supporting the political status quo and used the Bible to legitimize and strengthen the state. Richard Hooker, for example, pointed to Israel's political and spiritual community as a model for England. The Anglican tradition also builds on other Old Testament resources, such as God's active use of Israel's military to achieve his purposes, to explain England's use of military force as appropriate and even God-ordained. Thus, the armed forces are part of the state and, like the rest of the political enterprise, can and should be peopled with Christians.

Readings of Paul's epistles that highlight the politically subversive content in the letters would raise questions about the power-friendly interpretations of the Anglican model. The life of Jesus as recorded in the Gospels suggests that Christ did not seek to establish a political movement and rejected the use of the sword. If following Christ includes conforming our lives to this model, what does that mean for Christian political involvement? Does this suggest that Christians should also shy away from organized political movements or participation in the state? Can Christians, in good conscience, serve in the modern state, which is, by definition, an organization with a monopoly of force? Was this just Christ's particular mission, or is it one in which Christians today should follow? The Anglican tradition has not historically explained its church-state relations with frequent references to Christ, so it does not directly address these questions. Although the church and individual Christians might criticize a particular government's decision to go to war, the Church of England has no theological objection to Christians working for the state's military.

The Church of England's close institutional ties with the state create a situation in which it is natural for politics to enter the worship of the church. For example, the Book of Common Prayer includes prayers for the nations and its leaders in the weekly liturgies. More controversially, homilies by church leaders may take positions critical or supportive of government policy. For example, Archbishop Rowan Williams preached in church against the British government's handling of the war in Iraq. In his address, Williams acknowledged an expectation that Christians would be politically loyal to the government, but he said that Christians had to first pay attention to truth and suggested that the government had not been fully truthful in its communication of the facts justifying military action in Iraq ("Iraq War Damaged UK" 2007), so criticism of the state was justified.

Despite the secularization of British society, the population is still open to the church's presence in the public sphere. Even today, with England's democracy well established, many people still expect the church to unite the nation by promoting "common values" or a shared sense of morality (Monsma and Soper 1997: 127–128). Secular British politicians are likely to have a "greater readiness to listen to, and possibly be moved by, religious argument than might otherwise be the case. In short, there is an expectation on their part that religion in general has an important part to play in English public life" (Moyser 1985: 7). An implicit part of the Church of England's initial and continuing mission is to build a common national identity. The Anglican tradition places few limits on the relationship between the church and the state and between individual Christians and the political realm.

The Anglican Tradition and Contemporary Politics

The Anglican political model is based on a dated conception of the state and nation. The Church of England originated in a monarchical political system when most observers believed that state-building required religious unity among the nation. This meant that the religion of the ruler was the religion of the ruled. Today, however, the modern state is well established, and we can point to examples, like the United States, to suggest that a state can exist even when citizens follow diverse religions. The normative triumph of religious pluralism and democracy make Anglican church-state relations difficult to implement today. Outside an established church context, the Anglican norm of bringing religion into public life and politics into the church seems odd and problematic. It may be that the traditional church-state model practiced by the Church of England is best suited to countries with nondemocratic regimes and a relatively homogeneous society.

The increase in the number of autonomous provinces of the Anglican communion, especially after the collapse of the British Empire, deteriorated the authority of the English model and stimulated a variety of localized practices. As the Church of England ventured into other countries, it had to adapt its church-state model to new political realities. Brief examples from two diverse provinces—the United States, a democracy with separation of church and state, and Nigeria, a religiously diverse country with a history of authoritarianism—illustrate this point.

In the United States, the National Cathedral demonstrates the complicated church-state relations that emerge when the partial establishment tradition of the Church of England is transplanted in the American context of separation between church and state. The National Cathedral describes itself as combin-ing "the roles served by three great churches in England—Westminster Abbey, the nation's sacred shrine; St. Paul's Cathedral, the cathedral for Britain's capi-tal city; and Canterbury Cathedral, the mother church for Anglicans in that country" (Lloyd 2007: 6). Although it's an Episcopal church, its mission is to be a national church because "it was built as a spiritual home for the nation" (Lloyd 2007: 6). When President Bush addressed the nation on the National Day of Prayer and Remembrance a few days after the September 11 terrorist attacks, he spoke not from the White House or his own church, but from the Episcopal National Cathedral.

The challenge for the Episcopal Church is to pair this close connection and loyalty to the state with the critical voice of reform that is possible in England. Although the Anglican leadership in the United States is free to criticize the gov-ernment,[12] it does not have the same privileged voice that the Church of England does. The media is not expected to ask Anglican leaders for their views on political issues, and in no way do the views of Episcopal leaders speak, even symbolically, for the Christian community of the country. This potentially weakens the Angli-can vision of Christian political engagement, which ideally includes a church that supports the state and a state that is held accountable by the church.

Another very different example is the Church of Nigeria, which operates in a political context distinct from both the United Kingdom and the United States. Nigeria was an authoritarian regime from the country's independence in 1960 to the adoption of a new constitution in 1999. Today, a quasi-democratic regime governs tenuously. Moreover, unlike England and the United States, Nigerian society is divided roughly equally between Muslims and Christians, and there is significant political tension between these two groups. An active parliament and Christian society assumed in the Church of England's position do not apply. Still, loyalty to the state has been promoted by the current Angli-can leadership in Nigeria.

Even in this context, Anglican Archbishop Akinola recognizes political leaders as placed in their position of authority by God: "All powers belong to God Almighty. . . . That's our position in the church of God. God gives power to whoever He calls to provide leadership at any point in time" (*The Guardian Interviews Archbishop* 2006). After the May 2007 election, Archbishop Akinola encouraged Nigerians to remain peaceful, whatever their opinion of the election outcome, "trusting in the love of the Almighty God to choose the best for us" (Akinola 2007: 1). The belief that God ordains state leaders is consistent with Anglican support for the state.

The Church of Nigeria, however, faces the same dilemma as the American Episcopal Church. How does the church speak critically to the state? Nigerian church leaders noted that in the past, "[t]he Church has been complacent and often silent on socio-political matters of the nation and does not take firm and informed stand on these matters" (The Church of Nigeria 2006). But in 2006, leaders of the Church of Nigeria met to craft a vision for the church to rouse it to political awareness and action. Now, "[w]hile regretting her political aloofness and inertia, the Church believes that the need to wrest politics out from the hands of hawks and predators into those of godly and patriotic Nigerians is urgent, imperative and compelling. . . . Political Education is to become part and parcel of the Church's mission and ministry" (Akinola 2006).

The Anglican Church has encouraged Christians to run for political office, believing that Christian officers will infuse the government with a Christian ethos (Adediran 1994: 132), a view similar to the Reformed perspective in which Christians transform the state. In addition, the Church of Nigeria encouraged parishioners to participate in the 2007 elections and to "vote in credible candidates . . . as doing so would usher in God's blessing and avert impending national disaster" (Owerri 2006). According to the 2006 statement on the church's political awareness, "shying away from active politics is both an anti social behaviour and an ungodly act" (Akinola 2006). This renewal of Anglican support for Christian political activity is perhaps related to the democratization of Nigerian politics. Christians can now participate in the state because it has the possibility of being more than the stronghold of a few authoritarian leaders. The Church of Nigeria currently plays a state-building role, much as the early Church of England did. However, Anglicans in Nigeria do not speak for all citizens of the religiously diverse polity, nor can they even speak for all Christians given the extensive diversity among Nigeria's Christians (Griswold 2008). Instead of the Church of Nigeria uniting all Nigerians under one religious identity, as the Church of England tried to do, the Church of Nigeria seeks to unify the nation by persuading its followers to support pluralistic democracy.

The Church of England's church-state practices bear little similarity to the realities in many Anglican provinces. But the death of the English model as the normative standard for Anglican engagement with politics does not necessarily mean the death of an Anglican approach. If the communion stays united and diverse, Anglicans could draw on the tradition's distinct theological comprehensiveness. Because Anglicanism has, from its origins, been a broad church, members have had to practice the Christian virtues of humility, patience, and long-suffering. Leaders had to prioritize unity above their own status and personal opinions. If these virtues were joined to craft an Anglican approach to politics, it could lead to a tradition that advocated dialogue and consensus building rather than majoritarian politics. Anglicans' approach to politics would focus on the Christian character of participation in the political process.

Rather than Anglicans supporting an established church, then, the constitutional framework they would advocate might be a corporatist one in which the state was required to consult with interest groups, including religious groups, when drafting legislation and where political parties cooperated as much as they critiqued one another. The Anglican model would be a system that institutionalizes cooperation among diverse groups in society. The church's message for individual Christians would affirm their participation in politics, but only to the extent that they could exhibit the biblical virtues of patience, grace, and humility, which would facilitate citizens' ability to engage, rather than dismiss, those with whom they disagree. Acting as a Christian while participating in politics would be more important than gaining power. This version of an Anglican model would create formal avenues for criticism of the state but still hold a high view of the state because it acknowledges it as a partner worthy of cooperation.

This is a possible foundation for a future Anglican model of politics, but it is not the current reality. To the extent that any one model can describe Anglicanism and the state, it is the English model's high view of the state and its encouragement of Christian and church participation in politics that still predominates among Anglicans.

Conclusion

The Anglican tradition calls the church to be both a force for political stability and a venue for political critique. Outside England, loyalty to the state often remains strong, but without establishment, these Anglican churches lack the Church of England's institutional platform from which to speak the gospel to the political powers. This could limit the ability of the Anglican model of politics to fully travel to other provinces. Anglicans outside England can either discard the example of the mother church or, perhaps, Anglicans could use their characteristic comprehensiveness as a foundation for a new Anglican approach to politics. The future of the Anglican tradition's approach to politics depends in large part on the future of the Anglican communion and the balance of power that develops within the global body in the next decades.

NOTES

1. Many readers may be more familiar with the term Episcopal, the particular name of the national Anglican churches in the United States and Scotland. The term highlights the Anglican practice of recognizing bishops, the episcopacy, with authority to govern the church. This contrasts with other traditions, such as Baptist,

that have a decentralized form of decision making and often privilege the laity in church governance. I use the term Anglican to refer generally to all churches in the Anglican communion, including Episcopal churches in the United States and Scotland.

2. The pope's inaction was not simply a theological disapproval of divorce. See Moorman (Moorman 1980: 161–165) for the political pressures that made the pope unwilling to release Henry from his marriage.

3. Despite his break from Rome, Henry was not a Reformer and had, in fact, composed a treatise critical of Martin Luther's ideas.

4. For a more detailed description of the historical evolution of these groups within the Church of England, see Nockles (1994: 44–103).

5. For a history of evangelicals' position within Anglicanism, see Manwaring (1985) and Hylson-Smith (1988).

6. Anglican clergy in the South were less likely to be Loyalists. Southern Anglican churches usually enjoyed a privileged position as the established church in their colony, which made Southern clergy less dependent on England's political and ecclesial leadership for resources and power (Hein and Shattuck 2004: 42–44).

7. For example, the 1930 Lambeth Conference Resolution on the Anglican Communion defined it as a fellowship of churches in communion with the See of Canterbury with the following characteristics: the churches propagate the faith as set forth in the Book of Common Prayer and as authorized by the national church, they promote within their territory a national expression of Christian faith, and they are bound by the "common counsel of the bishops in conference." The structure of church government, or episcopacy, is another area often identified as central to Anglicanism. Bishops who wield significant power over the church, as opposed to a decentralized form of church governance driven by lay participation, is part of the Anglican identity. However, decision-making procedures vary throughout the Anglican communion, as does the type of authority exercised by the bishops (Norris 1998: 333–346).

8. Controversial issues, such as predestination (Article 17), were worded to allow several interpretations and a variety of doctrinal perspectives to appear in the articles. The text sides with Protestantism against Catholicism in affirming the authority of scripture and justification by grace through faith in Christ (Article 11), rather than through works (Article 12). Those with Catholic sensibilities could appreciate the Articles' respect for tradition and the use of a liturgical style that all churches in England were required to follow (Long and Noll n.d.: 14–15).

9. The Scottish Episcopal Church was the first Anglican church outside England to issue its own prayer book in 1764, followed by the American Episcopal Church in 1789 and the Church of Ireland Prayer Book in 1878 (Stevenson 2006: 133; Buchanan 2006: 229).

10. There are many books that probe the details of this conflict. One recent example is Radner and Turner (2006). For the purposes of this essay, it is most important to explain how this issue touches on the larger issue of Anglican comprehensiveness.

11. See, for example, Paul Avis's defense of establishment (2001) or the work of N. T. Wright (2003), a prominent Anglican bishop and New Testament scholar who supports the maintenance of the British monarchy and church establishment.

12. Historically, Episcopal leadership remained silent on pressing political issues, such as slavery and the Civil War, and when the church did take an active public role, it tended to construct voluntary institutions to alleviate the suffering of the poor and marginalized, rather than challenge government policy on these issues (Hein and Shattuck 2004: 65–66, 76–80, 96–99).

BIBLIOGRAPHY

Adediran, 'Biodun. 1994. "The Church and Politics." In *The Anglican Church in Nigeria (1842–1992)*, ed. A. Omoyajowo. Lagos: Macmillan Nigeria.

Akinola, Peter J. 2006. "Message to the Church and Nation Arising from the Political Awareness Seminar Held for the Bishops of the Church of Nigeria (Anglican Communion)." http://www.anglican-nig.org/PH2006messageonPol.htm. Accessed December 10, 2006.

Akinola, Peter J. 2007. "Abp. Akinola on Nigerian Elections, Holiness, and Other Issues." http://www.anglican-nig.org/abujasynod_pressbrief07.htm. Accessed October 9, 2008.

Avis, Paul. 1998. "What Is 'Anglicanism'?" In *The Study of Anglicanism*, eds. S. Sykes et al. London: SPCK/Fortress Press.

Avis, Paul. 2001. *Church, State and Establishment*. London: SPCK.

Bebbington, David. 1992. *Evangelicalism in Modern Britain: A History from the 1730s to the 1980s*. Grand Rapids, MI: Baker Book House.

Buchanan, Colin. 2006. "The Winds of Change." In *The Oxford Guide to The Book of Common Prayer: A Worldwide Survey*, eds. Charles Hefling and Cynthia Shattuck. New York: Oxford University Press, 229–238.

The Church of Nigeria: Anglican Communion. 2006. *Vision of the Church of Nigeria*. http://www.anglican-nig.org/vision.htm. Accessed December 10, 2006.

Cornwell, Peter. 1983. *Church and Nation*. Oxford: Basil Blackwell.

Cornwell, Peter. 1985. "The Church of England and the State: Changing Constitutional Links in Historical Perspective." In *Church and Politics Today: The Role of the Church of England in Contemporary Politics*, ed. G. Moyser. Edinburgh: T. and T. Clark.

Elizabeth's Act of Uniformity (1559). 1921. In *Documents Illustrative of English Church History*, eds. H. Gee and W. J. Hardy. London: Macmillan.

Elizabeth's Supremacy Act, Restoring Ancient Jurisdiction, A.D. 1559. 1921. In *Documents Illustrative of English Church History*, ed. H. Gee and W. J. Hardy. London: Macmillan.

Griswold, Eliza. 2008. "God's Country." *The Atlantic Monthly*. http://www.theatlantic.com/doc/200803/nigeria. Accessed November 20, 2008.

The Guardian Interviews Archbishop Peter Akinola. 2006. The Church of Nigeria: Anglican Communion, 2006. http://www.anglican-nig.org/akinolaGurdn_interview.htm. Accessed December 10, 2006.

Hefling, Charles. 2006. "Introduction: Anglicans and Common Prayer." In *The Oxford Guide to the Book of Common Prayer*, eds. Charles Hefling and Cynthia Shattuck. Oxford: Oxford University Press.

Hein, David, and Gardiner H. Shattuck Jr. 2004. *The Episcopalians*. Westport, CT: Praeger.

Hylson-Smith, Kenneth. 1988. *Evangelicals in the Church of England: 1734–1984*. Edinburgh: T. and T. Clark.

Hylson-Smith, Kenneth. 1996. *The Churches in England from Elizabeth I to Elizabeth II*. vol. 1, 1558–1688. London: SCM Press.

"Iraq War Damaged UK—Archbishop." 2004. *BBC News*. http://news.bbc.co.uk/2/hi/uk_news/3644609.stm. Accessed June 13, 2007.

Lake, Peter. 1988. *Anglicans and Puritans? Presbyterianism and English Conformist Thought from Whitgift to Hooker*. London: Unwin Hyman.

Lloyd, Samuel T. 2007. *A New Century, A New Calling*. Washington, DC: Washington National Cathedral. http://www.cathedral.org/cathedral/pdfs/Vision2007.pdf. Accessed June 2007.

Long, Kathryn, and Mark Noll. n.d. "Reformation Tradition and Protestant Theology I." Unpublished manuscript, Wheaton College, Wheaton, IL.

Manwaring, Randle. 1985. *From Controversy to Co-existence: Evangelicals in the Church of England 1914–1980*. Cambridge: Cambridge University Press.

Monsma, Stephen V., and J. Christopher Soper. 1997. "The Challenge of Pluralism: Church and State in Five Democracies." In *Religious Forces in the Modern Political World*, ed. A. D. Hertzke. New York: Rowman and Littlefield.

Moorman, J. R. H. 1980. *A History of the Church in England*. 3rd ed. Harrisburg, PA: Morehouse.

Morris, Jeremy. 2005. "The Future of Church and State." In *Anglicanism: The Answer to Modernity*. 2nd ed., eds. Duncan Dormor et al. New York: Continuum, 161–185.

Moyser, George. 1985. "The Church of England and Politics: Patterns and Trends." In *Church and Politics Today: The Role of the Church of England in Contemporary Politics*, ed. G. Moyser. Edinburgh: T. and T. Clark.

Nockles, Peter B. 1994. *The Oxford Movement in Context: Anglican High Churchmanship, 1760–1857*. New York: Cambridge University Press.

Norris, Richard A. 1998. "Episcopacy." In *The Study of Anglicanism*, eds. S. Sykes et al. Minneapolis, MN: Fortress Press.

Owerri, Amby Uneze. 2006. *Election 2007: Look at the Candidates Not the Political Party—Anglican Bishop*. http://www.anglican-nig.org/crediblelect.htm. Accessed December 10, 2006.

Pickering, W. S. F., et al. 1998. "Sociology of Anglicanism." In *The Study of Anglicanism*, eds. S. Sykes et al. Minneapolis, MN: Fortress Press.

Radner, Ephraim, and Philip Turner. 2006. *The Fate of Communion: The Agony of Anglicanism and the Future of a Global Church*. Grand Rapids, MI: William B. Eerdmans.

Sachs, William. 1993. *The Transformation of Anglicanism: From State Church to Global Communion*. Cambridge: Cambridge University Press.

Stevenson, Kenneth. 2006. "The Prayer Book as 'Sacred Text.'" In *The Oxford Guide to The Book of Common Prayer*, eds. Charles Hefling and Cynthia Shattuck. New York: Oxford University Press.

Sykes, Stephen. 1995. *Unashamed Anglicanism*. Nashville, TN: Abingdon Press.

Thomas, Philip H. E. 1998. "Doctrine of the Church." In *The Study of Anglicanism*, eds. S. Sykes et al. Minneapolis, MN: Fortress Press.

Thomas, W. H. Griffith. 1930. *The Principles of Theology: An Introduction to the Thirty-Nine Articles*. 2nd ed. New York: Longmans, Green.

Whalon, Pierre W. 2006. "The Future of Common Prayer." In *The Oxford Guide to the Book of Common Prayer*, eds. Charles Hefling and Cynthia Shattuck. Oxford: Oxford University Press.

Wright, N. T. 2003. "God and Caesar, Then and Now." In *Festschrift for Dr. Wesley Carr*. http://www.ntwrightpage.com/Wright_God_Caesar.pdf. Accessed November 19, 2008.

7

For the Sake of Conscience: Some Evangelical Views of the State

Timothy Samuel Shah

Evangelicalism is not a church, sect, or denomination. It has no formal membership and no headquarters. It has no capital or sacred center, no Rome or Mecca. Evangelicals have no pope, no authoritative magisterium. Evangelicalism is, rather, a transdenominational Protestant movement whose defining characteristic is to insist that authentic Christianity requires more than formal ecclesial membership or adherence. Instead, authentic Christian faith demands a belief that the Bible enjoys an authority that trumps other sources of authority, such as reason or tradition; personal and inward acceptance of the gospel message that Christ has atoned for humanity's sins on the cross and has thereby won eternal salvation for believers; and outward mission on the part of all believers, lay and clerical alike, to share the good news of salvation with others.

Evangelicalism's defining imperatives are thus "Believe" (in the ultimate authority of the Bible), "Be born again" (by trusting in the salvific power of Christ's sacrifice on the cross), and "Share the good news" (of salvation in Christ with others). While no single imperative necessarily distinguishes evangelicals from numerous other Christians, the evangelical label can be meaningfully applied whenever Christians (almost always Protestants) embrace all these imperatives as a package, which, historians believe, probably began in the late seventeenth century, though possibly earlier (Bebbington 1989: 1–19; Williams 1992: 681–753; Ward 2004: 11–13).

Given evangelicalism's diffuse and polycentric character and the variety of its forms and expressions over more than three hundred years and across the dozens of countries in which evangelicalism has become a significant presence, any attempt to define the evangelical view of the state would be foolhardy. As a broad movement rather than a denomination or tradition, evangelicalism lacks an elaborate doctrinal center. Consequently, evangelicals are often criticized (with the chief critics often being evangelicals themselves) for lacking a principled and unified body of political thought that is the equivalent of, say, Catholic social thought and for a consequent tendency toward a simplistic, fragmentary, and reactionary approach to politics (Noll 1994: 149–175; Sider and Knippers 2005: 9–11; Weeks 2006: 126).

What coherence evangelicalism possesses derives from its conceptually parsimonious tendency to resist ecclesial formalism in exchange for an experiential biblicism that by its nature is simple and hence widely accessible and adaptable. "It was best to preach the new birth, and the power of godliness," declared Anglican priest and itinerant evangelist George Whitefield in 1740, "and not to insist so much on the form: for people would never be brought to one mind as to that; nor did Jesus Christ ever intend it" (Noll 2003: 13–15). Both the power and the weakness of evangelicalism lie precisely in this parsimony and flexibility, which give it a tremendous ability to adapt to a wide variety of cultural contexts but also a tremendous inability to think and act as a unified movement or to construct a coherent tradition. Evangelicalism has thus assumed an astonishingly broad spectrum of successful forms, from Pietism to Methodism to Pentecostalism (the last of which, though treated in a separate chapter in this book, I insist on treating as a member of the evangelical family, following other scholars [Freston 2001]).

However, I argue that evangelicalism has generated a set of sophisticated and historically consequential views of the state that bear an organic relationship to the very nature of evangelicalism and its distinctive theological emphases. My exposition of these views proceeds chronologically, which serves the purpose of suggesting the historical trajectory both of evangelicalism and of its views of the state. Along the way, I provide some indication of the political consequences of the evangelical views of the state I describe. Above all, I emphasize that evangelical approaches to the state are consistently governed by a concern for the integrity and authority of individual conscience in two senses: evangelicals characteristically seek to liberate the consciences of believers and nonbelievers alike from top-down, state-initiated interference so they can enjoy maximum personal freedom to fulfill the imperatives of the gospel, and they seek to serve as the moral conscience of the political community in order to galvanize the bottom-up, individual-initiated reform of state and society. Douglas

Petersen observes that Latin American Pentecostals have seldom formulated a sophisticated social ethic, but they nonetheless practice one (Petersen 1996: 186, 227–233). In fact, both Pentecostal and non-Pentecostal evangelicals have sometimes been unwilling or unable to formulate sophisticated political philosophies, but their activism has nonetheless frequently generated distinctive, compelling, and influential doctrines of the state and its proper functions.

Evangelical Views of the State, 1675–1900

Scholars generally hold that the proper history of evangelicalism begins with Lutheran Pietism in the late seventeenth century (Ward 2004: 13; see also Noll 1998). The first Pietists exhibited thoroughly evangelical theological tendencies, including an emphasis on the importance of personal conversion. In important respects, the very nature of Pietist teaching bore important implications for politics and the state. In 1675, Lutheran pastor Philip Jakob Spener published a small book, *Pia Desideria, or Heartfelt Longing for a God-Pleasing Reform of the True Evangelical Church*, which in many ways marked the beginning of the Pietist movement (Spener 1964 [1675]). In the wake of the increasing control continental European states imposed on churches in the aftermath of the 1648 Treaties of Westphalia and in the context of a growing intellectualism in Lutheran theology, Spener advocated a fourfold program of church reform: intensive Bible study, both individual and in small-group "class meetings" (the *collegium pietatis*); greater emphasis on lay ministry; the active relating of Christian faith to daily life; and the evangelism of unbelievers through compassion and positive example rather than state coercion (Shenk 1998).

For our purposes, Pietist discomfort with state coercion merits special emphasis. Although Pietists, unlike Anabaptists, believed in working as much as possible within the structures of the state-established church, they began to insist that true and saving religion belonged to an entirely voluntary sphere outside the state's capacity to control. While they did not deny that the state had a legitimate interest in encouraging true religion, they were more skeptical than the Reformers—whether Lutheran, Calvinist, or Anglican—of the power of the state to effect a true spiritual reformation. "What had always been understood by reform," writes W. R. Ward, "had been action from above by the state" and particularly "the public disciplining of the irreligious" (Ward 2004: 13–14). In contrast, Spener held that the renewal of a sterile church establishment could come only from ordinary believers meeting in groups that operated outside state sponsorship. From the beginning, in other words, evangelicalism distanced itself from what had been a broad Reformed and indeed classical

Christian doctrine that the state played a crucial role in the advancement of true religion. Partly through his invocation of the gospel imperative, "Compel them to come in" (Luke 14: 23), St. Augustine launched this doctrine by explicitly and elaborately advocating the application of coercive political pressure to draw the Donatists and other heretics and schismatics back into the true church (Atkins and Dodaro 2001). Pietists, on the other hand, embraced a characteristically evangelical view of Christianity—hinging on voluntary inner conversion and "new birth," nurtured in small groups independent of the state-sponsored church—that by its nature rendered the state and state action essentially irrelevant to the religious sphere.

Also in the second half of the seventeenth century, evangelical tendencies appeared in England and America in many of the dissenting or nonconformist churches, especially the Baptists, and these tendencies also generated distinctive views of the state and its proper domain. In fact, the same emphasis on a religion of the heart and inner conversion evident in Spener's 1675 *Pia Desideria* appears in *Pilgrim's Progress,* published by Baptist preacher John Bunyan in two parts in 1678 and 1684 (Noll 1998). Evangelical beliefs and practices—in personal interpretation of scripture; in the indispensability of individual, voluntary access to faith; in evangelistic preaching—made many Baptists and other Dissenters the persistent objects of state persecution, with Bunyan himself serving a long prison sentence for unlicensed preaching between 1660 and 1672 (Hill 1990). The tireless resistance of Baptists and other Dissenters to state suppression of religious dissent—which surprised and impressed many observers, including John Locke—helped bring about the English Toleration Act of 1689 (Kraynack 1980).

On the other side of the Atlantic, the dissenter Roger Williams, who closely aligned himself with New England Baptists (though he ultimately refused to join any denomination), founded Providence Plantation in 1636 as "a lively experiment [for] full liberty in religious concernments" (Witte 2000: 20). The evangelical emphases that led Williams into close sympathy and cooperation with Baptists—belief in individual appropriation of scripture and personal, adult conversion—helped lay the foundations not only for his insistence on religious liberty but also for his advocacy of "a wall of separation between the garden of the Church and the wilderness of the world," as he famously formulated it in 1643. Where the two have been confounded, the result has been a disastrous corruption of faith. "The practising [of] civil force upon the consciences of men," Williams wrote in refutation of Cotton Mather's defense of state discipline of the ungodly, "is so far from preserving religion pure, it is a mighty bulwark or barricado [sic], to keep out all true religion" (quoted in Backus 1773).

For much of the seventeenth century, Anglo-American evangelicalism had essentially been confined to the dissenting churches. In the first half of the 18th century, however, the growing international reach of Lutheran Pietism, as well as its missionary offshoot, the Moravian Brethren, increasingly carried evangelical influences into the heart of the dominant established church of the English-speaking world, the Anglican Church. At a Moravian meeting in 1738, Anglican minister John Wesley "felt [his] heart strangely warmed" as he experienced a profoundly personal assurance that Christ "had taken away *my* sins, even *mine*, and saved *me* from the law of sin and death" (quoted in Noll 1998; emphasis in the original). Wesley founded the Methodists to inspire a personal acquaintance with God's grace, holy living, and evangelism by means of itinerant preaching. As long as Wesley lived, however, Methodism never broke formally from the established Church of England but was intended to serve as an *ecclesiola* in *ecclesia*—"a tight-knit religious fellowship within a broader church" (Bebbington 1989: 40).

Particularly until Wesley's death in 1791, Methodism hewed to a view of the state and politics that reflected the establishment location and commitments of its founder. Wesley insisted on a "no politics" rule, proscribing agitation on "controverted questions" within the movement, although he violated his own rule when he published, in 1775, a short pamphlet on the highly controverted question of American colonial resistance to the British Crown (Wesley 1775). The substance of the pamphlet, however, was highly conventional (it was largely plagiarized from Samuel Johnson, as Wesley later admitted) and proestablishment, arguing that the colonists had no legitimate grievance but merely sought an unfair and illegal exemption from parliamentary taxation. Wesley's views on the colonies probably reflected his own particular distrust of popular participation in politics but also a more general tendency among some 18th-century British evangelicals toward political "quietism and loyalism" (Bebbington 1989: 72). "I meddle not with the disputes of party," wrote the former slave trader and convert to evangelical faith John Newton in 1775, "nor concern myself about any political maxims, but such as are laid down in scripture" (in Bebbington 1989: 72–73). For their conception of the state, Newton, Wesley, and many other 18th-century evangelicals were largely content with the political maxims of the New Testament that enjoined believers to fear God, honor the king, and pay their taxes.

Evangelical political views were more diverse and complicated, however. In fact, in a striking departure from a quietist and loyalist posture, most evangelicals on both sides of the Atlantic were strong supporters of the American Revolution. According to Bebbington, the evangelical wings in the Church of Scotland, most Baptist ministers in America and all but two in London, and most Scottish evangelicals all backed the American cause (Bebbington 1989: 73). Many British evangelicals were so far from being strict loyalists, in other words, that they openly broke with their own government concerning the conflict with the colonies. Perhaps the most famous of all evangelical supporters of the revolution was John Witherspoon, the Scottish evangelical who had become principal of Princeton and who was the only clergyman to sign the Declaration of Independence (Bebbington 1989: 73; West 1996: 26–36).

Many evangelicals supported the revolution because they opposed political tyranny but also feared "that true religion was under threat" from anti-Protestant forces (Bebbington 1989: 73). More broadly, several scholars argue that the First Great Awakening, which began in Northampton, Massachusetts, in 1735 and was stimulated and defended by the great evangelical theologian Jonathan Edwards, fostered social and cultural attitudes that over the long run proved conducive to the American revolutionary spirit. According to William G. McLoughlin, for example, the Great Awakening prompted increasing numbers of ordinary individuals to consider both church and state creatures of the people and subject to their authority (McLoughlin 1977). Furthermore, despite a general conservatism, Wesley himself bucked much elite and mass opinion on both sides of the Atlantic with his uncompromising opposition to slavery, from 1743 onward, and his increasing insistence that the state act to suppress it (Dayton 1988: 73–74).

Even more than on the American Revolution, there was wide evangelical consensus on the question of religious liberty. Particularly noteworthy is that a commitment to broad religious liberty was not restricted to evangelical Dissenters, who stood to gain the most from a policy of religious toleration. Thomas Scott, Anglican curate and evangelicalism's greatest 18th-century commentator on the Bible, wrote of "the vast obligation" owed to John Locke for his liberal views on religious toleration (Bebbington 1989: 73). George Whitefield, Anglican minister and Methodist itinerant preacher, pressed for a robust respect for liberty of conscience and a profoundly ecumenical spirit (Witte 2000: 28). Wesley favored broad religious tolerance and liberty of conscience (though he believed Catholic disabilities should remain—only because the Catholic Church was theologically committed to persecution). The Methodist leader Adam Clarke turned this principle into a general view of the state: "Of all forms of government," he wrote, "that which provides the greatest portion of civil liberty to the subject, must be most pleasing to God, because most like his own" (Bebbington 1989: 73).

Unquestionably, however, evangelicals outside the established churches—Baptists, above all—were the most active and influential advocates of liberal and separationist views of the state vis-à-vis religion. One premise of this advocacy is a foundational and consistent evangelical political emphasis: the state possesses neither the right nor the competence to settle religious questions on behalf of its citizens; therefore, any assumption on its part of religious tasks and functions amounts to a direct interference in the unique prerogatives of God. Insofar as there many religions in the community, "[i]t was for God, not the state, to decide which of these religions should flourish and which should fade" (Witte 2000: 29). To make the state the sponsor of one particular form of religion was thus to usurp the sovereign authority of the Almighty. "We view it to be our incumbent duty, to render unto Caesar the things that are his," wrote the indefatigable Baptist pamphleteer and evangelical preacher Isaac Backus in 1773, "but that it is of as much importance not to render unto him any thing that belongs only to God, who is to be obeyed rather than man. And as it is evident to us, that God always claimed it as his sole prerogative to determine by his own laws, what his worship shall be, who shall minister in it, and how they shall be supported; so it is evident that this prerogative has been, and still is, encroached upon in our land" (Backus 1773). Whatever else evangelicals have articulated about the state, they have advocated few propositions more forcibly or consistently than the proposition that the state must never assume the authority and functions of God.

A closely related premise of evangelical advocacy of religious freedom and church-state separation concerned the divine origin and prior importance of religious freedom. Dissenting evangelicals were of the opinion that "[r]eligious liberty is a divine right, immediately derived from the Supreme Being, without the intervention of any created authority," in the words of evangelical preacher Israel Evans (Witte 2000: 29). Furthermore, they held that such religious rights are inviolable because the religious duties God imposes on individuals are of supreme and eternal importance. God gives reason, freedom, and conscience to individuals as a kind of trust, and individuals are responsible to God—and God alone—for their proper use. "Every man must give an account of himself to God, and therefore every man ought to be at liberty to serve God in that way that he can reconcile it to his conscience," wrote Baptist leader John Leland in 1791. "It would be sinful for a man to surrender to man [that] which is to be kept sacred for God" (Witte 2000: 40). John Jay, probably the most prominent evangelical statesman of the founding era as New York governor, author of five of the Federalist Papers, and later the first chief justice of the Supreme Court, declared in 1771 that "the rights of conscience and private judgment . . . are by nature subject to no control but that of the Deity" (West 1996: 55). States have a duty to respect the freedom of individuals to discharge their prior duties to God.

In addition, a strong conception of true religion as personal and voluntary led evangelicals to argue that any state coercion or control of individual freedom on religious matters negated the very possibility of true religion achieving real influence over the hearts and minds of citizens. State coercion designed to advance religion is instead doomed to corrupt religion. Wherever state intrusions on religious groups have been permitted over the long history of Christianity, wrote Isaac Backus, "tyranny, simony, and robbery came to be introduced and to be practiced under the Christian name" (Witte 2000: 30). In other words, late-18th-century Baptist evangelicals argued that state action in the religious sphere was not only irrelevant or insufficient for the promotion of true religion, which had been the conviction of late-17th-century Pietist evangelicals, but also destructive of genuine piety. Conversely, 18th-century evangelicals believed that the best way to purify religion and ensure its widest possible influence in state and society was to free it from both the coercive pressures and the corrupting supports of the state (Witte 2000: 30). They supported disestablishment not for the sake of privatizing religion, in other words, but for the sake of empowering it.

These radical views generated radical political conclusions. Dissenting evangelicals pressed not only for expansive state protections for religious liberty and diversity but also for the disestablishment of religion and the strict separation of church and state. In 1794, Baptist preacher John Leland proposed a sweeping amendment to the Massachusetts Constitution that would have forbidden the legislature from "establish[ing] any religion by law, giv[ing] any one sect a preference to another, or forc[ing] any man in the commonwealth to part with his property for the support of religious worship, or the maintenance of the gospel" (Witte 2000: 29). For many evangelical Baptists, this radical separationism entailed a nonconfessional state. Leland, for example, swept centuries of Christian political thought off the table by boldly proclaiming that "[t]he notion of a Christian commonwealth should be exploded forever." Of course, since at least Pope Gelasius I, Christians had frequently argued that temporal authority was distinct from spiritual authority and that the two should not be confounded, but they had just as frequently argued that the two authorities should closely cooperate to form a unified *res publica Christiana*. Evangelicals increasingly rejected this notion in favor of a more differentiated view of political society, partly because of their voluntaristic conception of religion but also partly because of their pessimistic view of the state, one that echoed Roger Williams's stark suggestion that the state belonged to a moral "wilderness" from which the "garden" of the church needed to take precautions to secure itself. The Baptist Isaac Backus, an admirer of Williams, wrote that "God has expressly armed the magistrate with the sword to punish such as work ill to their neighbors, and his faithfulness in that work and our obedience to such authority, is enforced [by the Bible]. But it is evident that the sword is excluded from the kingdom of the Redeemer" (Witte 2000: 30). Any admixture of these distinct realms would undermine the Lord's purposes for both, not least by bringing the corrupting spirit of the state into the pure spiritual realm of the church.

In the young American republic, evangelical views of the proper relationship between state and religion yielded crucial political consequences. At one strategic moment, Baptist evangelicals made their firm commitment to religious liberty known to James Madison, who (like other Federalists) initially opposed a constitutional bill of rights. When his Baptist constituents threatened to support his opponent (James Monroe) during his campaign for a seat in the First Congress in 1788–1789, Madison promptly shifted gears, issuing a statement to a Baptist minister declaring his support for "the most satisfactory provisions for all essential rights, particularly the rights of Conscience in the fullest latitude." Baptist leaders responded by supporting Madison, who went on to win the election by a few hundred votes, enabling him to sponsor the Bill of Rights as a member of the First Congress (Labunski 2006). As Michael McConnell notes, were it not for religious activists like these Baptist evangelicals, "We might not have a First Amendment" (McConnell 1999: 645–646).

Toward the end of the 18th century and in the early decades of the 19th century, evangelicalism was a dynamic and rapidly growing force in both Britain and America. In Britain, evangelicalism went from being an essentially lower-class movement outside the mainstream of the established church (a divide that was reinforced by the formal fissure between the Church of England and the Methodist "Connexion" that followed Wesley's death) to having a secure place within both the Church of England and upper-class society by 1830 (Brown 1961; Bebbington 1989: 97). In America, according to one estimate, evangelical churches represented about 17 percent of all mainline churches in 1780 but had jumped to nearly 49 percent by 1820 and 61 percent by 1860 (the same periods saw corresponding decreases for all other major Protestant groupings, i.e., Anglican, Calvinist, and Lutheran) (Witte 2000: 99; Hatch 1989).

One consequence of evangelical growth in the United States was that "state policies of patronizing a public religion became increasingly difficult to maintain," as constitutional scholar John Witte notes. "Many Evangelical churches, both Baptist and Methodist, insisted that states adhere more firmly to principles of disestablishment and separatism; in a number of states, they gained the political power to revise the constitutions accordingly" (Witte 2000: 100). In addition, evangelicalism's growth in status and sheer numbers, on both sides of the Atlantic, led to a marked broadening of its political agenda.

Although virtually all Anglo-American evangelicals had decisively rejected the idea that the state could be an appropriate vehicle of religious reform, they increasingly came to view the state as an essential vehicle of moral and social reform. Many evangelicals, such as Lyman Beecher, remained skeptical of partisan politics and continued to believe, with Williams and Backus before them, that an excessive entanglement between religion and state would endanger the evangelical cause. "[W]ith the annual detail of secular policy, it does not become Christians to intermeddle, beyond the unobtrusive influence of their silent suffrage," warned Beecher in a sermon in 1824. "The injudicious association of religion with politics, in the time of Cromwell, brought upon evangelical doctrine and piety, in England, an odium which has not ceased to this day." But in the same sermon Beecher carved out an exception: "When great questions of national morality are about to be decided, such as the declaration of war; or, in England, the abolition of the slave trade; or the permission to introduce Christianity into India by Missionaries; it becomes Christians to lift up their voice, and exert their united influence" (West 1996: 131).

In fact, Beecher's sermon neatly represents a twofold political tendency that was widespread among both American and British evangelicals in the 19th century and, in fact, among many evangelicals to this day. On one hand, evangelicals generally favored a sharply limited political role for themselves, as well as a sharply limited role for the state. On the other hand, evangelicals believed that the state was an appropriate and necessary instrument for the redress of moral and social evils they perceived to be significant. The "remarkable measure of consistency" in the political reform movements mounted by 19th-century British evangelicals, notes David Bebbington, was that their "object of attack was wickedness" (Bebbington 1989: 133). The observation applies equally well to 19th-century American evangelicals.

According to Bebbington, "three broad classes of wickedness" stirred evangelicals into political action. The first he calls obstacles to the gospel—"[a]nything that prevented human beings from hearing the gospel was a threat to their salvation that must be hateful to God" (Bebbington 1989: 133). British evangelicals mounted a political assault on slavery in the West Indian colonies in the 1830s "because it began to be seen, for the first time, as an absolute barrier to missionary progress in the Caribbean" (Bebbington 1989: 133). Similarly, some evangelicals began to seek parliamentary regulation of the factory workday when they perceived that workers had no time to attend religious meetings. A second class of evils Bebbington terms substitutes for the gospel—religious or secular systems of belief that competed with true, biblical faith. Roman Catholicism, Masonry, Darwinism, Marxism, socialism, Hinduism in British India, and even Thomas Jefferson's alleged atheism (a major issue in the U.S. presidential elections of 1800) all provoked sometimes furious evangelical political activism on one side of the Atlantic or the other at various points in the 19th century. A broad range of personal sins against the gospel constituted the third class. These sins included dueling, Sabbath breaking, prostitution, gambling, and alcohol consumption (West 1996: 79–170; Bebbington 1989: 132–137).

The ideas that inspired these forms of evangelical political activism include one I have already noted as a cardinal evangelical principle of the state: that the state should protect the religious liberties and freedoms of individuals. However, 19th-century evangelicals began to embrace a more expansive conception of how states could and should protect religious freedom. It was not enough for states to formally protect such rights in written constitutions and to refrain from directly impinging on such rights by religious laws or establishments. British and American evangelicals began to articulate the idea that states should avoid promoting any ideas or promulgating any laws that directly or indirectly interfere with the promotion, acceptance, and practice of the gospel. Acting on this principle, British evangelicals fought to remove restrictions on the entry of missionaries into British India, which they succeeded in doing by an act of Parliament in 1813, and they fought to stop British government and East India Company support for Hindu temples (Neill 1966: 89–93; van der Veer 1999: 27–30). American evangelicals fought for a ban on Sunday mail delivery, at least partly because it indirectly burdened evangelical conscience and the integrity of evangelical practice by compelling thousands of postal workers—many of them believers—to labor on the Sabbath (West 1996: 143).

Evangelicals also embraced another political idea that motivated their increasing activism for moral reform: the proposition that the integrity and prosperity of republican government required a virtuous citizenry (Noll 2002). "So long . . . as our people remain virtuous and intelligent," declared Baptist divine Francis Wayland, "our government will remain stable" (West 1996: 118). Conversely, "a people [without virtue] are neither fit to enjoy, nor able to assert and maintain their liberties," insisted Congregationalist Nathanael Emmons (West 1996: 119). In a highly influential address entitled "The Practicality of Suppressing Vice by Means of Societies Instituted for That Purpose," Lyman Beecher argued in 1803 that the nation was doomed without moral reform because "sin is in its nature anti-social. It will sunder the ties of society; lead us to bite and devour; to be hateful, and to hate one another" (West 1996: 86). According to John West's apt summary, the ideas underlying evangelical moral reform efforts were: "Morality is necessary for republican government; religion is necessary for morality; therefore, religion is necessary for republican government" (West 1996: 117).

Beecher's 1803 call for a moral reformation gained considerable momentum in the immediate aftermath of the famous duel on July 11, 1804, between Alexander Hamilton and Vice President Aaron Burr, resulting in Hamilton's death the next day. Though the duel provoked national revulsion, evangelicals viewed it with special horror and as a particularly alarming sign of the country's moral degradation because Burr was the son of an evangelical minister, the grandson of Jonathan Edwards, and the first cousin of the evangelical president of Yale, Timothy Dwight. Beecher's response to the tragedy suggested his view of the state and a salutary role for politics: he argued that the Bible excludes duelists from public office because it demands that those at the reins of state power be just men who fear God, and he urged citizens to refuse to support candidates who have participated in duels (West 1996: 88–92). Just as significant, the antidueling issue prompted evangelicals to seek reform through voluntary organizations and grassroots mobilization, a trend that accelerated after 1812. By 1828, the United States had seen the formation of some four hundred temperance societies. The same year saw the establishment of the General Union for Promoting the Observance of the Christian Sabbath. In 1834, evangelicals such as businessman Lewis Tappan were instrumental in the formation of the American Anti-Slavery Society, which soon became the nation's largest anti-slavery organization (West 1996: 112). On a variety of issues, these evangelical campaigns led to important changes in public opinion and the law—including, at long last, a congressional ban on dueling in the District of Columbia in 1839 (West 1996: 94–97). The way to reform state and society, in other words, is not by commandeering the state and forcing change from above but by mobilizing society and inspiring change from below—change that would, in due course, sweep across both state and society.

However, Bebbington's otherwise insightful typology of the kinds of "wickedness" that motivated evangelical political reform omits one important category: great social injustices. In fact, a number of such social evils—such as slavery, the oppression of Native Americans, and widow burning in India—motivated evangelicals to vigorously press for state intervention in the 19th century. Furthermore, *contra* Bebbington, who denies that any broad "humanitarian" impulse animated evangelicalism, these evils motivated an evangelical political response even where they did not erect any particular barrier to mission or evangelization. They were considered evil, pure and simple, and stimulated a concerted response primarily because they involved the infliction of gross and gratuitous cruelty on particular human beings.

- Pioneering evangelical missionary to India William Carey first pressed British authorities to stop *suttee*—the custom of immolating Hindu widows on the funeral pyres of their husbands—in 1804, and numerous other missionaries followed suit, although deference to indigenous religious sensibilities delayed serious action until 1829. What was their motive? As authoritative scholar of Christian missions in India Stephen Neill underscores, "[t]he plea of the missionaries . . . [was] not so much Christian as human . . . no direct appeal to the principles of the Gospel was necessary" (Neill 1966: 95).

- Evangelicals such as Jeremiah Evarts, corresponding secretary for the American Board of Commissioners for Foreign Missions (ABCFM), and Theodore Frelinghuysen, senator from New Jersey, urged the federal government to prevent the forcible removal of the Cherokee nation from Georgia in the 1820s and 1830s. Evarts and Frelinghuysen believed that the Cherokee, equal with whites in the sight of God, were perfectly entitled to retain possession of land they had long occupied, and that America's founding ideals (not to mention its treaty commitments) imposed on it a solemn duty to respect Cherokee self-government and independence (West 1996: 171–206).

- William Wilberforce and other British evangelicals undertook a long campaign first to end British involvement in the slave trade (which they succeeded in securing in 1807) and then to ban slavery throughout the British Empire (which they succeeded in securing in 1834, shortly after Wilberforce's death). Wilberforce considered it his "duty to endeavour to deliver these poor creatures from their present darkness and degradation," both from concern for their well-being and from concern that Britain would otherwise suffer the chastisements of Providence. Slavery also seems to have been abhorrent to Wilberforce because it was the "symbolic opposite" of his strong belief in free human agency under God (Hilton 1988: 209–211). The motives of evangelical abolitionists in America were much the same (Carwardine 1993; Young 2006).

The motives of these different movements were diverse, to be sure, but none of them had much to do with the displacement of the gospel or with sins of sex and alcohol, which, on Bebbington's account, are the almost exclusive engines of evangelical political activism. They had much more to do with the sheer magnitude and cruelty of various forms of human suffering and with evangelicals' belief that they would be complicit in such enormities if they failed to persuade their governments to suppress them.

Though evangelicals periodically engaged in morally charged political campaigns that demanded some form of state action, they tended to embrace the principle that, as a rule, the state should preserve and protect the free agency of individuals, which amounted to a political theory of laissez-faire and sharply limited government. Consider the Clapham Sect evangelicals and their most famous member, Wilberforce. Even as they struggled to step up government intervention to suppress slavery, Wilberforce and his evangelical colleagues were animated by a near-fanatical insistence on "little government" and a conviction that state activism should be severely limited, particularly in the economic sphere (Hilton 1988: 205; Brown 1961). They were in favor of free trade and hostile to policies that smacked of economic paternalism, such as the minimum wage, usury laws, and what we would today call corporate welfare—government bailouts of businesses that found themselves in trouble. But some scholars make a good case that Wilberforce's antislavery campaign and political and economic laissez-faire were perfectly compatible insofar as both slavery and state paternalism violated his strong conviction that human beings should be treated as free agents ultimately responsible to God alone (Hilton 1988: 206–207).

The Evangelical Tradition and Contemporary Politics

In the course of the 20th century, evangelicalism experienced dramatic decline in Britain and continental Europe, continuing strength in the United States and to a lesser extent Canada, and dramatic expansion in the global South. In fact, at the beginning of the 21st century, the global South was home to nearly 600 million of the world's approximately 800 million evangelical Protestants, or about 75 percent of all evangelicals (Shah 2004: 131 n. 10). Only about 1 percent of the global South population was Protestant in 1900 and only about 4 percent as recently as 1970, yet more than 10 percent is Protestant today (Barrett et al. 2001: 4, 13–15; Woodberry and Shah 2004: 49). Despite evangelicalism's rapid growth and increasing global reach, it continued to insist on limited government and the state's duty to protect religious freedom, and it also exhibited a characteristic concern to mobilize the state to rectify great social evils.

The early part of the 20th century, however, proved inauspicious for evangelical politics. In the final decades of the 19th century and early decades of the 20th century, several trends prompted Western evangelicals to de-emphasize the state and political engagement and to adopt a defensive posture of social withdrawal: the urgent revivalism of D. L. Moody, the loss of evangelical leadership and influence in historic Protestant denominations, the rise of "higher" biblical criticism in many churches and seminaries, the promotion of a Social Gospel by modernist Protestants, and the intellectual ascendancy of Darwinism in society as a whole (Green 2005: 15–21). These trends, which fueled the conflict between fundamentalism and modernism that increasingly affected both the United States and to a lesser extent Britain between 1900 and 1930 (Bebbington 1989: 181–182), led many evangelicals to reject all forms of "modernism," which for some included concerted efforts at social and political change. "Social reform," wrote British evangelical Presbyterian Scott Matheson in 1893, "ought never to draw the Church aside from her proper work of saving men." The "red scare" following the 1917 Russian Revolution intensified the feeling on both sides of the Atlantic that "tampering with the social order was inopportune" (Bebbington 1989: 211, 215). The result was what David O. Moberg has termed the "great reversal": a widespread abandonment by evangelicals of their historic engagement with society and politics (Moberg 1972).

Despite this trend, various social evils and putatively anti-Christian ideologies motivated fervent evangelical activism. In the United States, from the founding of the Women's Christian Temperance Union in 1873 to the implementation of the prohibitionist Eighteenth Amendment in 1920, temperance was a continuing focus of evangelical political mobilization on the grounds that alcohol was both sinful and destructive of family and society, particularly for the vulnerable poor (Smith 1987: 22; Pegram 1998; Timberlake 1963). Beginning in 1921, evangelical Presbyterian and progressive Democratic politician William Jennings Bryan helped lead a political campaign to ban the teaching of Darwinian evolution in public schools, aided by the main fundamentalist organization, the World Christian Fundamentalist Association, started in 1919. Antievolution legislation was introduced in numerous states, and between 1923 and 1928, five Southern states passed such legislation. Tennessee passed the strictest law, occasioning the Scopes trial in 1925. Though the trial resulted in a conviction for John Scopes, a public school teacher who had deliberately violated the law by teaching evolution, H. L. Mencken and other journalists succeeded in portraying the fundamentalist opponents of evolution—personified by Bryan, who prosecuted Scopes—as obscurantists. The sense that evangelicals had won a Pyrrhic victory was deepened by Bryan's death five days after the trial (Green 2005: 19).

Success on Prohibition deprived evangelicals of what had been one of their primary motives for political combat for several decades, while their public relations debacle on evolution robbed them of political self-confidence and enthusiasm (Green 2005: 19). In addition, a premillennialist expectation of Christ's imminent return—particularly in the influential formulation of English Plymouth Brethren theologian John Nelson Darby—suggested to evangelicals on both sides of the Atlantic that social reform and political action were futile (Balmer 1999: 51; Judis 2005: 6). Evangelical premillennialists, including the growing ranks of Pentecostals, believed "not that the development of the Kingdom will bring the King, but that the King Himself must come to establish the Kingdom; and that He, not man, is to make the Kingdom fit for men to live in" (in Bebbington 1989: 194). Consequently, evangelicals largely detached themselves from public affairs by 1930, particularly in the United States (Green 2005: 19).

Still, the much-noted fundamentalist withdrawal was much less complete and enduring than is often assumed. In the 1930s, Canadian-born Aimee Semple McPherson, the Pentecostal evangelist and frequent spokesperson for fundamentalist causes, supported evangelical involvement in politics in both the United States and Canada and even favored at least some government programs to assist the poor (Elliott 1994: 363–364). Many other evangelicals publicly attacked the Social Gospel of Walter Rauschenbusch and other liberal Protestants, as well as Franklin Roosevelt's New Deal, as akin to communism. Earlier, evangelicals mobilized to oppose the presidential candidacy of Al Smith, the Catholic and anti-Prohibitionist Democratic nominee in 1928, probably costing him votes in some Southern states and to a lesser extent in a few Northern states such as New York (Green 2005: 20–21).

Already by the early 1940s, however, the tide had begun to turn back toward a more vigorous and better organized evangelical thrust into politics and public life (Green 2005: 21–22). Self-described traditionalist and separatist fundamentalists led by Carl McIntire founded the American Council of Christian Churches (ACCC) in 1941 and the International Council of Christian Churches (ICCC) in 1948. However, their main aim was not to offer a positive political program but to counter the "modernism" of the Federal (now National) Council of Churches and later the World Council of Churches, and their political pronouncements were restricted almost exclusively to virulent anticommunism. But this exclusivist and narrow strand of evangelicalism was in decline by 1969 (Green 2005: 21–22, 23). In 1942, fundamentalists who were quickly labeled "new" or "neo" evangelicals founded the more inclusive National Association of Evangelicals (NAE), which from the beginning threw itself open to Pentecostals, Anabaptists, Holiness, and other nonfundamentalist Protestants (Smith 1998: 11; Cizik 2005: 35–38). Neo-evangelicals went beyond the fundamentalist goal of doctrinal purity to adopt a posture of "engaged orthodoxy": a determination to apply the gospel to every facet of private and public life, including the state and political affairs. Spurred by evangelist Billy Graham and theologian Carl Henry, neo-evangelicals established an array of institutions to equip evangelicalism to engage the wider society, including Fuller Seminary in 1947 and *Christianity Today* in 1956 (Carpenter 1997; Smith 1998: 1–15; see also Budziszewski 2006: 39–44). During the same period, Anglican priest and theologian John R. W. Stott promoted a similarly engaged and intellectually serious evangelicalism in Britain and throughout the Anglican communion (Bebbington 1989: 266–269).

Politics was a prominent concern of neo-evangelicals from the beginning. The NAE was founded in large part to counter the influence of secularism, communism (which it saw as but an extreme form of secularism), and Catholicism in American politics (Smith 1998: 122–123). Through much of the 1950s and 1960s, it advocated antisecularist constitutional amendments declaring the accountability of the U.S. government to Jesus Christ as Savior and "ruler of the nations" while strenuously opposing government aid to Catholic schools on the basis of strict separationism (Cizik 2005: 42). The NAE also opposed proposals to establish diplomatic relations with the Vatican (a feat Ronald Reagan accomplished only in 1983, by which time evangelicals had dropped their opposition); indirectly expressed doubts during the 1960 presidential campaign that John Kennedy, if elected, "would resist fully the pressures of the [Catholic] ecclesiastical hierarchy"; and sharply criticized Catholic countries such as Italy, Spain, and Colombia that restricted evangelical missionary activity (Cizik 2005: 40–41, 45). And throughout the Cold War, the NAE used various emphatic formulations to express its "unalterable opposition to every form of atheistic Communism," as its "25th Anniversary Manifesto" declared in 1967 (Cizik 2005: 46). In addition, the NAE adopted an official statement in 1956 condemning racial discrimination, which it deplored as a hindrance to the propagation of the gospel (Cizik 2005: 42).

In the widespread evangelical view of the state that the NAE represented, a system of ordered liberty can endure only insofar as the state secures the widest possible evangelical liberty to proclaim the gospel—which alone brings true order and true freedom to both individuals and societies—while it also refuses to support nonevangelical substitutes for the gospel, whether communism, secularism, Catholicism, or racist doctrines of white superiority (Cizik 2005: 21–22; Weeks 2006: 135).

On economic matters, neo-evangelicals gradually abandoned knee-jerk condemnations of government efforts on behalf of the poor as "socialistic" in favor of what George Marsden termed a "Christianized version of Republicanism": a limited acceptance of New Deal-style welfare programs (Marsden 1991: 74, cited in Green 2005: 24). That a solid majority of evangelicals backed Lyndon Johnson in 1964—not only 67 percent of Southern evangelicals but also 56 percent of northern evangelicals—provides some indication of a shift in evangelical views of the state and state intervention (Green 2005: 25). Between the 1970s and the 1990s, evangelicals were increasingly influenced by various evangelical leaders such as Vinay Samuel, Ronald Sider, Samuel Escobar, Rene Padilla, Jim Wallis, and Nicholas Wolterstorff to support a greater role for the state on behalf of the poor. For example, more than one hundred evangelicals from across the global North and South signed a declaration on Christian faith and economics in January 1990 affirming the duty of the state to provide "sustenance rights" to the poor while also concluding that "economic power is diffused within market-oriented economies to a greater extent than in other systems" (Schlossberg et al. 1994: 27, 28).

Building on an instinctive and long-standing distrust of concentrated state power, evangelicals in the United States and elsewhere have increasingly adopted the view that the state should play a real but limited supporting role concerning poverty alleviation that avoids an expansive central-government paternalism. Instead, diverse evangelicals such as Marvin Olasky, Amy Sherman, and James Skillen have pressed for government policies and programs that help grassroots groups such as churches address poverty by drawing on their proven ability to encourage individual responsibility and behavioral change among the poor (Schaefer 2003; Sherman 2003).

Just as in the 19th century, moral and social evils continued to motivate evangelical political activism, and evangelicals continued to believe that the state often played an indispensable role in curbing or eliminating such evils. On the domestic front, shortly after the U.S. Supreme Court's *Roe v. Wade* decision in 1973, evangelical thinkers and activists such as Francis Schaeffer, C. Everett Koop (who served as Ronald Reagan's surgeon general), and Harold O. J. Brown mounted a broad antiabortion campaign, including demands for government restrictions on abortion (Schaeffer 1981; Koop and Schaeffer 1983 [1979]; Green 2005: 26). Schaeffer in particular encouraged evangelicals to adopt the political principle of "co-belligerency"—that is, a willingness to work closely with like-minded nonevangelicals to oppose abortion, euthanasia, and other fruits of "secular humanism." Schaeffer's nonsectarian approach to political advocacy exercised a strong influence on self-described fundamentalist and formerly apolitical leader Jerry Falwell and his founding in 1979 of the Moral Majority, which sought to mobilize a wide variety of evangelicals, mainline Protestants, Catholics, and Jews on moral issues like abortion, homosexuality, and pornography, as well as other issues, such as support for Israel and the Jewish people (Dobson 1987: 3–5). Gross violations of human rights by communist governments continued to stir a fierce anticommunism on the part of evangelicals (Dobson 1987).

On the international front, American evangelicals became so concerned about the widespread persecution of their fellow believers in Sudan, China, India, Indonesia, Egypt, and numerous other countries beginning in the mid-1990s that they provided the "main grassroots energy" behind the passage of the International Religious Freedom Act in 1998. Evangelicals also successfully pushed for legislation on the Sudanese civil war and international human trafficking. In these instances, too, evangelicals worked in close partnership with a broad range of religious and nonreligious "co-belligerents" (Hertzke 2003, 2004; Mead 2006).

The rapid expansion of evangelical churches in the global South generated not only American evangelical activism on their behalf but also growing political activism by global South evangelicals themselves. In a few cases, such as Brazil and Nicaragua, evangelicals entered politics at least partly because of moral issues such as abortion (Freston 2001: 21–23; Llana 2006). In many other cases, such as Chile, Nigeria, Burma, Indonesia, India, and China, a primary objective of evangelical political activism has been to secure religious freedom and full legal and political equality at both national and provincial levels (Poblete 1999; Freston 2001: 182–184; Freston 2004: 30–33). Without lobbying by Christians, including a broad spectrum of Protestants, India would probably lack its present constitutional protection of "the right freely to profess, practise and propagate religion" (Smith 1963: 100–134, 495–499; Kim 2003: 37–58).

An evangelical consensus that the state has a duty to curb social evils and refrain from religious persecution was sharpened in 1974 at the First International Congress on World Evangelization that gathered in Lausanne, Switzerland. Of the 2,700 evangelicals representing about 150 countries, more than 50 percent were from the global South. According to *Time* magazine, the Congress was "a formidable forum, possibly the widest-ranging meeting of Christians ever held" (http://www.lausanne.org/about/lausanne.html). Under the chairmanship of John Stott, the "Lausanne Covenant" that emerged included a statement on evangelical social responsibility that provides some indication of global evangelical thinking on the state and politics.

Though the Lausanne Covenant sharply distinguished "salvation" from "political liberation," it elevated politics by insisting that "evangelism and socio-political involvement are both part of our Christian duty." And in contrast with a fundamentalist separation of salvation from social and political concerns, it insisted that the message of salvation entails an adverse judgment on "every form" of alienation, oppression, and discrimination, all of which are departures from the reconciliation between God and human persons Christ brought about on the cross. The Lausanne Covenant added a ringing summons "to denounce evil and injustice wherever they exist" (First International Congress on World Evangelization 1974: 5). The covenant's social teaching inspired evangelicals in countries as diverse as Kenya, Brazil, and Peru to place greater emphasis on social justice and political activism (Freston 2001: 34–36, 150, 242).

Toward the end of the Lausanne Covenant, a paragraph on "Freedom and Persecution" begins with a brief statement on the state: "It is the God-appointed duty of every government to secure conditions of peace, justice and liberty in which the Church may obey God, serve the Lord Jesus Christ, and preach the gospel without interference." Significantly, Lausanne's only statement on the state focuses on its divinely ordained duty to establish those conditions without which the church cannot fulfill its divinely ordained duty: to obey God, serve Christ, and preach the gospel without interference. The clear emphasis is on the duty of the state to provide the widest possible berth for religious freedom. If any specific form of political evil and injustice is most on the minds of the Lausanne evangelicals, in other words, it is religious persecution in all its forms. Both the Lausanne Covenant itself and Stott's commentary on it focus their concern on "all who have been unjustly imprisoned," not only Christian believers (First International Congress on World Evangelization 1974: 13; Stott 1975). Yet no one could accuse the Lausanne drafters of investing too much hope in politics. "We . . . reject as a proud, self-confident dream the notion that people can ever build a utopia on earth," the covenant declares (15). Lausanne's political vision is fixed on egregious injustices evangelicals are duty-bound to mitigate now, not on social dreams they might hope to fulfill in the far-off future.

Evangelicals have generated coherent and consistent perspectives on the state, but they have not managed to produce a detailed political program, consistent political style, or unified political front. In part, this is because of ethnic and racial divisions; white, black, and Latino evangelicals in the United States, for example, are animated by different political agendas and exhibit distinct party affiliations and voting behaviors. Such differences notwithstanding, some observers attribute a robust theocratic agenda to the evangelical movement as a whole, which originates partly in the "dominion" theology or "theonomic reconstructionism" developed by American theologians R. J. Rushdoony and Gary North (Balmer 1999: 100; Goldberg 2006). Others attribute a social and political quiescence to evangelicals, born of an alleged hyperspiritual otherworldliness (Lalive D'Epinay 1969). Of course, both observations cannot be true of evangelicals—or at least not of the same group of evangelicals at the same time—for the obvious reason that one cannot simultaneously be indifferent to the state and intent on capturing it. The reality is that evangelical political activists, whether in the global North or the global South, seldom look much like Islamist militants or Amish separatists, falling instead into rather mainstream patterns of political involvement.

A few evangelicals, like theonomic reconstructionists, as well as some neo-Pentecostal political activists in Guatemala and Zambia, believe it is their evangelical right and duty to capture the state in order to implement a top-down, biblically mandated reform and cleansing of society (Phiri 2008; Samson 2008). And surveys show that some Pentecostal evangelicals support constitutional amendments to make their countries officially "Christian," much as the NAE supported such constitutional amendments in the United States over many years. Frederick Chiluba, the openly evangelical president of Zambia from 1991 to 2002, declared the country "Christian" in a private ceremony in December 1991 and forced legislation through parliament in 1996 officially altering the preamble to the constitution to designate the Republic of Zambia a Christian nation (Phiri 2008: 102–107).

While these apparently theocratic tendencies provoke considerable hostility and hysteria in some quarters (Balmer 2006; Harris 2006), nowhere in the world has a theocratic agenda ever mobilized a significant number of evangelicals, let alone unified them into a common political front over a sustained period of time. The truth is that Chiluba ended up dividing rather than unifying Zambia's evangelical community and left office deeply unpopular (Phiri 2008). In several surveys, samples of Pentecostals—who probably constitute the world's most intense and numerous subgroup of evangelicals—consistently embrace church-state separation over Christian nationalism. Only in Nigeria, South Africa, and the United States do majorities or pluralities of Pentecostals surveyed express support for the idea that the state should make their country a "Christian nation" (and even in those countries the percentages are relatively low, at 58 percent, 45 percent, and 52 percent, respectively) (Pew Forum on Religion & Public Life 2006).

Consistent with this limited evangelical support for theocratic politics in even a mild form, neither the political field nor the religious landscape in most countries, including the United States, has favored candidates or movements perceived as practicing "Christian identity" politics or promoting a specifically evangelical political agenda. From Pat Robertson in 1988 to Mike Huckabee in 2008, presidential candidates emerging from the evangelical movement and making their evangelical identity a central element in their campaigns have fallen far short of attracting monolithic evangelical support. George W. Bush attracted strong evangelical support, but he was not a "movement evangelical," and his personal faith was but one element in (what used to be) his broad appeal (Rozell 2003; Green 2008). Huckabee, in contrast, never enjoyed overwhelming evangelical support. Less than ten days after winning the Iowa caucuses, Huckabee enjoyed only slightly more white evangelical support than McCain (34 percent to 27 percent), according to the Pew Research Center. By the end of February, 47 percent of white evangelicals surveyed backed McCain, while only 37 percent backed Huckabee (Pew Research Center for the People and the Press 2008). Though Huckabee managed to win primaries in caucuses in a few states with large evangelical populations, such as Alabama, Georgia, Louisiana, Kansas, and Iowa (in the last of which, a remarkable 60 percent of Republican caucus-goers were evangelicals), McCain won numerous states across the country, including a few with large evangelical populations, such as South Carolina and Florida. The pattern is similar outside the United States: evangelical politicians running largely on evangelical or Christian platforms, such as Rios Montt in Guatemala, Nevers Mumba in Zambia, and Jerry Gana in Nigeria, have seldom performed well in free and fair electoral contests (Imo 2008; Phiri 2008; Samson 2008).

If evangelicals tend to shy away from the maximalist politics of theocracy, they also tend to shy away from the minimalist politics of withdrawal and quiescence. Survey research conducted by Timothy Steigenga in Guatemala and Costa Rica found that evangelicals are not monolithically conservative or politically quiescent. Though Steigenga found that all those with more conservative religious beliefs, including evangelicals, are less likely to criticize public officials or engage in conflictual political activity, religious conservatives are more likely to vote and engage in voluntary community work than religious liberals or the religiously unaffiliated (Steigenga 2001). In the Pew Forum's 2006 survey of Pentecostals, Pentecostals and charismatics surveyed were no less likely than others to be involved with voluntary organizations (Pew Forum on Religion & Public Life 2006).

In a historical parallel with communism, one phenomenon that has given evangelical political activism somewhat greater unity and focus in recent years is the real and perceived threat of radical Islam. As noted before, evangelicals in a variety of countries have sought to mobilize their governments to oppose radical Islam in various ways: evangelicals joined other religious groups to mobilize the U.S. government to resist the worldwide persecution of Christians, often by governments or groups animated by radical Islam; evangelicals have tended to give President Bush and the War on Terror higher approval ratings than other Americans do; evangelicals have tended to support the Iraq war at higher levels than other Americans (60 percent versus less than half of other Americans) on the belief that it is a front in the War on Terror (Cox 2007); and evangelicals have mobilized strongly in Nigeria, Kenya, and other countries to try to prevent Muslim political activists from establishing or expanding Muslim personal law (Ranger 2008). Given the widespread evangelical belief that Islam is a false substitute for and/or a dangerous obstacle to the gospel (to use Bebbington's categories), such political mobilization is understandable.

An Evangelical View of the State

With remarkable consistency over more than three hundred years, evangelicals have offered a view of the state that has systematically repudiated the longstanding tendency of the Western Christian political tradition to view "statecraft as soulcraft," to borrow George Will's felicitous formula (Will 1983). According to this classic tendency, the state plays a central role in the moral and spiritual formation of individuals. Indeed, the core function of political authority is to assist individuals in the acquisition of those virtues without which they cannot know and achieve the *summum bonum*. Princes on this view were above all seen as benevolent teachers whose central duty was to exercise a fatherly care over the moral and spiritual well-being of their subjects. The "magisterial" Reformers Luther and Calvin embraced this view with much the same conviction and vigor as Augustine and Aquinas.

Evangelicals have propounded a radically different approach to the state and politics that can perhaps best be summarized as "soulcraft as statecraft." On this view, states, no matter how decent and just, cannot "make men moral" (George 1993), but rather moral men make decent and just states. And what makes men moral is voluntary, inward conversion to the gospel, one person at a time. Evangelicals believe that fundamental moral, social, and political change comes not through top-down, state-centered legal and policy schemes but through the bottom-up transformation and mobilization of individuals (Hollinger 1983).

The moral and spiritual priority of personal conversion entails the overriding political priority of religious freedom. As God's ministers under God's sovereignty, states are under the most solemn duty to ensure that individuals enjoy the maximum freedom to respond to God's gracious offer of salvation in Jesus Christ. While evangelicals around the world and across history, from Kuyperian Calvinists to American neo-evangelicals to Zambian Pentecostals (Freston 2001: 154–164), have sometimes urged states to formally acknowledge God's sovereignty through various legal instruments and civic rituals, their convictions and denominational diversity have almost always prevented them pressing for any particular form of church establishment or any restrictions on the religious freedom of nonevangelicals. In contrast to some liberal political theories, however, which seek to liberate the state from religious influence so that public life can be as secular as possible, the evangelical conception of religious freedom liberates religion from state interference so that it can exert the greatest possible influence on public as well as private life.

Evangelical skepticism of the state's authority and capacity in the realms of morality and religion characteristically generates a wider view that the best state is a limited, watchman state that is more like a police officer or at most an umpire than a moral tutor or benevolent father (Weeks 2006: 131). From the evangelical view, then, the primary task of the state is to defend the innocent and vulnerable—by harsh means, if necessary—against the criminality of the wrongdoer (Romans 13: 4), whether the slave trader, widow burner, Indian hater, liquor seller, abortion provider, or persecutor of religion. A decidedly secondary though still important task of the state is to support nonstate, civil society actors such as churches in their independent and voluntary efforts to help the poor.

Though clearly different from some versions of liberalism, evangelicals' stripped-down, suspicious view of the state resembles in important respects the "liberalism of fear" of the late Harvard political theorist Judith Shklar in its assumption "that some agents of government will behave lawlessly and brutally in small or big ways most of the time unless they are prevented from doing so" (Shklar 1989: 28). Particularly after a century in which state-sponsored schemes of social engineering and human transformation wrought such spectacular destruction, many evangelicals join Shklar in concluding that the best way to prevent this besetting political danger is to insist that states abandon utopian ambitions in favor of the narrower and more necessary task of defending the most vulnerable human beings from the worst evils and injustices (Marshall 2005: 321–322).

NOTE

I thank Sandra Joireman for the kind invitation to write this chapter, Sarah Baggé for outstanding research assistance, and Paul Marshall for encouraging and helpful feedback.

BIBLIOGRAPHY

Atkins, E. M., and Robert Dodaro, eds. 2001. *Augustine: Political Writings*. Cambridge: Cambridge University Press.

Backus, Isaac. 1773. "An Appeal to the Public for Religious Liberty." In *Political Sermons of the American Founding Era, 1730–1805*, ed. Ellis Sandoz. Indianapolis, IN: Liberty Press, 327–368.

Balmer, Randall Herbert. 1999. *Blessed Assurance: A History of Evangelicalism in America*. Boston: Beacon Press.

Balmer, Randall Herbert. 2006. *Thy Kingdom Come: How the Religious Right Distorts the Faith and Threatens America, an Evangelical's Lament*. New York: Basic Books.

Barrett, David B., George T. Kurian, and Todd M. Johnson. 2001. *World Christian Encyclopedia*. 2nd ed. New York: Oxford University Press.

Bebbington, D. W. 1989. *Evangelicalism in Modern Britain: A History from the 1730s to the 1980s*. London: Unwin Hyman.

Brock, Peter. 1972. *Pacifism in Europe to 1914*. Princeton, NJ: Princeton University Press.

Brown, F. K. 1961. *Father of the Victorians: The Age of Wilberforce*. Cambridge, Cambridge University Press.

Budziszewski, J., with John Bolt, Michael Cromartie, William Edgar, Jean Bethke Elshtain, David L. Weeks, and Ashley Woodiwiss. 2006. *Evangelicals in the Public Square: Four Formative Voices on Political Thought and Action*. Grand Rapids, MI: Baker Academic.

Carpenter, Joel A. 1997. *Revive Us Again: The Reawakening of American Fundamentalism*. New York: Oxford University Press.

Carwardine, Richard. 1993. *Evangelicals and Politics in Antebellum America*. New Haven, CT: Yale University Press.

Cizik, Richard. 2005. "A History of the Public Policy Resolutions of the National Association of Evangelicals." In *Toward an Evangelical Public Policy: Political Strategies for the Health of the Nation*, eds. Ronald J. Sider and Diane Knippers. Grand Rapids, MI: Baker Books, 35–63.

Cox, Dan. 2007. "Young White Evangelicals: Less Republican, Still Conservative." Pew Forum on Religion & Public Life, Washington, DC, September 28. http://pewfo rum.org/docs/?DocID=250. Accessed April 30, 2008.

Dayton, Donald W. 1988. *Discovering an Evangelical Heritage*. Peabody, MA: Hendrickson.

Dobson, Edward. 1987. "The Bible, Politics, and Democracy." In *The Bible, Politics, and Democracy*, ed. Richard John Neuhaus. Grand Rapids, MI: William B. Eerdmans, 1–18.

Elliott, David R. 1994. "Knowing No Borders: Canadian Contributions to American Fundamentalism." In *Amazing Grace: Evangelicalism in Australia, Britain, Canada, and the United States*, eds. Mark A. Noll and George A. Rawlyk. Montreal: McGill-Queen's University Press, 349–374.

First International Congress on World Evangelization. 1974. "The Lausanne Covenant." http://www.lausanne.org/lausanne-1974/lausanne-covenant.html. Accessed July 18, 2007.

Freston, Paul. 2001. *Evangelicals and Politics in Asia, Africa, and Latin America*. Cambridge: Cambridge University Press.

Freston, Paul. 2004. "Evangelical Protestantism and Democratization in Contemporary Latin America and Asia." *Democratization* 11(4): 21–41.

George, Robert P. 1993. *Making Men Moral: Civil Liberties and Public Morality*. Oxford: Clarendon Press.

Goldberg, Michelle. 2006. *Kingdom Coming: The Rise of Christian Nationalism*. New York: W. W. Norton.

Green, John C. 2005. "Seeking a Place." In *Toward an Evangelical Public Policy: Political Strategies for the Health of the Nation*, eds. Ronald J. Sider and Diane Knippers. Grand Rapids, MI: Baker Books, 15–34.

Green, John C. 2008. "Does McCain Need Evangelical Voters?" Q and A with Mark O'Keefe. Pew Forum on Religion & Public Life, Washington, DC, February 8. http://pewforum.org/events/?EventID=166. Accessed April 30, 2008.

Harris, Sam. 2006. *Letter to a Christian Nation*. New York: Knopf.

Hatch, Nathan O. 1989. *The Democratization of American Christianity*. New Haven, CT: Yale University Press.

Hertzke, Allen D. 2003. "Evangelicals and International Engagement." In *A Public Faith: Evangelicals and Civic Engagement*, ed. Michael Cromartie. Lanham, MD: Rowman and Littlefield, 215–235.

Hertzke, Allen D. 2004. *Freeing God's Children: The Unlikely Alliance for Global Human Rights*. Lanham, MD: Rowman and Littlefield.

Hill, Christopher. 1990. *A Tinker and a Poor Man: John Bunyan and His Church, 1628–1688*. New York: W. W. Norton.

Hilton, Boyd. 1988. *The Age of Atonement: The Influence of Evangelicalism on Social and Economic Thought, 1795–1865*. Oxford: Clarendon Press.

Hollinger, Dennis P. 1983. *Individualism and Social Ethics: An Evangelical Syncretism*. Lanham, MD: University Press of America.

Imo, Cyril. 2008. "Evangelicals, Muslims, and Democracy: With Particular Reference to the Declaration of Sharia in Northern Nigeria." In *Evangelical Christianity and Democracy in Africa*, ed. Terence O. Ranger. Evangelical Christianity and Democracy in the Global South, ed. Timothy Samuel Shah. Oxford: Oxford University Press, 37–66.

Judis, John. 2005. "The Chosen Nation: The Influence of Religion on U.S. Foreign Policy." Policy Brief 37 (March). Washington, DC: Carnegie Endowment for International Peace.

Kim, Sebastian C. H. 2003. *In Search of Identity: Debates on Religious Conversion in India*. New Delhi: Oxford University Press.

Koop, C. Everett, and Francis A. Schaeffer. 1983 [1979]. *Whatever Happened to the Human Race?* Westchester, IL: Crossway Books.

Kraynak, Robert P. 1980. "John Locke: From Absolutism to Toleration." *American Political Science Review* 74 (March): 53–69.

Labunski, Richard E. 2006. *James Madison and the Struggle for the Bill of Rights*. Oxford: Oxford University Press.

Lalive d'Epinay, Christian. 1969. *Haven of the Masses: A Study of the Pentecostal Movement in Chile*. London: Lutterworth.

Llana, Sara Miller. 2006. "Evangelicals Flex Growing Clout in Nicaragua's Election." *Christian Science Monitor*, November 2. http://www.csmonitor.com/2006/1102/p01s02-woam.html. Accessed October 30, 2008.

Marsden, George M. 1991. *Understanding Fundamentalism and Evangelicalism*. Grand Rapids, MI: William B. Eerdmans.

Marshall, Paul. 2005. "Human Rights." In *Toward an Evangelical Public Policy: Political Strategies for the Health of the Nation*, eds. Ronald J. Sider and Diane Knippers. Grand Rapids, MI: Baker Books, 307–322.

McConnell, Michael W. 1999. "Five Reasons to Reject the Claim That Religious Arguments Should Be Excluded from Democratic Deliberation." *Utah Law Review* 3: 639–657.

McLoughlin, William Gerald. 1977. "'Enthusiasm for Liberty': The Great Awakening as the Key to the Revolution." *Proceedings of the American Antiquarian Society* 87: 69–95.

Mead, Walter Russell. 2006. "God's Country?" *Foreign Affairs* 85(5): 24.

Moberg, David O. 1972. *The Great Reversal: Evangelism versus Social Concern*. Philadelphia: Lippincott.

Neill, Stephen. 1966. *Colonialism and Christian Missions*. London: Lutterworth.

Noll, Mark A. 1994. *The Scandal of the Evangelical Mind*. Grand Rapids, MI: William B. Eerdmans.

Noll, Mark A. 1998. "Defining Evangelicalism." In *A Global Faith: Essays on Evangelicalism and Globalization*, eds. Mark Hutchinson and Ogbu Kalu. Macquarie Centre,

N.S.W.: Centre for the Study of Australian Christianity, Robert Menzies College, Macquarie University.

Noll, Mark A. 2002. *America's God: From Jonathan Edwards to Abraham Lincoln.* New York: Oxford University Press.

Noll, Mark A. 2003. *The Rise of Evangelicalism: The Age of Edwards, Whitefield, and the Wesleys.* Downers Grove, IL: InterVarsity Press.

Pegram, Thomas R. 1998. *Battling Demon Rum: The Struggle for a Dry America, 1800–1933.* Chicago: Ivan R. Dee.

Petersen, Douglas. 1996. *Not by Might, nor by Power: A Pentecostal Theology of Social Concern in Latin America.* Oxford: Regnum Books International.

Pew Forum on Religion & Public Life. 2006. "Spirit and Power: A 10-Country Survey of Pentecostals." Pew Forum on Religion & Public Life, Washington, DC. http://pewforum.org/surveys/pentecostal/. Accessed April 30, 2008.

Pew Research Center for the People and the Press. 2008. "McCain's Support Soars, Democratic Race Tightens." Pew Research Center for the People and the Press, Washington, DC, February 3. http://people-press.org/reports/display.php3?ReportID=392. Accessed April 30, 2008.

Phiri, Isabel Apawo. 2008. "President Frederick Chiluba and Zambia: Evangelicals and Democracy in a 'Christian Nation.'" In *Evangelical Christianity and Democracy in Africa,* ed. Terence O. Ranger. Evangelical Christianity and Democracy in the Global South, ed. Timothy Samuel Shah. Oxford: Oxford University Press, 95–129.

Poblete, Martín. 1999. "Chile: From the *Patronato* to Pinochet." In *Religious Freedom and Evangelization in Latin America: The Challenge of Religious Pluralism,* ed. Paul Sigmund. Maryknoll, NY: Orbis Books, 220–234.

Ranger, Terence O. 2008. "Afterword." In *Evangelical Christianity and Democracy in Africa,* ed. Terence O. Ranger. Evangelical Christianity and Democracy in the Global South, ed. Timothy Samuel Shah. Oxford: Oxford University Press, 231–242.

Rozell, Mark J. 2003. "The Christian Right: Evolution, Expansion, Contraction." In *A Public Faith: Evangelicals and Civic Engagement,* ed. Michael C. Cromartie. Lanham, MD: Rowman and Littlefield, 31–49.

Samson, C. Mathews. 2008. "From War to Reconciliation: Guatemalan Evangelicals and the Transition to Democracy, 1982–2001." In *Evangelical Christianity and Democracy in Latin America,* ed. Paul Freston. Evangelical Christianity and Democracy in the Global South, ed. Timothy Samuel Shah. Oxford: Oxford University Press, 63–96.

Schaefer, Kurt. 2003. "Evangelicals, Welfare Reform, and Care for the Poor." In *A Public Faith: Evangelicals and Civic Engagement,* ed. Michael Cromartie. Lanham, MD: Rowman and Littlefield, 125–156.

Schaeffer, Francis A. 1981. *A Christian Manifesto.* Westchester, IL: Crossway Books.

Schlossberg, Herbert, Vinay Samuel, and Ronald J. Sider. 1994. *Christianity and Economics in the Post–Cold War Era: The Oxford Declaration and Beyond.* Grand Rapids, MI: William B. Eerdmans.

Shah, Timothy Samuel. 2004. "The Bible and the Ballot Box: Evangelicals and Democracy in the 'Global South.'" *SAIS Review* 24(2): 117–132.

Shenk, Wilbert R. 1998. "The Theological Impulse of Evangelical Expansion." In *A Global Faith: Essays on Evangelicalism and Globalization,* eds. Mark Hutchinson and Ogbu Kalu. Macquarie Centre, N.S.W.: Centre for the Study of Australian Christianity, Robert Menzies College, Macquarie University.

Sherman, Amy L. 2003. "Evangelicals and Charitable Choice." In *A Public Faith: Evangelicals and Civic Engagement,* ed. Michael Cromartie. Lanham, MD: Rowman and Littlefield, 157–172.

Shklar, Judith N. 1989. "The Liberalism of Fear." In *Liberalism and the Moral Life,* ed. Nancy Rosenblum. Cambridge, MA: Harvard University Press, 21–38.

Sider, Ronald J., and Diane Knippers, eds. 2005. *Toward an Evangelical Public Policy: Political Strategies for the Health of the Nation.* Grand Rapids, MI: Baker Books.

Smith, Christian. 1998. *American Evangelicalism: Embattled and Thriving.* Chicago: University of Chicago Press.

Smith, Donald Eugene. 1963. *India as a Secular State.* Princeton, NJ: Princeton University Press.

Smith, Timothy L. 1987. "A Shared Evangelical Heritage." In *Evangelicalism: Surviving Its Success,* vol. 2, *The Evangelical Round Table,* ed. David Fraser. St. Davids, PA: Eastern College and Eastern Baptist Theological Seminary, 12–28.

Spener, Philip Jakob. 1964 [1675]. *Pia Desideria.* Philadelphia: Fortress Press.

Steigenga, Timothy J. 2001. *The Politics of the Spirit: The Political Implications of Pentecostalized Religion in Costa Rica and Guatemala.* Lanham, MD: Lexington Books.

Stott, John R. W. 1975. *The Lausanne Covenant: An Exposition and Commentary.* Minneapolis, MN: World Wide.

Timberlake, James H. 1963. *Prohibition and the Progressive Movement, 1900–1920.* Cambridge, MA: Harvard University Press.

Van der Veer, Peter. 1999. "The Moral State: Religion, Nation, and Empire in Victorian Britain and British India." In *Nation and Religion: Perspectives on Europe and Asia,* eds. Peter van der Veer and Hartmut Lehmann. Princeton, NJ: Princeton University Press, 15–43.

Ward, W. R. 2004. "Evangelical Identity in the Eighteenth Century." In *Christianity Reborn: Evangelicalism's Global Expansion in the Twentieth Century,* ed. Donald M. Lewis. Studies in the History of Christian Missions. Grand Rapids, MI: William B. Eerdmans, 11–30.

Weeks, David L. 2006. "Carl F. H. Henry on Civic Life." In *Evangelicals in the Public Square: Four Formative Voices on Political Thought And Action,* eds. J. Budziszewski, with John Bolt, Michael Cromartie, William Edgar, Jean Bethke Elshtain, David L. Weeks, and Ashley Woodiwiss. Grand Rapids, MI: Baker Academic, 123–139.

Wesley, John. [1775] 1991. "A Calm Address to Our American Colonies." In *Political Sermons of the American Founding Era, 1730–1805,* ed. Ellis Sandoz. Indianapolis, IN: Liberty Press, 409–420.

West, John G. 1996. *The Politics of Revelation and Reason: Religion and Civic Life in the New Nation.* Lawrence: University Press of Kansas.

Will, George F. 1983. *Statecraft as Soulcraft: What Government Does*. New York: Simon and Schuster.

Williams, George Huntston. 1992. *The Radical Reformation*. Sixteenth Century Essays and Studies, vol. 15. Kirksville, MO: Sixteenth Century Journal Publishers.

Witte, John. 2000. *Religion and the American Constitutional Experiment: Essential Rights and Liberties*. Boulder, CO: Westview.

Woodberry, Robert Dudley, and Timothy Samuel Shah. 2004. "The Pioneering Protestants." *Journal of Democracy* 15(2): 47–61.

Young, Michael P. 2006. *Bearing Witness against Sin: The Evangelical Birth of the American Social Movement*. Chicago: University of Chicago Press.

8

Pentecostalism: Holy Spirit Empowerment and Politics

Stephen M. Swindle

More than half a billion people throughout the world adhere to Pentecostalism in some form, and today the movement is often referred to as the "third force" of Christendom, with Roman Catholicism and Protestantism. Adherents can be found in almost every traditional denomination, they are widespread in the emerging nondenominational congregations, and some subset of them ascribe to almost every other Christian doctrine that we have. In addition, though its expansion in the United States has been significant, Pentecostalism has enjoyed its widest popularity and most explosive growth overseas. Understanding how this pervasiveness and diversity will affect the role of the church in modern politics is therefore essential.

The discussion of Pentecostalism and its relationship to the state and citizenship presents two immediate challenges. The first is one of definition and classification. Like the Anabaptist and evangelical traditions already discussed, Pentecostalism is not a denomination per se but rather a loosely organized group of churches that emphasize a set of similar faith positions. Most significant in this regard is its emphasis on a second (or third) work of grace, which is most frequently accompanied and evidenced by speaking in tongues. This "second baptism" is seen as essential to the empowering of the Christian for ministry through the divine bestowing of the gifts of the Holy Spirit. Though other diverse theological commitments may surround this belief in a second baptism, this distinctive theological center is the motivation for treating Pentecostalism as a tradition worthy of separate treatment in this book.

The second challenge is the behavioral freedom that such a theological commitment provides. This emphasis on the active working of the Holy Spirit hampers the potential for theological and behavioral consistency in at least two ways. First, the active presence of the Holy Spirit and possibility of ongoing revelation creates a historical hesitancy to canonize any specific theological statements that might restrict such revelation. Consequently, identifying a set of core theological commitments beyond the baptism in the Holy Spirit is nearly impossible.[1] Second, the expectation of, and respect for, personal revelation can provide justification for almost any specific behavior. Personal revelation is provided a status of authority almost equivalent to scripture and therefore is rarely challenged by other Pentecostals, who, though their own personal revelations may be different, respect, accept, and even expect such revelations. Consequently, perspectives on the appropriate relationship between the Christian citizen and the state are almost limitless, as are understandings of appropriate political behavior.

This chapter is organized into four major sections. I begin with a fairly detailed exploration of the historical roots of Pentecostalism in America, focusing initially on its Wesleyan and Holiness roots, through the defining event of Azusa Street, and then concluding with the organizational evolution after Azusa and a few of the significant denominational splits that have occurred since that time.[2] In the second part of the chapter, I then discuss the theological distinctive of the movement—Holy Spirit baptism and its evidences. In the third part, I then turn to the discussion of how this theological distinctive shapes how Pentecostals view the state and Christian citizenship. And finally in the fourth part, I explore the expressions of contemporary politics. Throughout most sections, the conversation transitions through four distinct components of the Pentecostal movement: its Holiness roots in America, denominational Pentecostalism, the charismatic movement, and Pentecostalism's expression overseas.

Historical Background

The American roots of modern Pentecostalism can be traced to the doctrinal teachings of John Wesley and the Holiness movement that emerged as an offshoot of Methodism in the 19th and early 20th centuries. For Wesley, the process of salvation involved two crises. The first, justification, freed the believer from the sins that he had committed, and the second, entire sanctification or full salvation, liberated the believer from his moral nature that caused sin. Wesley believed that through the perfection process of loving the Lord God with all one's heart, soul, and mind, it was possible for the believer to live without conscious or deliberate sin—in a state of holiness.

Not surprisingly, it was within the Methodist Church that Holiness theology gained its initial foothold in the United States. However, just as this perfectionist theology was gaining momentum, several events began to erode Methodism's central role. First, the theology of denominational leadership began to slowly shift away from its Holiness roots, and a declining emphasis on Wesley's teaching of entire sanctification occurred. As more and more members of the denomination became dissatisfied with what they perceived to be a "liberal shift" in theological focus, the denomination itself became internally embattled, resulting ultimately in two formal splits: the Wesleyan Methodists in 1843 and the Free Methodists in 1860. Second, the Civil War split the Methodist Church over the issue of slavery. In addition to losing the staunchly abolitionist Wesleyan Methodists and Free Methodists, in 1845, Southern leaders within the denomination formally left the Methodist Episcopal Church and formed the Methodist Episcopal Church, South.[3] Although a Holiness revival within the Methodist Church occurred immediately following the war, the Methodist Church would never fully recover from the numerous and significant splits of this era. And finally, an increasing number of Holiness evangelists and nondenominational associations gradually weakened mainline Methodism's central role in the Holiness movement. As independent Holiness denominations and congregations began to appear, the schism between the Holiness movement and Methodism widened, and tensions began to escalate as Methodist practice drifted further and further away from the traditional Wesleyan doctrines of Christian perfection and began to embrace more ecumenical and social agendas.

It was not until the late 1800s that the first distinctively Pentecostal churches began to appear. Examples include the predominantly African American Church of God in Christ (1897), the Pentecostal Holiness Church (1898), and the Church of God of Cleveland, Tennessee (1906). Though these early Pentecostal churches largely emerged from the Holiness movement and generally retained their perfectionist teachings, the establishment of separate Pentecostal denominations paved the way for the divergence that was to occur between the Holiness movement and Pentecostalism, a distinction that would be crystallized by the events at Bethel Bible College and Azusa Street.

Most modern Pentecostals trace their roots to Bethel Bible College in Topeka, Kansas. Charles Fox Parham, an ex-Methodist minister and Holiness adherent, was the founder of the college and is usually identified as the instrument through which the modern Pentecostal movement was begun. He was born in 1873, became a preacher at the age of about fifteen, and largely distanced himself from traditional denominations early in his ministry. His decision to start a Bible College of his own was driven by what he saw as the "falling short" of early Pentecostal experiences and his desire to experience the accounts of the early church in Acts. In his own words, "[W]hile many had obtained real experience in sanctification and the anointing that abideth, there still remained a great outpouring of power for the Christians who were close to this age" (Nienkirchen 1992: 30).[4]

Early on in the school's history, after exhaustively studying the scriptural context of baptism in the Holy Spirit, Parham and his students came to the conclusion that scripture taught that speaking in tongues was biblical evidence of the baptism in the Holy Spirit. At the watch night service of December 31, 1900, student Agnes N. Ozman requested that hands be laid on her so that she might receive the baptism in the Holy Ghost. In her own words, "[I]nstantly, the Holy Spirit came upon me, and I began to speak in other tongues, and to glorify God. I talked several languages, and it was clearly manifest when a new language was spoken." Other students, and eventually Parham himself, received the baptism as well, and the practice of glossolalia (speaking in tongues) began to spread. Modern Pentecostalism was born.

If the Bethel Bible College experience represents the genesis of the modern Pentecostal movement, it is the Azusa Street revival of 1906 through 1909 that is commonly viewed as the catalyst from which the movement was launched. As Parham traveled, spreading the message of glossolalia, he came across and became the teacher of another Holiness preacher, William J. Seymour. Seymour embraced Parham's teaching of Apostolic Faith,[5] eventually was asked to move to Los Angeles to pastor a local church there, and began preaching the message of Apostolic Faith to the local congregation. Though not immediately well received, eventually local leaders of the Holiness Association embraced Seymour's perspective, and through a series of events, many began to be baptized in the Holy Spirit and speak in tongues. As the meetings grew, they eventually moved to an old church at 312 Azusa Street, where the Pentecostal revival exploded. People from all over the country came to the tiny church on Azusa Street to receive the baptism in the Holy Spirit, and soon the Pentecostal doctrine began to spread extensively throughout the country.

At first, the Pentecostal doctrine spread mainly in Holiness churches and other individual congregations. However, both within and outside those circles, the doctrine of glossolalia met with significant resistance. One of the earliest and bitterest critics of the events surrounding Azusa was Alma White (1949), leader of the Pillar of Fire Church, who in 1936 compiled her opinions of the movement in a book titled *Demons and Tongues,* where she describes Parham and Seymour as "rulers of spiritual Sodom," speaking in tongues as "satanic gibberish," and Pentecostal services as "the climax of demon worship." Respected Bible preacher G. Campbell Morgan called the Pentecostal movement "the last vomit of Satan," and Reuben A. Torrey stated that it was "emphatically not of God, and founded by a Sodomite"[6] (Synan 1971: 143–144). In addition, several Holiness churches—including the Church of the Nazarene, the Wesleyan Methodist Church, the Salvation Army, the Pilgrim Holiness Church, and the Free Methodist Church dissociated themselves completely from the Pentecostal movement (Synan 1971: 146).

Division within the fledgling Pentecostal movement was also soon to emerge. At the center of this controversy was the traditional Holiness teaching of Wesleyan sanctification as a second work of grace. Because most of the early leaders of Pentecostalism were prominent in the Holiness movement, early on, the doctrine of Christian perfection was almost universally accepted. However, as glossolalia spread among non-Holiness congregations, most notably Baptist, the Wesleyan doctrine of Christian perfection was seen as an unnecessary component of the Christian experience. At the forefront of this controversy was William H. Durham and his "finished work" theory, which emphasized sanctification as a progressive work, with baptism in the Holy Spirit following as a second blessing. For this group, the Christian experience involved two steps, conversion and then baptism in the Holy Spirit. In 1914, the first national Pentecostal organization—the Assemblies of God—was formed and adopted the Durham position as part of its theology. The Assemblies of God soon became the largest Pentecostal denomination, and most subsequent Pentecostal movements were based on its model.

Conflict continued in the early history of Pentecostalism. In what was to become known as the "Oneness" or "Jesus Only" controversy, several leading Pentecostal ministers—most prominently Frank J. Ewart—rejected the traditional notion of the Trinity and focused instead on the singular personality of Jesus Christ. The Trinitarian versus Unitarian battle was waged most significantly within the denominational leadership of the newly founded Assemblies of God. Though the Trinitarians ultimately prevailed—and consequently set Pentecostalism on a decidedly Trinitarian path—a significant number of early Pentecostals formed Unitarian churches, such as the Pentecostal Assemblies of the World and the United Pentecostal Church.

Two final offshoots of the Pentecostal movement are worth mentioning before moving on to a more detailed discussion of its theological distinctives. Though inroads into mainstream denominations were slow, the charismatic movement of the 1960s and 1970s—what is also sometimes referred to as neo-Pentecostalism—served to legitimate the baptism in the Holy Spirit and speaking in tongues within traditional churches. First within the Episcopal Church—through the ministry of Dennis Bennett—and subsequently in Lutheran, Presbyterian, and Catholic circles, traditional denominations began to experience and accept the doctrine of baptism in the Holy Spirit. These "new Pentecostals" largely remained in their traditional congregations and worked to "renew" them by their continued presence from within (hence the phrase "charismatic renewal"). Consequently, the charismatic movement is much broader, more inclusive, and less doctrinally consistent than traditional Pentecostalism. As the *Dictionary of Pentecostal and Charismatic Movements* (1988) describes, the charismatic movement is "[t]he occurrence of distinctively Pentecostal blessings and phenomena, baptism in the Holy Spirit with the spiritual gifts of I Corinthians 12:8–10, outside a denominational and/or confessional Pentecostal framework" (130).

In recent years, a "third wave"[7] of Pentecostalism has emerged that focuses less on glossolalia and more on the other gifts of the Holy Spirit, particularly prophecy and divine healing. This movement stresses what has come to be called "power evangelism," whereby the gospel is shared and spread through the demonstration of supernatural signs and wonders. Though predominantly emphasized in nondenominational circles, the centrality of Holy Spirit baptism has drawn adherents not only from charismatic circles but also from both traditional and new Pentecostalism as well.

Though there are isolated reports of glossolalia events in many parts of the world prior to Azusa, the spread of Pentecostalism throughout the world did not occur in earnest until after the Azusa revival.[8] However, despite its largely American origins, today well over three-quarters of all Pentecostals live outside the United States, the vast majority in the developing world.[9] In addition, the multifaceted expressions of Pentecostalism in these regions of the world have further diversified both the theology and practice of Pentecostalism, making it even more difficult to specifically categorize and summarize the movement. A brief exploration of Pentecostalism's roots and growth in Latin America, Asia, and Africa, therefore, can provide some additional insight into the nature of Pentecostalism and its variants.

The spark of Pentecostalism in each of these regions appears to be the result of the almost simultaneous appearance of local revivals and the arrival of Western Pentecostal missionaries. In Asia, for example, the arrival of Azusa missionaries Alfred and Lillian Garr (who went to India because they believed that they had spoken Bengali upon receiving the baptism in the Holy Spirit) coincided almost perfectly, both temporally and geographically, with a Pentecostal revival that broke out at a girls' orphanage run by Fanny Simpson, a

Methodist missionary from Boston. In Latin America, the movement began in Chile, where local Pentecostal experiences were given leadership and voice by the arrival of Willis Collins Hoover, a missionary from the Methodist Episcopal Church in Chicago. Likewise, a few years later in Brazil, the arrival of Daniel Berg and Gunnar Vingren gave rise to the Brazilian Assemblies of God, today the largest national Pentecostal movement in the world. And finally, in Africa, the origins of Pentecostalism are largely associated with the work of John Graham Lake, a Methodist preacher who went to South Africa in 1908.[10]

There are countless other examples of local revivals and missionary activity that together birthed national Pentecostal movements throughout the world. Each is significant in its own right, but an exhaustive inventory of such events is unnecessary for the task of this chapter. What should be emphasized, however, is the extent of the growth of the Pentecostal movement that has occurred in the last century. It is estimated that more than 10 percent of today's Latin American population is Pentecostal, with the highest country-specific figures (roughly 30 percent) in Guatemala, Chile, and Brazil. In addition, it is believed that Pentecostals make up more than 90 percent of the Protestant population in the region (Martin 1994). In Africa, best estimates also suggest that roughly 10 percent of the population is Pentecostal, with its strongest presence in Zimbabwe, Kenya, Nigeria, Ghana, and Zambia. And finally, Pentecostalism is enjoying its most rapid growth in Asia, particular in Indonesia, China, and South Korea. As startling as these current numbers may be, what lies ahead may actually be even more startling. It is estimated that approximately nineteen million new converts to Pentecostalism are occurring annually, and that by the middle of this century, Pentecostalism will be not only the most powerful religious force on the globe but also potentially its most potent political force as well (Barrett 1998).

Theological Distinctive: Baptism in the Holy Spirit

As the historical overview suggests, identifying a set of core Pentecostal theological commitments is not a simple task. In response to what it perceived to be the apostasy of the Christian church, many early leaders of the movement rejected creedal statements. It was their belief that creeds focused the believer's attention on right belief rather than on a right relationship with Jesus Christ and that creeds had the potential to become more important than the leading of the Holy Spirit and one's own conscience (Tomlinson 1913). For neo-Pentecostalism, it is its ecumenical nature, or transdenominational appeal, that presents the obstacle to such a task. Pentecostals can be found in almost every theological tradition, with little more than a similar understanding of the power of Holy Spirit baptism unifying them. Not only does the similar understanding of Holy Spirit baptism provide the unifying theme within the various strands of Pentecostalism but also it most starkly distinguishes Pentecostalism from other Christian traditions—including the far more loosely defined evangelicalism of the last chapter. And finally, all Pentecostal variants tend to focus on the experiential aspects of faith rather than a set of scriptural or intellectual faith commitments. This places scripture in a unique position within the Pentecostal tradition and strongly contrasts it with Christian traditions emphasizing *sola scriptura*.

For Pentecostals, baptism *in* the Holy Spirit is a distinctive work separate from salvation and is evidenced by the manifestation of various Holy Spirit gifts, or charisma, operating through Christian believers. This second definitive work provides the believer with a dimension of spiritual power that goes beyond the baptism *of* the Holy Spirit that occurs at salvation. Baptism of the Holy Spirit provides the believer with regeneration, conviction, and a confidence to witness, but only after baptism in the Holy Spirit can the believer truly experience the power of God in its fullness.

Though all Pentecostal variants distinguish between baptism of the Holy Spirit and baptism in the Holy Spirit, within the movement there is some variation in terms of the timing and effect of Holy Spirit baptism. Many non-Pentecostal churches trace their heritage to the 19th-century American Holiness movement.[11] For these churches, baptism in the Holy Spirit represents a significant and distinctive second work of grace, which provides the believer with the realization of Christian perfection. Sanctification occurs instantaneously, is usually evidenced by speaking in tongues, and has the purpose of ushering in sinless perfection. There is also a Pentecostal variant of this second blessing group, but in this case sanctification is seen as an ongoing, lifelong process, not an instantaneous work at Holy Spirit baptism.[12] Again, baptism is often evidenced by speaking in tongues, but its purpose is empowerment for the believer to witness boldly and minister spiritual gifts. And finally, another Pentecostal variant are those churches that view baptism in the Holy Spirit as a "third blessing" distinct from both justification *and* sanctification.[13] Baptism in the Holy Spirit may or may not occur simultaneously with the other two, but when it does, the evidence is speaking in tongues, and its purpose is the same as for the "second blessing" Pentecostals.

A second common characteristic of all Pentecostal traditions is the primary focus on the believer's experience with God and His power. First and foremost, Pentecostalism is experiential as much as, if not more than, it is doctrinal. Pentecostals are a group of people who have a common shared experience, baptism in the Holy Spirit, and they have little use for doctrine or theology that challenges the validity of that experience. It is not that they are fundamentally anti-theological, but they do fear elevating theology above the active and personal working of the Holy Spirit. Theology that is formalized and purely intellectual potentially inhibits the powerful experiential nature of the Holy Spirit.

The primacy of personal revelation through the Holy Spirit also places the Pentecostal tradition in contrast to those denominations committed to the doctrine of *sola scriptura*. For example, as discussed by Timothy Lomperis for the Lutheran tradition in chapter 3, the principle of *sola scriptura* simultaneously frees and binds the Christian citizen. The Christian citizen is free to the extent that disobedience is justified when civic authority transgresses into the spiritual realm without biblical authorization or when civic demands contradict the divine demands of scripture. Christian citizens are also bound, however, to the extent that their own actions must be justified by scripture. For the Pentecostal tradition, scripture lacks this final authority. That is, freedom is justified not only by scriptural reference but also through personal revelation. In consequence, the Pentecostal tradition also lacks the same sense of being bound to scripture in any specific sense. In this regard, Pentecostals are more easily aligned with those denominations that emphasize *prima scriptura,* the centrality of scripture, but believe that scriptural understanding can be improved by reference to other sources, in this case the personal revelatory voice of the Holy Spirit.

A Pentecostal Perspective on the State

Lacking the specific creedal commitments associated with the other traditions in this book, Pentecostalism has a less definitive position on the state and citizenship than the others. To combat this problem, this section focuses on the tensions that shaped early Pentecostal views of the state and citizenship prior to Pentecostalism's widespread incorporation into traditional denominations that clouds its more contemporary expressions. This focus on the foundational eras of Pentecostalism allows a more lucid discussion of basic political commitments without distraction from the plethora of commitments that can be found today. Those complexities are addressed in the final section of the chapter.

The earliest Pentecostal perspectives on the state and citizenship were grounded in the movement's theological commitment to Christian perfection, and it is varying perspectives on the implications of Christian perfection that provide the central tension in the Pentecostal movement in terms of appropriate social and political behavior. On the one hand, the doctrine of Christian perfection is often viewed as an entirely individually focused doctrine, which removes the individual from collective concerns. From this perspective, holiness occurs when the individual is transformed into a life of particular virtues. This individual focus narrows the believer's concern to their own immediate problems and provides a theological justification for isolation from society and from community concerns. Political and social activism, therefore, were not essential to Christian behavior. The focus of Christian behavior was evangelism and personal spiritual growth. Social and political change was possible only, and would occur only, through the transformation of individuals to Christian perfection, one at a time.

On the other hand, the communal aspects of Christian perfection were essential to the Wesleyan tradition. For Wesley and his followers, holiness was "communal Holiness." Because love is the essence of holiness and love is fundamentally relational, one could not be holy in isolation. For Wesley, the spreading of scriptural holiness entailed "the transformation of the economic and political order, the establishment of Pentecostal commun(al)ism and the abolition of war" (Jennings 1990: 153). Holiness was about a "new creation," both individually and collectively. Social and political change was mandated. Christian perfection was impossible without a transformation of the world around the believer. The holiness believer was to be dissatisfied with surrounding injustices and committed to an alternative vision of the world and society.

In many ways, these two strands of Pentecostal-Holiness are similar to the tension in Anabaptism identified by Sandra Joireman in chapter 5. In both traditions, there are adherents who are reticent toward social activity and others who see social activity as an essential expression of Christian faith. For the reticent Anabaptist, it is the hierarchical placement of the church over the state and the primacy of heavenly citizenship that compels Christians to distance themselves from politics. For the reticent Pentecostal, it is an emphasis on personal holiness that leads one to the same conclusion. For the more activist variants of both traditions, faith requires action. For the Anabaptist, activism creates an environment in which the church can flourish and more effectively carry out its tasks. For the Pentecostal, actions of social justice are a natural and necessary expression of individual holiness. Though the theological impetuses for passivity and activity in each tradition are distinct, the political behaviors they motivate are essentially the same.

It is the second of these perspectives, political activism, that seems to more accurately describe the perspective of the early Pentecostal-Holiness movement. In the beginning, the relationship between perfectionist thought and political activism was extensive and intentional. The extension of personal perfection into societal perfection was straightforward and intuitively appealing.

With strong support from the Pentecostal-Holiness churches, many reform movements began to perfect American life, such as women's rights, the abolition of slavery, anti-Masonry, and Prohibition.[14]

Accompanying this social activism, however, was an intense antagonism toward the state. As Grant Wacker has noted, early Pentecostals refused any allegiance to the state because the state was an "earthly" creation. "Like the Tower of Babel, the State signaled human presumption at best, the enthronement of godlessness, immorality, greed, and violence at worst" (Wacker 2001: 217). Many early Pentecostal leaders actively preached against nationalism in general and against U.S. patriotism specifically. Positions ranged from the basic incompatibility of the Kingdom of God and the kingdoms of this world, to seditious and treasonous statements against the state.[15] For the early Pentecostals, individual identity was found in Christ, and therefore, a believer's nationality was Christian, rather than American or affiliated with some other state.

Once again, we see a similarity in perspective linking the Anabaptist and Pentecostal-Holiness traditions. For both, the spiritual and eternal focus of the kingdom of heaven must necessarily supersede, and in many cases annul, the fleshly and temporal focus of the kingdom of man. As citizens of heaven, Christians should employ spiritual "weapons" as they seek change, not fleshly weapons like politics. In contrast, Lomperis suggests in chapter 3 that the Lutheran conception of the two kingdoms "created an extra burden of Christian responsibility to politics and government." Though politics was still to play no role in advancing one's personal agenda, it was viewed as an appropriate, and perhaps even effective, means by which justice could be created for others. And because "Christians enjoy the experience of God's grace . . . they are qualified above all others for service in secular government." This perspective seems to be completely absent in early Pentecostalism.

Finally, as an offshoot of this antistate perspective, early Pentecostal roots were pacifistic—once again linking it closely to the Anabaptist tradition. Though early leaders allowed individual members to pursue their own consciences, they also believed that scripture taught conscientious objection. Early Pentecostal leaders such as Charles Fox Parham and Frank Bartleman preached forcefully against Christian participation in war. In fact, in 1917, the Assemblies of God USA sent a statement officially declaring itself a pacifist church to President Woodrow Wilson. The basic argument was that if an intercultural, interracial, and gender-inclusive unity in Christ was experienced, a Pentecostal could not go to war against a Christian brother or sister.[16]

The transition from Holiness to denominational Pentecostalism was largely accompanied by a shift from the communal understanding of Christian perfection to a more individually focused perspective. An increasing emphasis on the baptism of the Holy Spirit and speaking in tongues altered the connection between society and Pentecostalism in several important ways. The direct relationship between the believer and God, provided through the Holy Spirit, advocated a much more vertical relationship between the individual and God, rather than a horizontal relationship between the believer and those around him or her. Consequently, Pentecostalism moved away from the social transformation agendas of its early heritage. As Pentecostalism distanced itself from its Holiness roots, it became largely apathetic toward significant social change and adopted a much more apolitical and asocial public agenda. This is not to suggest that the Pentecostal movement disconnected completely from society, but rather that its primary motivation and agenda shifted. Because of the "disinherited" nature and lower socioeconomic composition of the early Pentecostal churches, a focus on social welfare—taking care of the less advantaged—had always been an important component of Pentecostal churches, and this continued to be the case even as the movement transitioned into its modern variant. Programs such as schools, orphanages, and retirement homes continued to be central to their social agenda.

Another change that occurred, as Pentecostalism moved away from its Holiness roots and toward a more direct focus on baptism in the Holy Spirit and speaking in tongues, was an energetic focus on mission work and world evangelism. Pentecostal theologian Frank Macchia has described Pentecostalism as "a paradigm shift from an exclusive focus on holiness to an outward thrust that involved a dynamic filling and empowering for global witness" (1999: 16). For many early Pentecostals, the gift of tongues was viewed not only as evidence of the baptism in the Holy Spirit but also as a miraculous means by which the gospel could be spread. The doctrine of xenoglossia, the spontaneous ability to speak in unknown foreign languages, was widely accepted. The divinely granted ability to speak in other languages was not for personal edification but rather for the purpose of efficiently proclaiming the gospel to peoples who had not yet had the opportunity to hear it in their own language. As more and more people received this ability, the Pentecostal churches became very aggressive in sending missionaries overseas to spread the gospel. Though few Pentecostals continue to view speaking in tongues exclusively in xenoglossiac terms, the initial impetus toward evangelism that it provided continues today.

In addition, the outpouring of all the gifts of the Holy Spirit—tongues, prophesy, miraculous healings, and others—is often interpreted as evidence that the end times are approaching. For many early Pentecostals, the outpouring of the Holy Spirit that they were experiencing was the fulfillment of the prophecy of Joel:

And it will come about after this that I will pour out my Spirit on all mankind; and your sons and daughters will prophesy, your old men will dream dreams, your young men will see visions. And even on the male and female servants I will pour out My Spirit in those days. And I will display wonders in the sky and on the earth, blood, fire, and columns of smoke. The sun will be turned into darkness, and the moon into blood, before the great and awesome day of the Lord comes. And it will come about that whoever calls on the name of the Lord will be delivered. (Joel 2: 28–32a, NASB)

Understanding this Holy Spirit outpouring as the evidence of Christ's imminent return impelled Pentecostals to embrace a worldview of evangelism. If Christ was coming soon, and His great commission was to be fulfilled, a sense of urgency for missionary work and a privileged place for the missionary call was inevitable.[17]

An additional implication of this global worldview was an increasing skepticism of nationalism and a growing sense of the multicultural aspects of the Christian faith. If Pentecostals were to fulfill the moral requirements of the global missionary mandate, they had to confront all forms of discrimination, including nationalism. The perspective of Gerrit Polman, a Pentecostal missionary pioneer, provides but one example of this perspective. For Polman, nationalism was one of the strongest threats to Christian unity, and he repeatedly emphasized the universal character of the gift of the Holy Spirit (van der Laan 1989: 15).[18] Holy Spirit baptism was the great leveler, and any sense of moral superiority or otherness was in direct conflict with that truth. Early Pentecostal missionary training, therefore, emphasized the importance of respecting the indigenous character of local churches, and strong central control from some Western or other foreign mission agency was avoided (Bundy 1989).

The Pentecostal Tradition and Contemporary Politics

As Pentecostalism moved into the mainline churches and the charismatic renewal took shape, it was accompanied by a significant shift in terms of political focus and activity. Once a largely marginalized and somewhat isolated Christian movement and perspective, Pentecostalism soon became assimilated into mainstream Christianity and was embraced as an active and important component of Christian evangelicalism; as the evangelical movement has become more active and visible in politics, so, too, has Pentecostalism. It is also at this point that a distinctive Pentecostal variant becomes harder and harder to identify.

Ironically, this shift toward a renewed sense of responsibility to reconstruct and reform society and politics returned Pentecostalism to a social and political perspective closer to its Holiness roots. The difference, however, is that the modern perspective is driven more by pragmatic concerns than it is with any return to a theological heritage and perspective that expects such behavior as an outgrowth of Christian perfection. As the social and political mores of modern society are perceived to move further and further away from God, Christians have increasingly adopted a perspective of social responsibility to actively work to counteract these forces, and increasingly, using the established processes of politics is viewed as a legitimate way of doing so. To the extent that political activity can be used effectively to accomplish Godly purposes, it is embraced. However, if conventional political activity is unsuccessful in accomplishing Godly purposes, it is discarded in favor of other strategies. This begs the question of whether what we currently observe—a renewed focus of the church on active political engagement—will continue into the future.

What has failed to accompany this renewed political activity, however, is a consensus of what that transformation should entail. For the charismatic Christian, the most important aspect of political theology is not an official doctrinal teaching about the state but rather the personal image of how Godly human association can be acted out in society through the actions of Christian believers. It is the Holy Spirit that leads in this regard, and it is a believer's specific personal revelation that defines the course of action to be taken.

Consequently, charismatic Christians adopt political perspectives across the entire range of possible relations to the state. On one end of the continuum are charismatic Christians who advocate Christian Reconstruction—the complete rebuilding and transformation of the state (and other social institutions) to reflect its biblical blueprint. On the other end of the continuum are charismatic Christians who advocate Christian anarchy—a perspective that challenges the legitimacy of all authority that is not God. In between are a myriad of more moderate perspectives advocating the use of the state to accomplish a variety of both liberal and conservative social and political agendas.

The variety of Pentecostal political perspectives is further expanded when we consider its variants outside the United States. The most explosive areas of Pentecostal growth occurred in the developing world, where its theology was widely embraced as the means by which the disenfranchised—economically, socially, and politically—could rise above their station in life through the power of the Holy Spirit.[19] Through its message of equality and prosperity, Pentecostalism became the "religion of the oppressed" and a "refuge for the masses" and provided a voice of political opposition against the excesses and corruption of existing social and political elites—including existing religious institutions and particularly the Catholic Church.

The earliest and largest explosion of Pentecostalism occurred in Latin America, and it is also in this region that we observe the most politically active Pentecostal elements. Though initially encouraged by church leaders to distance themselves from the "inevitable moral staining of the world" and to be content with keeping their faith to themselves, today Latin American Pentecostals are actively engaged in politics at the highest levels. They have historically voted in large numbers and with the mind-set of "brother voting for brother." Consequently, explicit Pentecostal electoral success has been significant throughout the region. For example, on two different occasions a Pentecostal has been elected to the presidency of Guatemala, on one occasion to the vice presidency of Peru, and to several prominent positions in Colombia and Brazil, and their legislative success throughout the region has been significant.[20] In addition to the simple act of voting and the accompanying electoral success, Latin American Pentecostals have begun to embrace a wider political agenda and in some instances have formed explicitly Pentecostal political parties to carry out that agenda.[21] Though most of these parties have had limited success, the decision of the Pentecostal movement to formally organize politically has represented an important departure from their strategy in other regions of the world.

The explosion of Pentecostal activism in the region has been puzzling to many social scientists, particularly given the movement's initial aversion to such engagement. In addition, there appears to be an absence of any theological foundation from which the activism has emerged, leaving the movement without a sense of coherence and a common agenda. Perhaps the most cogent explanation is offered by Edward Cleary, who suggests that pragmatism is largely responsible.[22] For Cleary, the changing socioeconomic status of Pentecostalism and its increasing numbers provided the movement with a set of unexpected political resources, which were in turn mobilized to achieve a variety of social and political agendas. In a sense, political activism has been providential more than it has been intentional. As Roland Ireland has suggested, the Pentecostal "[p]olitical challenge spills over as an unintended consequence from Pentecostal religious life" (Ireland 1998: 125).

In the 1970s, a decade or so after the Latin American explosion, a similar explosion of Pentecostalism occurred in Africa. Again, its primary appeal was its theology of individual prosperity and what many saw as an access point to the benefits of modernity that many Africans felt had previously been denied to the continent. For African Pentecostals, politics continues to be viewed as an arena dominated by the principalities and powers of the world and has been left largely untouched by organized Pentecostal activism. The connection of

Pentecostalism to the state is largely one of mediation. That is, in the face of weak states, political corruption, indebtedness, and clientelism, churches have become alternative communities that wield power against the state through nongovernmental organizations and other forms of social organization (Martin 2002).

The Asian story is more complex. In most cases, politics and Pentecostalism in Asia do not meet. In India, for example, emphasis is placed on corporate and individual discipline, accompanied by an expectation of the supernatural in the everyday lives of believers (Bayly 1994). In the Muslim states of Malaysia and Indonesia, Pentecostal energies are more about basic acceptance and social survival than they are about grand political agendas. In South Korea, where Christianity has enjoyed a prominent role for nearly a century among the middle class and the educated, Pentecostalism has been a vehicle for the survival and advancement of the poor. And finally, in China, Christianity operates largely underground in home churches and through lay ministry, which has made Pentecostalism an attractive theology, with its emphasis on personal revelation through the Holy Spirit, but has obviously kept it distant from any form of political activity.

Conclusion

To suggest that Pentecostalism has a specific understanding of the state and citizenship is to misrepresent the extraordinary diversity that defines the movement. Though the commitment to, and centrality of, the doctrine of baptism in the Holy Spirit does provide its members with a common starting point, the doctrine itself requires an acceptance of a wide range of possible social and political perspectives. The expectation of, and respect for, personal revelation makes it difficult to privilege one perspective over another. God's revelation is evolving and it is personal. His gifts and callings are diverse. To constrain and limit the specific way in which individual Christians walk their faith, therefore, is inappropriate.

NOTES

1. The use of the phrase "baptism *in* the Holy Spirit" (sometimes also phrased as "baptism *with* the Holy Spirit") is intentional and is used to distinguish it from "baptism *of* the Holy Spirit" (sometimes also phrased "baptism *by* the Holy Spirit"). For Pentecostals, baptism *of* or *by* the Holy Spirit occurs at conversion and is common to all believers, whereas baptism *in* or *with* the Holy Spirit occurs subsequently (Pentecost).

2. Although this chapter focuses on the development of Pentecostalism in North America, there is a growing body of literature on Pentecostal events in other places around the world prior to the 20th century, most famously, the Korean Revival of 1903, which spread into China, but also African, Indian, and Latin American indigenous Pentecostal movements. See Kalu (2008) for African and George (2001) or McGee (1996) for Indian Pentecostalism. For details of Pentecostal experiences around the world, see Stanley M. Burgess and Edward M. van der Mass (2002).

3. The Northern and Southern branches formally reunited in 1939 under the Methodist Protestant Church. In 1940, some Southerners who continued to remain strongly segregationalist formed the Southern Methodist Church.

4. Opinions about Parham and his ministry vary widely. Supporters view him as a watershed figure in the history of the Christian church, a man whose desire was to experience the "Full Gospel" of Jesus Christ, and the vessel through which God chose to impart a second, modern Pentecost. His detractors portray him as a heretic, a racist, a man of self-righteousness, and one of the most destructive influences in the modern church.

5. Apostolic Faith refers to the belief that the "signs and wonders" associated with the ministry of Christ's disciples, as portrayed in Acts, are active today and imparted to the Christian believer through the baptism in the Holy Spirit (in modern parlance, what some would call the "Full Gospel" of scripture). This position is in contrast to those believers who embrace the cessastionist view that all extraordinary acts of God have ceased or, at least, that all miraculous gifts of the Spirit have ceased.

6. The statement "founded by a Sodomite" is in reference to Charles Parham, who, in 1907, was charged with the sodomy of young boys. Though he was never convicted, many have used this charge as evidence against the legitimacy of both Parham and the movement he initiated.

7. As far as I am aware, the term "third wave" was first used by C. Peter Wagner in his article "The Third Wave?" in *Pastoral Renewal,* July–August 1983.

8. Though this sentence is empirically accurate, many have argued that the focus on Azusa and its missionaries has resulted in the Americanization of the Pentecostal movement and inappropriately underplayed the important role of numerous Asian, African, Latino, and Caribbean Pentecostal pioneers.

9. The reason for the appeal of Pentecostalism in the developing world has been widely studied and will not be explored extensively here. The two most common explanations of its appeal focus on its sociological and ecumenical dimensions. Even in the United States, Pentecostalism has been disproportionately embraced by the lower classes of society, who see its theology as providing equality in the spiritual realm that does not exist for them either economically or socially. Likewise, the ease with which baptism in the Holy Spirit and glossolalia can be merged with existing faith commitments has provided flexibility for the movement that many traditional denominations do not enjoy.

10. As an interesting aside, most of the missionaries listed here were from in or around Chicago and to one extent or another were influenced by the leadership of William H. Durham.

11. Churches in this tradition include the Church of the Nazarene, Wesleyan, and Free Methodist.

12. Churches in this tradition include the Assemblies of God and Church of the Foursquare Gospel.

13. Churches in this tradition include Church of God (Cleveland, TN), Church of God in Christ, Pentecostal Holiness Church, and Church of God of Prophecy.

14. As an interesting aside, the rise of political populism and the creation of Holiness denominations seem to parallel each other in terms of both time and geographic region.

15. For a more detailed overview with specific quotes from early church leaders, see Paul Alexander's "Historical and Contemporary Pentecostal Critiques of Nationalism," a paper presented at the 34th Annual Meeting of Pentecostal Studies.

16. Other arguments brought forward were less theological but rather more economic in nature, focusing on the fact that war would only benefit the rich at the expense of the poor (Beaman 1989: 52ff.).

17. If there is one common theme in the archival research of Pentecostal publications, it is the consistency with which there is a focus on the end times and calls to evangelism. When referenced, international events are discussed only in terms of their evidence of Christ's eminent return and the Christian's duty toward intentional evangelism.

18. Polman was also an adherent and advocate of Pentecostal pacifism. For Polman and those like him, pacifism was part of the church's redemptive witness to the world; the moral integrity of pacifism was to be a sign of the restoration of apostolic faith (see Dempster 1989).

19. Initially, the social and economic appeal of Pentecostalism was far greater than its political appeal. Early on, Pentecostals tended to retreat from politics because they viewed it as a realm "beyond their reach" and under the control of the elites who had worked to repress them. Only after Pentecostalism enjoyed a period of significant growth and acquired a level of social legitimacy did their attention turn to the political arena.

20. The highest level of national legislative success occurred in Brazil in 1986, when eighteen Pentecostal deputies were elected to the National Assembly.

21. For example, the Universal Church of the Kingdom of God (IURD) in Brazil, the Authentic Renovating Organization (ORA) in Venezuela, and the National Solidarity Movement in El Salvador.

22. Interestingly, it is for reasons of pragmatism that Cleary suggests that Pentecostal activism will eventually lose its force. Though explicit political activity has provided the Pentecostal movement with some initial success, the likelihood of the Pentecostal movement succeeding beyond a peripheral force in politics is unlikely. Consequently, as they begin to experience political failure, Cleary expects that they will move out of politics and engage in alternative strategies.

BIBLIOGRAPHY

Anderson, Allan. 1992. *Bazalwane: African Pentecostals in South Africa*. Pretoria, South Africa: Unisa Press.

Anderson, Allan. 2004. *An Introduction to Pentecostalism*. Cambridge: Cambridge University Press.

Barrett, David. 1998. "World Growth at 19 Million a Year." *Christianity Today* 42(13).

Bartleman, Frank. 1980. *Azusa Street: The Roots of Modern-day Pentecost*. Plainfield, NJ: Logos International.

Bayly, Susan. 1994. "Christianity and Competing Fundamentalisms in South Indian Society." In *Accounting for Fundamentalism*, eds. Martin Marty and R. Scott Appleby. Chicago: Chicago University Press, 726–769.

Beaman, Jay. 1989. *Pentecostal Pacifism: The Origin, Development, and Rejection of Pacific Belief among Pentecostals*. Fresno, CA: Center for Mennonite Brethren Studies.

Boardman, William E. 1858. *The Higher Christian Life*. Boston: Henry Hoyt.

Bundy, David. 1989. "Bishop William Taylor of Methodist Mission: A Study in Nineteenth Century Social History." *Methodist History* 27(4): 197–200; 28(1): 2–21.

Burgess, Stanley M., and Edward M. van der Mass, eds. 2002. *The New International Dictionary of Pentecostal and Charismatic Movements*. Grand Rapids, MI: Zondervan.

Cleary, Edward L., and Hannah W. Stewart-Gambino, eds. 1998. *Power, Politics, and Pentecostals in Latin America*. Boulder, CO: Westview.

Cox, Harvey. 1996. *Fire from Heaven: The Rise of Pentecostal Spirituality and the Reshaping of Religion in the 21st Century*. London: Cassell.

Dayton, Donald W. 1981. *Theological Roots of Pentecostalism*. Grand Rapids, MI: Zondervan/Francis Asbury Press.

Dempster, Murray W. 1989. "'Crossing Borders': Arguments Used by Early Pentecostals in Support of the Global Character of Pacifism." *EPTA Bulletin* 8(1): 64.

Dictionary of Pentecostal and Charismatic Movements, eds. Stanley M. Burgess and Gary B. McGee. 1988. Grand Rapids, MI: Regency Reference Library.

Ewart, Frank J. 1947. *The Phenomenon of Pentecost*. Houston, TX: Herald.

Flower, J. Roswell. 1915. "What Will the Harvest Be? Article in Last Week's *Evangel* Receiving Just Criticism." *Weekly Evangel*, August 14.

George, A. C. 2001. "Pentecostal Beginnings in Travancore, South India." *Asian Journal of Pentecostal Studies* 4: 215–237.

Hollenweger, Walter J. 1981. *Pentecostalism: Origins and Developments Worldwide*. Peabody, MA: Hendrickson.

Ireland, Rowan. 1998. "Pentecostalism, Conversion, and Politics in Brazil." In *Power, Politics, and Pentecostals in Latin America*, eds. Edward L. Cleary and Hannah W. Stewart-Gambino. Boulder, CO: Westview, 123–189.

Jennings, Theodore W. 1990. *Good News to the Poor: John Wesley's Evangelical Economics*. Nashville, TN: Abingdon Press.

Kalu, Ogbu. 2008. *African Pentecostalism: An Introduction*. New York: Oxford University Press.

Leoh, Vincent. 2005. "Toward Pentecostal Social Ethics." *JAM* 1: 39–62.

Macchia, Frank D. 1999. "The Struggle for Global Witness: Shifting Paradigms in Pentecostal Theology." In *The Globalization of Pentecostalism: A Religion Made to Travel*, eds. Douglas Peterson, Murray W. Dempster, and Byron D. Klaus. Carlisle, UK: Regnum Books International, Paternoster.

Martin, David. 1994. "Evangelical and Charismatic Christianity in Latin America." In *Charismatic Christianity as a Global Culture,* ed. Karla Poewe. Columbia: University of South Carolina Press.

Martin, David. 2002. *Pentecostalism: The World Their Parish.* Malden, MA: Blackwell.

McGee, Gary. 1996. "Pentecostal Phenomena and Revivals in India: Implications for Indigenous Church Leadership." *International Bulletin of Missionary Research* 20.

Nienkirchen, Charles W. 1992. *A. B. Simpson and the Pentecostal Movement.* Edinburgh: Hendrickson.

Paloma, Margaret M. "The Spirit Bade Me Go: Pentecostalism and Global Religion." Paper prepared for presentation at the Association for the Sociology of Religion annual meetings, August 11–13, 2000, Washington, DC.

Robeck, Cecil M., Jr. 1992. "The Social Concern of Early American Pentecostalism." In *Pentecost, Mision and Ecumenism: Essays on Intercultural Theology,* ed. Jan A. Jongeneel. Frankfurt: Peter Lang, 97–106.

Smidt, Corwin. 1989. "'Praise the Lord' Politics: A Comparative Analysis of the Social Characteristics and Political Views of American and Evangelical Christians." *Sociological Analysis* 50 (Spring): 53–72.

Synan, Vinson. 1971. *The Holiness-Pentecostal Movement.* Grand Rapids, MI: William B. Eerdmanns.

Tomlinson, A. J. 1913. *The Last Great Conflict.* Cleveland, TN: Press of Walter E. Rodgers; reprinted 1984, Cleveland, TN: White Wing.

Van der Laan, Cornelius. 1989. "The Theology of Gerrit Polman: Dutch Pentecostal Pioneer." *EPTA Bulletin* 8(1): 15.

Wacker, Grant. 2001. *Heaven Below.* Cambridge, MA: Harvard University Press.

White, Alma. 1949. *Demons and Tongues.* 4th ed. Zeraphath, NJ: Pillar of Fire.

Wogaman, J. Philip. 2000. *Christian Perspectives on Politics.* Louisville, KY: Westminster John Knox Press.

9

Concluding Reflections

Mark R. Amstutz

The preceding chapters have presented distinctive features of major theological traditions of Western Christianity. The book covers four classical traditions—Catholic, Lutheran, Reformed, and Anabaptist,[1] along with three other influential perspectives: Anglicanism, Pentecostalism, and evangelicalism. The latter two movements have become the fastest growing Christian churches in recent decades, accounting for most of the growth of Christianity in Africa, Asia, and Latin America. Although estimates of the number of Christians at the beginning of the new millennium vary considerably, we can assume that almost two billion persons, or nearly a third of the world's population, considers itself part of Western Christian churches.

A major aim of this book is to illuminate how diverse Christian traditions approach politics, government, and the state. In this concluding chapter, I review several key themes that have been addressed implicitly or explicitly in the chapters. My aim is to highlight similarities and differences in the political theology of different Christian traditions and perspectives. I do so by focusing on four fundamental issues: the relationship of spiritual life to temporal life, the relationship of church and state, the legitimacy of the state, and the purpose of the state. In describing and assessing how different Christian groups address politics and government, we must remember that traditions are dynamic, continuously adapting to new challenges. Thus in developing an understanding of how different churches approach political concerns and global political challenges, we must keep in mind the contemporary practices and beliefs of believers, not the historic conflicts and divisions that have given rise to different theological traditions.

Even though Christians approach politics from different theological perspectives, they nonetheless share many core beliefs about faith and political action, such as assumptions about human nature and the priority of divine authority over temporal power. In the chapter's second section, I therefore explore some shared norms of Christian political ethics. I focus on four principles: the dignity of person, the universality and persistence of human sin, the need for a limited state, and the church's priority of proclaiming the gospel.

Major Themes in Political Theology

Spiritual Life versus Temporal Life

How should Christians conceive of their religious faith relative to the social, economic, and political obligations and necessities of life? Should faith be concerned only with spiritual life, or should it also structure economic, social, and political life? In the words of H. Richard Niebuhr, how should Christ relate to culture? And when conflicts arise between spiritual responsibilities and the demands of temporal life, which should take precedence?

Although Christians have been divided on how to conceive of the relationship of spiritual life to temporal life, there is wide agreement, based on biblical teaching, that when conflict arises between the two realms, obedience to God must take precedence over any temporal responsibilities. When Peter and other apostles are brought before the Jewish Council (Sanhedrin) for teaching allegedly false doctrines, they declare that their first responsibility is to God, not the state. Peter boldly declares: "We ought to obey God rather than men" (Acts 5: 29). Jesus himself says that his disciples should first pursue the "kingdom of God" and then fulfill other desires and obligations (Matthew 6: 33).

One way of resolving the tension between temporal and spiritual authority is to pursue a strategy of detachment and withdrawal, with monasticism serving as the ultimate expression of such an option. But Jesus commands his followers to be in the world but not of it (John 17: 15, 16). Believers are to work and serve Christ in the temporal city while maintaining their ultimate allegiance to God. One of the most perceptive descriptions of how believers fulfill their dual responsibilities to the temporal and heavenly kingdoms was set forth in the third century, when Roman authorities were persecuting Christians. The anonymous Letter to Diognetus states in part:

Christians are indistinguishable from other men either by nationality, language or customs. They do not inhabit separate cities of their own, or speak a strange dialect, or follow some outlandish way of life. . . . With regard to dress, food and manner of life in general, they follow the customs of whatever city they happen to be living in, whether it is Greek or foreign. And yet there is something extraordinary about their lives. They live in their own countries as though they were only passing through. They play their full role as citizens, but labor under all the disabilities of aliens. Any country can be their homeland, but for them their homeland, wherever it may be, is a foreign country. Like others, they marry and have children, but they do not expose them. They share their meals, but not their wives. They live in the flesh, but they are not governed by the desires of the flesh. They pass their days upon earth, but they are citizens of heaven.

As the chapters in this book make plain, Christians have addressed the challenge of dual citizenship in a variety of ways. Some have done so by emphasizing responsibilities to the heavenly kingdom and minimizing, if not denigrating, responsibilities to the state and political life. Often the priority of spiritual life has been expressed by an emphasis on religious practices, discipleship, and evangelism. For Pentecostalism, this has involved giving priority to personal holiness, while de-emphasizing, if not opposing, political responsibilities. For Anabaptists, this has meant even greater disregard for the state, making religious concerns paramount. And evangelicals have expressed the primacy of the spiritual realm by focusing on evangelism and global missionary activity.

Although the Catholic, Lutheran, and Reformed traditions also affirm the priority of spiritual authority in the religious domain, they acknowledge the importance of the state in developing and sustaining societies that affirm the common good. Since human beings are by nature social creatures, the state has an important function in providing a safe and stable environment where persons can achieve their full humanity. According to Robert Shelledy, because government can be an instrument of either justice or injustice, the Roman Catholic Church has historically emphasized the responsibility of using temporal power to serve the common good. In the Anabaptist tradition, by contrast, the role of the state is more limited, providing order so that the church can carry out its mission. Although Lutherans believe that the state should promote a humane political order, they assume that only partial justice can be realized because of the pervasiveness of sin. The Reformed tradition shares with Lutheranism a belief in the universality and totality of sin, but unlike Lutheranism, it assumes that temporal power, like all realms of God's creation, is under divine authority. As James Skillen observes, the task of the state is not simply to restrain evil but to be an instrument of justice and reconciliation through Christ.

The Legitimacy of the State

A second related issue is the moral significance of nations and states. For believers who assume that the only important citizenship is membership in the Kingdom of God, the state is not morally significant. The division of the world into distinct sovereign states, after all, is not a necessary part of the divine plan for the world. Since nation-states emerged as a means to regulate political life and contain international violence, they arose providentially as a means to facilitate social order. Thus, for Holiness churches, Mennonite communities, fundamentalists,[2] and Pietist groups, allegiance to the universal Kingdom of Christ must take precedence over any temporal political affiliations. As a result, patriotism and nationalism are potentially inimical to the universal body of Christ because such allegiances can impair the unity of believers. Indeed, to the extent that nationalism impairs the transnational unity of the body of Christ, it is contrary to the divine will. This is why Sandra Joireman notes that some Mennonites claim that excessive attachment to one's state is idolatry.

The Lutheran and Reformed traditions have been far more accepting of the legitimacy of the state in carrying out the tasks of maintaining civic order and promoting people's well-being. Indeed, Luther argued that Christians must not only support the state but also participate in its decision making in order to protect communities from evil developments. Christians were not to use politics for personal gain, however, but were to advance public justice. As Timothy Lomperis notes, the vocation of politics provides a means for walking "the extra mile of the Sermon on the Mount."

The Reformed tradition affirms an even more important role for politics and government, because believers are called to influence the structures and policies of government. But Skillen, too, warns that excessive attachment to one's own nation can be morally problematic. He observes that some believers, using Reformed theological concepts and emphasizing Old Testament law, have viewed their nation as a fulfillment of the "new Israel." Using the old covenant between God and Israel and the new covenant between Christ and his church, some believers—such as some Dutch Reformed Christians in South Africa and fundamentalists in the United States—have viewed their nation as God's chosen people. But the "new Israel," as Skillen notes, cannot be applied to individual states but rather to the international or transtemporal body of Christ. Besides pursuing domestic justice, Christians must also foster the reformation and transformation of global politics. According to Skillen, because God's sovereignty extends to the whole world, Christians must be prepared to consider global governance models that circumscribe state sovereignty in order to advance global justice.

Although the Catholic Church opposed the rise of the sovereign nation-state in the mid-17th century,[3] it has historically supported a strong political engagement, developing a substantial body of moral teaching appropriate to this task. This body of knowledge—known as Catholic social thought—has played an important role in influencing ideas about political life, such as the sanctity of life, citizenship, human rights, democracy, and war. At the same time, Catholicism, like other traditions, has called attention to the dangers of nationalism and the need for transnational solidarity in pursuing the common good.

According to Leah Anderson, Anglicanism "has the highest view of the state" among Christian traditions. Because of the political nature of the origins of the church, the state not only regulated public affairs but also served as the ultimate decision-making authority over the church (Church of England). As a result, Anglicanism's Erastianism contributed to a fused conception of spiritual and temporal authority, with the church serving as an instrument of the status quo.

The Purpose of Government

There is general consensus among Christians that government is a divinely ordained institution. In First Peter, Paul tells believers to "accept the authority of every human institution," and in Romans 13, he calls on them to "be subject to the governing authorities" because God himself has instituted government. Believers are not admonished to establish their own political institutions but to obey established authorities. From a biblical perspective, therefore, the state is a divinely ordained institution—a part of God's created order. As Nicholas Wolterstorff has noted, governmental authority belongs "to God's providential care for human beings."[4] This means that God's sovereignty extends through the church, as well as the state. More particularly, this means that Christ is the head of not only the church but also the state. Consequently, "the Christian is under the rule of Christ not only in the church but also in the state."[5]

Despite the widespread consensus among Christians of the divine role of government, believers have historically held many different views about the scope and purpose of government. These differences arise not simply from different interpretations of the scriptures but also from diverse conceptions about the role of government for believers and nonbelievers alike. For Pietist traditions, including Holiness churches, Mennonite communities, and fundamentalist groups, for example, the task of government is relatively insignificant, providing a fundamental order in which the church can carry out its mission. Government was not established to fulfill God's Kingdom on earth but to maintain order in a fallen world. Pietists have therefore assumed that believers should focus their energies on service to Christ by proclaiming the gospel, modeling righteousness, and tangibly demonstrating love by caring for those in need. When government institutes policies that are contrary to the Christian faith, believers must resist public authority. The decision to publicly oppose the state is especially strong within the Anabaptist tradition, particularly when the state resorts to violence. Because Mennonites are committed to nonviolence, they refuse to participate in a state's armed forces—a position that, according to Joireman, "is the most visible evidence of the Mennonite belief regarding the responsibilities of the church and the state."

Other Christians, notably Lutherans and evangelicals, have also held a constrained view of the state. For them, the primary task of government was negative—to restrain evil and maintain public order. Promoting human rights and fostering public justice were not regarded as feasible initiatives because of the inordinate impact of sin in government. Nevertheless, politics is important for both Lutherans and evangelicals. As Lomperis notes, Luther, following Augustine, believed that Christians are called to live and serve in both the heavenly kingdom of Christ and the temporal kingdom of the earth. Although believers should live according to the "uncoercive Word of God," they also have a responsibility to care for neighbors—a responsibility that leads them to participate in temporal affairs, using the coercive force of the state to advance public justice and protect the innocent from attack. For Lomperis, the two kingdoms were not totally separate, disjointed realms of responsibility but rather a "fused paradox." The fusion of faith and politics is captured in Lomperis's assertion that believers "should not help themselves through politics, but through politics they are called to serve and fight injustice for others."

Evangelicalism has also contributed to the clarification of the proper role of the government in advancing public justice. The conventional wisdom about evangelicals, however, is that because of their excessive concern with spiritual life and more particularly with the priority of evangelism, they have contributed little to public life. Although evangelicalism has never developed a sophisticated doctrine of the state, it has nevertheless developed a framework that has been conducive to limited government, as well as social justice. According to Timothy Shaw, although evangelicalism has subordinated politics to missionary activity, it has ironically contributed to a conception of statecraft that bases the pursuit of public justice and the common good on the integrity and virtue of people. As a result, the foundation for a humane society is not so much based on devising appropriate public policies but on "soulcraft"—that is, the moral development of persons. Evangelicalism has therefore been skeptical of top-down, state-centered policies to advance human welfare. Instead, it has supported "bottom-up transformation and mobilization of individuals" to achieve lasting reforms.

The Catholic and Reformed traditions and, to a lesser degree, Anglicanism have a far more positive conception of the role of government. For them, the purpose of the state not only includes the constraining tasks of maintaining public order and enforcing the law but also includes the positive tasks of fostering the common good—of promoting and protecting human rights and establishing structures and policies that contribute to a community's social, economic, and cultural well-being. For Catholics, political community is natural, since human beings are unable to fulfill their true humanity apart from social associations. As Shelledy notes, the Catholic perspective therefore views the state as an institution that can advance the common good. For Reformed believers, government is similarly an important institution in God's redemptive plan. As part of the original created order, the state functions not only to restrain conflict but also to foster a structure where human beings can live and work in communion with each other. As Skillen notes, "[C]reation comes first, sin comes second." The central task of government, however, is not to impose Christian norms on citizens, but rather to uphold public justice.

Church versus State

A fourth issue that Christians have faced over the centuries has been how to specify loyalties and boundaries between temporal and spiritual authority, between obligations to the state and those to the church. Ever since the Pharisees asked Jesus whether it was lawful to pay taxes to Caesar, Christians have struggled to define the appropriate boundaries between the altar and the throne, between faith and politics. Jesus' answer—that we should "render to Caesar the things that are Caesar's and to God the things that are God's"—did not provide a conclusive answer because he did not specify the boundaries of the temporal realm. As a result, Christians have historically interpreted the boundaries of Caesar's coin in a variety of ways.

Some have argued that since God is sovereign and the church is concerned with the soul, the religious realm allows little room for Caesar. For Anabaptists and Pentecostals, for example, the state has a negligible claim on believers. Indeed, for many of them faithfulness to the Kingdom of God involves minimal engagement with public life in general and even less direct contact with government itself. Some Anabaptist communities even refuse to vote. Given

the historic tension between church and state, it is not surprising that Mennonites not only refuse to serve in the military but also refuse positions of political
authority. Although Mennonites and Pentecostals have continued to emphasize the primacy of the church over the state, a growing number of believers
in these traditions have become more engaged in public affairs. As Swindle
observes, a number of Pentecostal leaders have assumed elective office in Latin
American countries.

Evangelicals have also historically pursued a separatist strategy that involved
modeling Christian disciplines and having limited concern with public affairs.
Ironically, the evangelical focus on piety and evangelism nevertheless contributed to a conception of politics rooted in the morality and virtue of individuals,
rather than in the justice of public policies themselves. The historic disregard
for politics among evangelicals, however, began to change in the United States
in the 1970s. When they concluded that a growing number of state practices
were inconsistent with a biblical worldview, they established well-organized
political action groups that sought to reform public policies and elect leaders
who were most likely to advance their political agenda.

Although Lutheranism may have been originally interpreted as calling
for a distinct separation between religion and the state, Lomperis argues that
Lutheran tradition celebrates the interpenetration or fusion of the earthly and
heavenly kingdoms. This interpenetration, or fused paradox, calls on believers
to integrate the demands of Christ with responsibilities in politics. In practice,
this means that Christians must apply the Sermon on the Mount to their individual behavior but must serve their neighbors in the political realm by calling
for peace and fighting for justice.

The Reformed tradition places even more demands on believers in reconciling their obligations to the church and the state. Because the political sphere
is an independent, distinct sphere under the sovereign judgment of God, it
functions entirely separately from the church. At the same time, believers who
are called into public life have a responsibility to bring the love of Christ into
the realm of public affairs in order to redeem and transform the structures and
policies of the state.

Historically, Catholicism and Anglicanism have both championed a strong,
integrated role of church and state. Although each of these traditions now supports a distinct separation of spiritual and temporal authority, in the past both
sought to fuse the two realms. In the medieval era, for example, popes sought
to control both the altar and the throne, while Anglicanism arose in Britain
with the monarch establishing control over the church. In time, both traditions
restored a balance between the two authorities, with the church emphasizing its distinctive contribution to the moral well-being of society and the state

providing a humane order that affirmed human rights, including religious freedom. Beginning in the 19th century, the Catholic tradition began developing a sophisticated theory of social and public life based on papal encyclicals, pastoral letters, and other teaching documents. This conceptual body of knowledge (Catholic social teaching) provides the most developed social and political thought of any Christian tradition and is a significant model of how to integrate biblical, moral reflection with the challenges of public life.

Because of its close fusion of church and state, the Anglican tradition emphasizes loyalty to the state and obedience to government. Unlike most Christian traditions that emphasize a clear separation of church and state, Anglicanism encourages support for government leaders and public policies. Historically, it has not regarded the church as an institution called to check the power of temporal authority or to lead in the reformation of public life. Rather, Anglicanism has encouraged a shared partnership between church and state, religious authority and temporal authority. As Anderson notes, to the extent that believers seek to transform public life, reform is carried out within the structures of church and state.

Core Principles of Christian Political Ethics

Despite different theological perspectives, there is widespread consensus on many core religious principles and beliefs that relate to the state and, more specifically, the role of Christians in public life. Four of the most important of these are the dignity of persons, the universality and persistence of sin, the need for a limited state, and the imperative for the church to be the church. In this section, I briefly examine each of these.

Human Dignity

The notion that human beings are entitled to dignity and respect is a widely accepted belief among Christians. This idea is rooted in the fact that humans are created in the image of God (*imago dei*) and therefore have infinite worth. Although human beings may differ in their social, economic, political, and intellectual capabilities, as bearers of God's image, they are fundamentally equal. From a Christian perspective, the dignity and glory of persons is based not on the rational or moral nature of humans but on God's unlimited and all-embracing love (agape). And because God's love is unconditional and all-inclusive, human dignity is universal, extending to every person regardless of age, race, gender, nationality, or professional status. The Apostle Paul powerfully expresses the universality and equality of persons when he writes that "there is neither Jew nor Greek, there is neither slave nor free, there is neither male nor female; for you are all one in Christ Jesus" (Galatians 3: 28).

Glen Tinder argues that the most fundamental premise of Western social and political theory is the notion of human dignity—which he defines as "the idea of the exalted individual."[6] According to Tinder, this idea not only is "the spiritual center of Western politics" but also provides the foundation for Christian political reflection and action. Catholic social thought similarly emphasizes the priority of persons. According to a group of leading American Catholic thinkers, the most basic principle of Catholic social teaching is "the inalienable dignity of every single human person."[7] This dignity, they stress, is not given by the state but is inherent in all persons. The papal encyclical *Peace on Earth (Pacem in Terris)* similarly notes that the foundation of well-ordered and productive societies is the belief that every human being is "a person who is endowed with intelligence and free will." The encyclical goes on to stress that the Christian faith reinforces the worth of persons: "If we look upon the dignity of the human person in the light of divinely revealed truth, we cannot help but esteem it far more highly; for men are redeemed by the blood of Jesus Christ, they are by grace the children and friends of God and heirs of eternal glory."[8]

The idea of exalted individuals is important because it provides the foundation for the claims of human rationality, sociability, creativity, and moral autonomy. Human freedom is an essential dimension of human dignity because without freedom there can be no responsible action—no authentic expressions of love, no pursuit of the common good, no creative labor, and no justice. In his encyclical *On Human Work (Laborem Exercens)*, Pope John Paul II notes that "man is the image of God partly through the mandate received from his Creator to subdue, to dominate, the earth. In carrying out this mandate, man, every human being, reflects the very action of the Creator of the universe."[9] Because creation is not finished, people can continue God's original creation as cocreators, using their freedom responsibly in fostering justice and promoting the common good. In particular, the creation mandate enables people to improve medical science, create new products, develop new technologies, devise new scientific theories, invent new marketing strategies, compose new music, create new works of art, and engage in similar creative acts. A group of Catholic laypeople makes this important claim about work and creation: "Humans become co-creators through discovery and invention, following the clues left by God. Yet human beings are creators not only in changing the world, but also in realizing their own inner possibilities. Every human being who works must be respected as a person."[10]

Human Sin

The glory of human beings is only a part of Christian anthropology. The other part is the belief in the totality and universality of human sin. Sin is total because it affects all aspects of people's lives—their minds, spirits, goals, and desires—and it is universal because it affects all human beings regardless of their education, wealth, moral disposition, or even spirituality. The Apostle Paul affirms this truth: "For all have sinned and come short of the glory of God" (Romans 3: 23). Although some believers have sought to minimize sin and temptation by pursuing disciplines of personal holiness or following a separatist strategy of minimal engagement in the world, it is important to stress that all persons—believers and nonbelievers—are always within the grip of sin. This is why confession is central to the Christian religion. The recognition of human frailty is expressed simply but powerfully in the so-called Jesus prayer of the Christian Orthodox Church: "Lord Jesus Christ, Son of God, have mercy on me, a sinner." Thus, to be human is to be subject to sin.

According to Reinhold Niebuhr, the Christian estimate of sin is serious because it places the root of sin in the human will. "This evil," he writes, "cannot be regarded complacently as the inevitable consequence of his finiteness or the fruit of his involvement in contingencies and necessities of nature. Sin is occasioned precisely by the fact that man refuses to admit his 'creatureliness' and acknowledge himself as merely a member of a total unity of life. He pretends to be more than he is."[11] Sin therefore arises from the misuse of human freedom by enthroning the self and displacing God. The result is self-debasement. Sin is therefore ironic: "[I]n trying to ascend, we fall."[12]

If sin is as pervasive in human beings as Christian doctrine alleges, then its impact on politics is likely to be all-encompassing. Because reason is tainted by sin, natural law, moral principles, or other rational goals can provide only a proximate, imperfect guide to action. Moreover, because the intellect can be an instrument of self-interest, collective decisions are often the result of group interest rather than of impartial morality. Even if reason could devise just political and economic policies, the implementation of any just policy can always be compromised by self-interest, partiality, and self-righteousness. Political action, especially morally inspired action, must be advanced with humility and tentativeness. The awareness that all human initiatives are incomplete or flawed does not mean, however, that moral judgments should not be made. Rather, it means that believers should use moral language with care, avoiding excessive reliance on moralistic language that defines issues in terms of justice and injustice, good and evil. Niebuhr wisely observed that "the Christian faith ought to persuade us that political controversies are always conflicts between sinners and not between righteous men and sinners."[13]

Although all Christian traditions affirm the universality and ubiquity of human sin, they differ on its nature and impact on social and political life. The Reformed and Lutheran traditions, for example, assert that human sin not only impairs communal action but also afflicts human reason. As a result, natural law is not considered a reliable guide to moral action. For the Catholic tradition, by contrast, natural law and moral reason are important sources of Christian political morality, providing truths and principles that reinforce and clarify biblical morality. Undoubtedly, one of the important insights to emerge from the notion of universal human sin is the need for accountability and checks and balances within government. Because sin and self-interest are ubiquitous and because the temptations for injustice are greatest as human influence and power increase, some Christian thinkers have emphasized the need for institutions that restrain human ambition. James Madison, the father of the U.S. Constitution, defended the principles of separation of power and checks and balances based on his "realistic" conception of human nature.[14]

The Limited State

A third significant principle in Christian political ethics is the imperative of a limited state. The need to delimit political authority derives from two fundamental biblical truths: first, since human beings are created in the image of God, they are entitled to dignity and respect, and second, since God is sovereign, temporal authority is ultimately answerable to a higher authority. The first truth means that governments may not trample on human rights. In particular, they may not make unlimited claims on their subjects, and in particular they may not circumscribe people's freedom of conscience. The fundamental task of the state is to serve the common good by using public authority to nurture and protect the fundamental rights of citizens.

The second truth—that God is sovereign—means that the state cannot make unlimited claims. Since temporal power is under divine judgment, the boundaries of state authority are circumscribed by higher law. This does not mean that the state should not exert final authority in temporal affairs; rather, it means that the sphere of government must be constrained. The idea of a strong but limited state is not only consistent with biblical faith but also consistent with modern democratic practices that emphasize the role of an energetic civil society. Civil society—comprised of such mediating institutions as churches, professional associations, unions, advocacy networks, and other nongovernmental organizations—is important because it nurtures cooperation and trust (social capital) and thereby fosters communal solidarity. Indeed, the efficacy of the state is as much dependent on its own institutions as it is on the values, habits, and nongovernmental institutions that provide the foundation for a vigorous society.

One way of delimiting the state is to view it as one of several institutions directly accountable to divine authority. In his famous Stone Lectures, Abraham Kuyper, the late-19th-century Dutch theologian and politician, argued that although God was sovereign over all the earth, his authority in the temporal realm was expressed in a differentiated manner through a variety of institutions, including the family, church, economic life, politics, and work. According to Kuyper, God entrusts direct responsibility for human welfare in each distinct sphere. Thus, the state is responsible in governmental life, while the church and family are responsible for religious and familial life.[15]

The church has an important function in maintaining a limited state. By asserting its responsibility in its religious sphere, the church can help prevent the state from encroaching on its area of responsibility. By the same token, a state that nurtures human freedom and protects religious freedom in particular benefits from stronger religious communities that can, in turn, foster the renewal of public morality.

As noted earlier, the diverse Christian traditions examined in this book establish widely different boundaries between church and state, spiritual and temporal life. Some, like Pentecostalism, give primacy to the spiritual realm and de-emphasize the role of faith in political life. Others, like Mennonites and other Anabaptist groups, emphasize the development of religious communities that model values and practices consistent with authentic religious commitment. Still others, like the Reformed and Roman Catholic traditions—emphasize the need for direct political engagement of believers.

The Task of the Church

As noted earlier, Christian traditions define the nature and temporal role of the church differently.[16] Some, like the Pentecostal, Anabaptist, evangelical, and Lutheran traditions, emphasize the spiritual task of evangelism and nurturing authentic Christian discipleship. For them, the church has a limited role in public affairs. And to the extent that the church engages in public life, it does so indirectly by modeling values and practices, individually and collectively. The Roman Catholic and Reformed traditions, however, regard the task of the church as not simply fostering religious faith but also nurturing social, economic, and political patterns that are conducive to a just, humane communal life. Although spiritual life is considered primary in these traditions, the task of the church is not simply saving souls or modeling Christian virtues. Rather, the church must secondarily contribute to the reformation and transformation of all of God's creation. Salvation, in other words, is an all-embracing responsibility that includes politics and government.

Regardless of how the various traditions approach the nature and role of faith, the church has an important institutional role in ensuring a delimited state. In "Christianity and Democracy," Richard Neuhaus observes that "the first and final assertion Christians make about all of reality, including politics is 'Jesus Christ is Lord.'" He goes on to note that because the church's major task is to proclaim this message, it must maintain a critical distance from all actual or proposed temporal initiatives. "Christians betray their Lord," he writes, "if, in theory or practice, they equate the Kingdom of God with any political, social or economic order of this passing time."[17]

If the church is to fulfill its obligation in proclaiming the Lordship of Christ, it must protect its independence from the state and must be careful not to engage in partisan politics. As Alexis de Tocqueville noted long ago, "[T]he church cannot share the temporal power of the state without being the object of a portion of that animosity which the latter excites."[18] The church must therefore not become identified with a political leader, party, or nation, because a close political affiliation will call into question the church's autonomy and impair its ability to bring judgment to bear in public life. Most important, if the church ceases to focus on its fundamental spiritual tasks, it will lose its capacity to identify and apply biblical and moral principles to temporal affairs.

How should the church remain true to its authentic mission while relevant to the affairs of state? It can serve as a moral teacher to the state. As a moral teacher, the church can help identify and clarify fundamental moral values and biblical norms that should guide political debates and analysis. Additionally, the church can help structure public policy debates by illuminating the nature and role of relevant moral values. In the early 1980s, the U.S. Catholic bishops illustrated the important role of the church as a moral teacher in "The Challenge of Peace," their pastoral letter on nuclear arms. Regardless of whether one agrees with the analysis, the letter is significant because it (a) addresses a major public policy issue in an authoritative manner, (b) illuminates relevant biblical and moral norms along with traditional church teaching about peace and war, and (c) offers prudential judgments in a provisional manner.[19] The bishops recognize that their competence does not lie in national security affairs. Nonetheless, they interpret the moral and religious wisdom of the Catholic tradition and apply it to the problem of nuclear deterrence. Although the letter offered a number of policy recommendations, the primary contribution of the study was its moral assessment of nuclear strategy in light of biblical and theological analysis.

In sum, the church must carry out those functions that it does best—namely, to apply a Christian worldview to political problem solving—and refuse to get involved in areas in which it does not have competence, namely, devising specific policies to solve contemporary political problems. In his study of politics of the World Council of Churches (W.C.C.), the late Paul Ramsey argued that the W.C.C. had become too closely aligned with political programs and had lost its capacity to grasp and proclaim transcendent truths. In his short book *Who Speaks for the Church?* Ramsey offered the following counsel: "Christian political ethics cannot say what should or must be done but only what may be done. In politics the church is only a theoretician. The religious communities as such should be concerned with perspectives upon politics with political doctrines, with the direction and structures of common life, not with specific directives. They should seek to clarify and keep wide open the legitimate options for choice, and thus nurture the moral and political ethics of the nation. Their task is not the determination of policy."[20]

Conclusion

As is evident from the chapters in this book and from my short sketch in the first part of this concluding essay, Christians have historically held different perspectives on the nature and purpose of the state. Each tradition can contribute important insights to Christian political ethics and, more specifically, to the task of bringing moral reformation to the world. But Christians have not always expressed appreciation for the contribution that distinct traditions can make to the witness of the church. Indeed, instead of unity, conflict and competition have characterized the relationships among different churches and diverse religious traditions.

It is therefore useful to recall H. Richard Niebuhr's admonition that no single tradition fully expresses the divine strategy of redemption. In his classic *Christ and Culture*—a study that explores major alternative theological traditions on the relationship of faith to temporal life—Niebuhr reminds readers than no single church, group, or individual can provide an authoritative voice for the work of Christ in the world because God's redemptive strategy is "in the mind of the Captain rather than of any lieutenants."[21] Because no tradition provides a complete answer to the question of "Christ and culture," believers should be humble and tentative in their political pronouncements, remembering that history will remain, to the end of time, inconclusive and indeterminate.

NOTES

1. Theologian H. Richard Niebuhr has felicitously defined these four traditions—Catholicism, Lutheranism, Calvinism, and Anabaptism—as Christ above culture, Christ and culture in paradox, Christ transforming culture, and Christ against culture. See H. Richard Niebuhr, *Christ and Culture* (New York: Harper Torchbooks, 1951).

2. The Christian fundamentalist movement in the United States emerged in the early 1920s in response to the growth of modernist, secular developments within mainline Protestant churches. Fundamentalists sought not only to reclaim the "fundamentals" of the faith but also to reinforce the need for separation from the world. Since both evangelicals and fundamentalists share a commitment to orthodox religious beliefs and to the authority of the Bible, the primary difference between evangelicals and fundamentalists is their approach to cultural engagement. Whereas fundamentalists demand separation and a rigid adherence to religious practices, evangelicals support engagement and a more flexible application of religious beliefs.

3. For a discussion of this point, see Daniel Philpott, *Revolutions in Sovereignty: How Ideas Shaped Modern International Relations* (Princeton, NJ: Princeton University Press, 2001).

4. Nicholas Wolterstorff, "Theological Foundations for an Evangelical Political Philosophy," in *Toward an Evangelical Public Policy*, eds. Ronald J. Sider and Diane Knippers (Grand Rapids, MI: Baker Books, 2005), 150.

5. Ibid., 152.

6. Glenn Tinder, "Can We Be Good without God?" *Atlantic Monthly* (December 1989): 71–72.

7. Lay Commission on Catholic Social Teaching and the U.S. Economy, *Toward the Future: Catholic Social Thought and the U.S. Economy* (New York: American Catholic Committee, 1984), 5.

8. Pope John XXIII, *Pacem in Terris*, part 1, paragraph 10. http://www.vatican.va/holy_father/john_xxiii/encyclicals/documents/hf_j-xxiii_enc_11041963_pacem_en.html.

9. Pope John Paul II, *Laborem Exercens*, paragraph 4. http://www.vatican.va/holy_father/john_paul_ii/encyclicals/documents/hf_jp-ii_enc_14091981_laborem-exercens_en.html.

10. *Toward the Future*, 25–26.

11. Reinhold Niebuhr, *The Nature and Destiny of Man: A Christian Interpretation*, Vol. 1 (New York: Charles Scribner's Sons, 1964), 16.

12. Tinder, "Can We Be Good," 77.

13. Reinhold Niebuhr, "Why the Christian Church Is Not Pacifist," in *The Essential Reinhold Niebuhr: Selected Essays and Addresses*, ed. Robert McAfee Brown (New Haven, CT: Yale University Press, 1986), 111.

14. See Alexander Hamilton, James Madison, and John Jay, *The Federalist Papers* (New York: New American Library, 1961). See especially Federalist Nos. 10 and 51 authored by James Madison.

15. Abraham Kuyper, *Lectures on Calvinism* (Grand Rapids, MI: William B. Eerdmans, 1961).

16. Even within the traditions themselves, believers manifest their faith commitments in different ways. Traditions do not establish uniform patterns but are themselves expressed in a variety of patterns. For example, although Pentecostalism emphasizes the doctrine of baptism in the Holy Spirit, this core belief, as Swindle notes, is expressed in widely different ways, theologically and politically, resulting in different levels of social and political engagement. Similarly, while Anabaptists give priority to core theological beliefs, such as nonviolence, the primacy of Christian commitments, and the global nature of the church, Joireman observes that Anabaptist groups express their fidelity to Christ in variety of ways.

17. Richard John Neuhaus, *Christianity and Democracy: A Statement of the Institute on Religion and Democracy* (Washington, DC: Institute on Religion and Democracy, 1981), 1.

18. Alexis de Tocqueville, *Democracy in America,* trans. Henry Reeve (New York: Appleton, 1904), 1: 334.

19. U.S. Catholic Bishops, "The Challenge of Peace: God's Promise and Our Response," A Pastoral Letter on War and Peace (Washington, DC: United States Catholic Conference, May 3, 1983.

20. Paul Ramsey, *Who Speaks for the Church?* (Nashville, TN: Abingdon, 1967), 152.

21. Niebuhr, *Christ and Culture,* 2.

Index